MA... I0021369

ADOBE PHOTOSHOP ELEMENTS 2024 USER GUIDE

"A Comprehensive Guide To Mastering Photoshop Elements 2024."

New in Premiere Elements 2024!   Copy from one photo to another   Create a Zoom Burst   Create a panorama

Explore the World of Photoshop Elements 2024

Efficient Organization with the Organizer

Mastering Filters And Camera Raw

Precision in Photo Editing with the Photo Editor

Pro Tips and Tricks

TODD LEMMINGS

TABLE OF CONTENT

INTRODUCTION

Make the most of your photo-editing experience by using this "Photoshop Elements 2024 User Guide" to its fullest. Your key to grasping Photoshop Elements 2024's most recent capabilities is this meticulously written book, which is appropriate for novices as well as seasoned users.

Discover the World of Photoshop Elements 2024:

Uncover the fundamentals with a perceptive overview of Photoshop Elements 2024, dispelling any confusion regarding its features and user interface. This book offers a strong basis for self-assured navigation, regardless of experience level.

Efficient Organization with the Organizer:

Discover how to use the Organizer's power to streamline your creative process. Effortlessly organize, classify, and arrange your images to improve productivity and maintain a spotless digital workspace.

Precision in Photo Editing with the Photo Editor:

Utilize the Photo Editor module to unleash your artistic side. This book walks you through every stage, from simple tweaks to sophisticated methods. With thorough instructions and practical examples, you can turn average images into exceptional pieces of art.

Mastering Filters and Camera Raw:

Become an expert editor by delving deeply into Camera Raw and Filters. Investigate a wide range of artistic possibilities to improve and style your photos. This part gives you the ability to express your own perspective by revealing the techniques behind editing at the professional level.

Pro Tips and Tricks:

Learn the insider strategies and tricks used by pros to accomplish amazing outcomes. You'll find a wealth of information in this section that will elevate your experience with Photoshop Elements 2024, from sophisticated methods to time-saving shortcuts.

What You Will Find

- Inside are comprehensive courses suitable for both novice and expert users.
- Useful illustrations to support your knowledge.
- Detailed instructions for effective photo management.
- Innovative methods for powerful picture manipulation.
- insider knowledge to make editing smooth and easy.

Take a trip through time-traveling magic with "Photoshop Elements 2024 User Guide." Learn the techniques for effective planning, accurate editing, and artistic expression, and see how your pictures come to life like never before. This book is your key to maximizing Photoshop Elements 2024's capabilities, regardless of your level of experience.

BOOK SECTION 1

INTRODUCTION TO PHOTOSHOP ELEMENTS 2024

CHAPTER ONE- CHAPTER TWO

❖ **GETTING STARTED**

❖ **THE BASICS I; WORKSPACE AND ENVIRONMENT**

CHAPTER ONE

GETTING STARTED; KNOWING PHOTOSHOP ELEMENTS 2024

Adobe Photoshop Elements 2024

In the history of Adobe, the first release of Photoshop Elements was in 2001. It was a less complicated and more reasonably priced substitute for Adobe Photoshop's professional edition. Photoshop Elements was referred to as a simpler and friendlier version of Adobe Photoshop. When it first came out, it worked with both Windows and Mac OS, and home users and photo enthusiasts soon started to favor it.

Photographers, videographers, image editors, graphic designers, and anybody else who wants to edit and create their photos or videos use Adobe Photoshop Element.

Adobe started selling Photoshop Elements in 2003 together with a video editing program called Adobe Premiere Elements. With this bundle, users can now start editing photos and videos at an even lower cost thanks to this bundle.

The most recent iteration of Adobe's widely used photo-editing program for home users is Adobe Photoshop Elements 2024. With a range of features that can assist users in editing, enhancing, and sharing their photos, it is made to be both inexpensive and simple to use. It was officially released on October 19, 2023

Adobe Photoshop Element can be purchased one time, and it doesn't need to be renewed regularly. Among the many tools in the Adobe Photoshop Element are AI-powered one-click subject selection, content-aware cropping, automatic image colorization, and skin smoothing. It can be used with Windows and Mac computers.

New Features/Updates In Photoshop Elements 2024

Similar to its earlier versions, Adobe Photoshop Element 2024 is a graphic editing program intended for creating and editing digital files such as pictures, videos, and photos. However, it has been improved with new features to provide a more efficient user experience. With instructions on how to quickly and easily create amazing image creations, effects, designs, prints, etc., it offers a simple way to get started.

- **AI-powered Color Match**: With this feature, the color and tone of one photo are automatically matched to another. This can be useful for making collages or matching a photo's color to a particular theme.

- **Auto Selections with One Click**: Selecting an automatic option makes it easy to improve or replace a selected area. This feature allows you to make selections with just a click.

- **Stylized Texts**: You can now make captivating texts for your designs and projects with this new feature. Open your photos, select **Basic**, *Guided Mode*, and *Add Text* to activate this feature.

- **Creating Photo Reels**: Featuring their text, effects, and graphics, photo reels quickly flip through your best photos. To facilitate sharing, save them as GIFs or MP4s. Your best pictures can be presented amazingly with this feature. Click *Create*, and select *Photo Reel*, after opening your images to use this feature. Finally, a layout can be chosen from the available sizes.

- **Quick Actions**: With just one click on Quick Actions, you can automatically adjust tone, eliminate backgrounds, adjust white balance, and more. Add images from a larger variety of files and folders on your phone as well. Open any of your photos and select the **Quick Action** panel in **Quick Mode** to activate this feature.

- **Free Access to Adobe Stock**: With Photoshop Elements, you can experiment with different backgrounds, create collages, or design motivational quote graphics using the thousands of gorgeous stock photos at your disposal. You can quickly and easily access thousands of free Adobe Stock images with this feature. You can change your background image by using the free image from Adobe Stock. The Quote Graphics also provides access to Adobe Stock. Navigate to the **File menu**, select **Adobe Stock Search**, and look through the library for the desired picture.

- **Improved UI layout**: The UI interface of Photoshop Elements 2024 has been updated to meet the aesthetic needs of the users. with this new update, explore eye-friendly modern fonts, icons, buttons, and colors. Additionally, select between light and dark mode options.

- **Web and Mobile Companion Apps:** The version comes with a mobile and web app. This allows you to perform one-click Quick Actions to automatically adjust tone, eliminate backgrounds, adjust white balance, and more. Moreover, import images from a larger variety of files and folders on your phone. With this, you can also sync across the Elements Organizer and the web and mobile companion apps.

 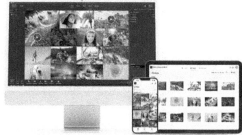

Other new updates include:

- **New Filters**: Filters like Black and White, and the Artistic Filter have been added to the software`s filter menu. An artistic effect equivalent to paintings or drawings is produced by an artistic filter. A black-and-white photo can be created with a black-and-white filter, which offers several ways to adjust the grayscale image's contrast and intensity.
- **Enhanced Organizer and Improved Performance:** With several enhancements to the program's speed and responsiveness, Photoshop Elements 2024 has been performance-optimized.
- **Support for New File Formats**: HEIC and HEIF are two of the new file formats that Photoshop Elements 2024 supports.

System Requirement Of Photo Elements 2024 On Windows And Mac.

Shown in the box below is the minimum requirement of Photoshop Elements 2024

Windows	macOS
Processor with AMD equivalent or Intel 6th Generation or later and support for SSE4.1.	Intel CPUs from the sixth generation or later.
Only 64-bit versions of Microsoft Windows 10 (version 22H2) or Windows 11 version 22H2) are supported; Windows 7 and Windows 8.1 are not.	Apple CPUs from the silicon M1 generation or later; macOS 12, macOS 13 (13.4 or later)
8 GB of RAM • 8 GB of free hard disc space for installing applications; extra space needed for temporary files and online content downloads during product installation and use (installs cannot be made on removable flash drives or volumes with case-sensitive file systems).	8 GB of RAM and 6 GB of free hard drive space are needed to install the application; extra space is needed for temporary files and online content downloads while the product is being installed and used (it cannot be installed on removable flash drives or volumes that use case-sensitive file systems).

Resolution of the display: 1280 x 800 (at 100% scale factor)	Resolution of the display: 1280 x 800 (at 100% scale factor)
Display driver compatible with Microsoft DirectX 12.	To activate the product and download features and online content, you must have an internet connection.
Internet connection necessary for product activation and feature and content downloads	

Downloading And Installing Photoshop Elements 2024
Follow the instructions below to install the software into your PC.

- Open your web browser page, and enter the URL link below to download Adobe Photoshop Elements
  https://helpx.adobe.com/download-install/kb/photoshop-elements-downloads.html
- Click on **Download** for either **Windows** or **Mac**

For Windows	For macOS
Download 64-bit	Download
Languages: Czech, Dutch, English, French, German, Italian, Japanese, Polish, Spanish, and Swedish	Languages: English, French, German, and Japanese

After downloading the software program, do the following to install it.

- The download file appears as an encrypted file on your PC, right-click on the file and extract the file to a folder.

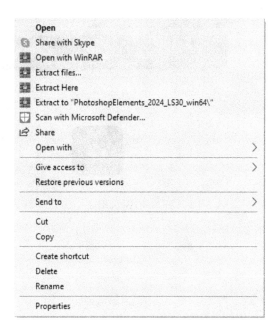

- After extraction, launch the software, and click **Continue** on the following screen that pops up.
- Choose your **Preferred Language** and **Installation Location** from the Installation Options screen, then click **Continue**.

- Choose your prior version of Photoshop Element from the screen that displays next, then click **Confirm**.

- To load the Adobe Photoshop Editor Workspace, select **Launch** The Photo Editor from the next screen that appears.

- Next, log in once more with your **Adobe ID** and **password**.

- Select "**Activate Now**" from the Welcome screen on the following page.

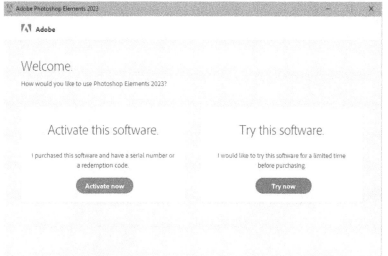

- Enter the serial number and select **Next** on the ensuing screen and the Photo Editor will automatically launch itself.

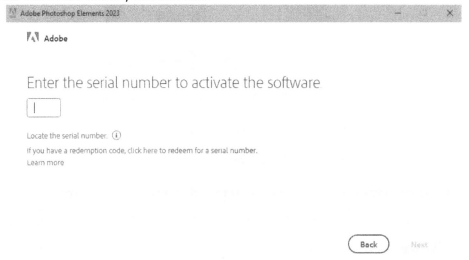

- Here, the Photo Editor has been effectively launched.

CHAPTER TWO

THE BASICS I; WORKSPACE AND ENVIRONMENT

The Photoshop Elements Workspace

The first user interface that appears on your screen when you launch Photoshop Elements is called the **Home Screen**.

The Home Screen

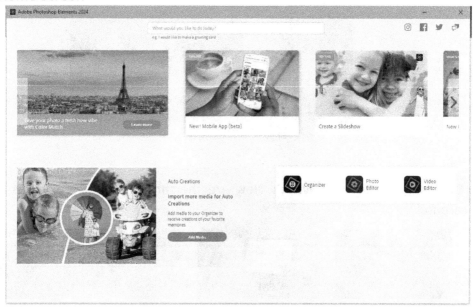

Contained in the Home Screen are created slide shows, motion pictures, and automatically generated images for its users to use with the imported media.

From the home screen, you can access recently opened files, find creative inspiration, switch workspaces, find entertaining editing projects, and ask the Adobe community for help.

Below are some of the buttons that help you interact effectively with the Home Screen.

- **The Search Bar**: This interface button is located at the top of the Home Screen and can be used to quickly search for help documents and tutorials for different features. To use the search bar, type the desired keyword into the search bar and press the Enter key on your keyboard and the pertinent results will appear as hyperlinks and thumbnails on the Home Screen.

- **Carousel of Cards**: A carousel of cards in the top section of the Home Screen gives users access to information about upcoming features, tasks, and motivational ideas. You navigate the carousel by clicking the arrows that appear on its left and right sides.

New in Premiere Eleme   New in Photoshop Elements 2024!

Explore, **Try This**, and **What`s New** are the three categories of cards in the carousel.

New in Photoshop Elements 2024!   New! Web App (beta)   Bring in your photos and videos   New in Premiere Eleme

- ○ **Explore**: With the help of this tag, you can explore specific features within the Photoshop Element program. Press the View button to use this feature.

EXPLORE

New! Web App (beta)

View, create, and share your photos & videos on any browser. Enjoy 2GB of free cloud storage. English-only beta.

View

13

- **Try This**: This blue tag provides information about new features in the Photoshop Element application. To utilize these resources, click the Open Link icon.

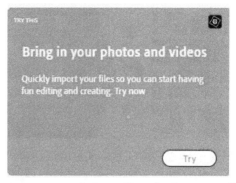

- **What's New**: There are many interesting features available to you when you click on this green tag. These features are displayed and updated based on the actions you take and the features you use in Photoshop Elements. To give any of these features a try, click the Try button.

- **Auto Creations**: These are created automatically by the program using the media that has been imported into the Elements, and they are located at the bottom of the Home Screen. You can add media to Auto Creations by choosing Add Media from the Auto Creation menu. You can view every auto-created project, including picture collages, slideshows, and video collages, by choosing View All or the number icon underneath the Auto Creations thumbnail.

- **The Organizer**: On the right side of the Home Screen is where you can find the Organizer. This is where you import, browse, and organize photos so that your collection remains efficient and well-organized. The Organizer has tools for rating, sorting, tagging, and finding your photos.

- **The Photo Editor**: This section contains the tools for creating and editing photographs. These comprise color, brightness, effect, image correction, and other tools.

- **The Video Editor**: This allows you to use the editing tools and videos in Photoshop Element.

- **Recent Files**: You can view the project files that have been worked on recently on the Home Screen. Using this symbol, you can pick up where you left off with the project right away. This window displays any open image in the Photo Editor.

Working With the Photo Editor

One of the most important tools in the Photoshop element is the Photo Editor.

With its many features, you can crop, resize, rotate, change the contrast and brightness, and add filters to your photos. Additionally, you can edit your photos with the Photo Editor by adding shapes and text. The Photo Editor offers options for applying effects, adjusting color and brightness, repairing photos, and more, as was previously mentioned.

Do the following to access the Photo Editor.

- On the right-hand side of the **Home Screen**, select the **Photo Editor** icon.

- The Interface of the Photo Editor displays automatically filled with professional tools for editing images; menus, options, and panels. By default, the Photo Editor is in the **Quick Mode**. An image of the Quick Mode is displayed below.

Ultimately, the Photo Editor is made up of three workspaces. The three editing modes available on the workspace are **Quick, Guided**, and **Advanced**.

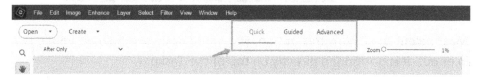

At the top of the workspace are options collectively called the **Menu Bar.** It is made up of *File, Edit, Image, Enhance, Layer, Select, Filter, View, Window, and Help.*

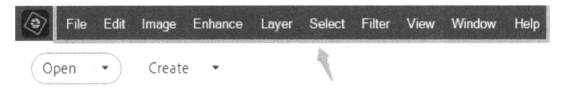

The main workspace of the Photoshop Element application is the **Image Window**. The image window at the top shows the many images that are opened and created.

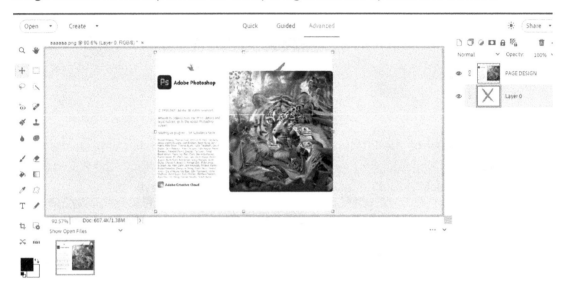

Let`s quickly some attachment features around the image window.

- **File Name**: The filename of each file that is opened in the image window is displayed in the *status bar* above the image window.

- **Scroll Bar**: The Scroll bar appears when you zoom in on an image. To move the image within the window image, use the Hand tool from the Toolbar, the scroll bar, or the scroll arrows.

- **Magnificent Box**: With this option, you can quickly see how an image is zoomed in or out. It is positioned directly on top of the Taskbar.

- **Information Box:** Position beside the magnificent box, with the information box, you can select the data that will be shown by selecting from a pop-up menu of possibilities. The following are the options accessible in the information box:

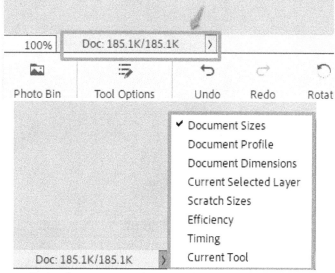

- o **Document Size**: This option shows information about the resolution and size of the stored files.
- o **Document Profile**: This option displays the color profile of the file.
- o **Document Dimension**: This shows the document's actual size in the unit of measurement of your choice, such as inches.
- o **Current Selected Layer**: By clicking and selecting a layer in the Layer panel, you can choose Current Selected Layer as a readout.
- o **Scratch Sizes**: This option displays the amount of Memory used by each open document.
- o **Efficiency**: This determines how many operations are carried out in contrast to using the scratch disk. When the value reaches 100 %, the RAM is used up. The scratch disk is utilized when the percentage falls below 100%.
- o **Timing:** This shows how long it took to finish the last task.

○ **Current Tools**: The tool name that was selected from the Touch panel appears here.

The right side of the workspace is where **Panels** are docked, in what is known as the Panel Bin. The panel shown below is the *Adjustment Panel*.

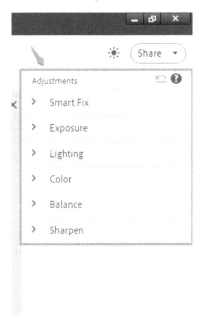

The workspace's left side is where you'll find the **Tools panel**.

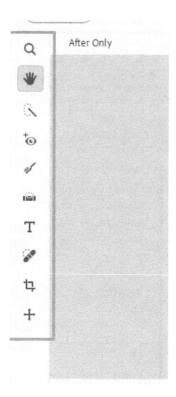

A wide range of options for editing, enhancing, and stylizing photos are available from the Tools panel when combined with objects in the Panel Bin and the tools inside. In the next section of this chapter, we will be learning about each part of the workspace in detail.

The Quick Mode

The Quick mode is the simplest workspace in the Photo Editor. It has fewer tools and editing options compared to the other workspaces.

The Menu Bar in Quick Mode is made of the following constituents: *File, Edit, Image, Enhance, Layer, Select, Filter, View, Window,* and *Help*. A grey display indicates which functions are marked as unavailable in the Menu bar and cannot be selected or accessed as shown in the Window Menu below.

The **Zoom Tool**, **Hand Tool**, **Selection Tools**, **Healing Brush Tool**s, **Red Eye Removal Tool**, **Whiten Teeth**, **Straighten Tool**, **Text Tool**s, **Healing Brush Tools**, **Crop Tool**, and **Move Too**l are the tools available in the Quick Mode.

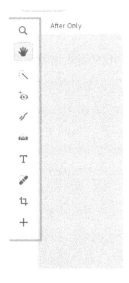

Located at the base of the workspace is another feature in the Quick Edit mode called the **Panel Bin**. Tools like Photo Bin, Tool Options, Rotate, Organizer, Element

Web, Adjustment, Effects, Quick Actions, Textures, and Frames are included in this section of the workspace.

Located directly below the **Image Windows** is the **Photo Bin**. The **Photo Bin** displays a preview version of the images that are currently opened in the Photo Editor. The two available options in this tab are **Show Open Files** and **Show Files Selected In Organizer**.

The Photo Bin can be used to rotate photographs, open and close photos, hide photos, and see file metadata, among other things. A thumbnail of each image that has been seen in the Image window is shown in the Photo Bin. With the Photo Bin, you can move a lot of open photos around. it appears when you open one or more images/photographs in the Photo Editor.

The Guided Mode

The Guided Mode is the second workspace in the Photo Editor. With this workspace, you can achieve a range of preset effects, that function like a wizard-like interface. With the Guided Edit mode, you can make simple decisions about your photos and let the computer handle the rest.

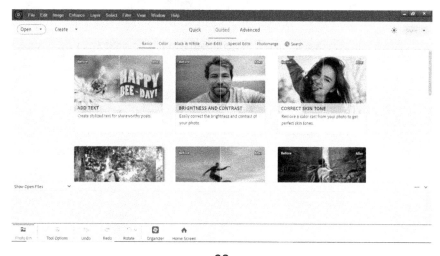

The Guided Edit mode is intended to walk you through a variety of editing tasks step-by-step, as its name suggests.

Select the **Guided Mode** from the three workspaces menu to access the Guided Mode.

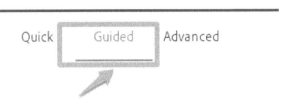

Guided Edits are arranged into six categories on the screen in guided mode and they are *Basic, Color, Black & White, Fun Edits, Special Edits,* and *Photomerge.*

Let`s quickly explore each of the categories.

- **Basic**: With this edit, you can adjust the images using features like levels, cropping, brightness and contrast, skin tone correction, and add text to a photograph.

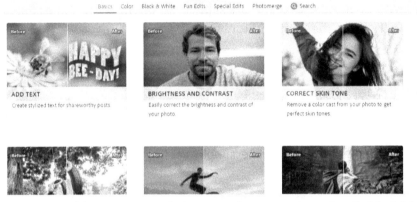

- **Add Text**: One of the new features that the Guided Mode has is this. You can use this to create stylized text for your images.

ADD TEXT

Create stylized text for shareworthy posts.

- **Brightness and Contrast**: This is a spectrum edit that allows you to change the amount of lightness and contrast in a photograph.

BRIGHTNESS AND CONTRAST

Easily correct the brightness and contrast of your photo.

- **Correct Skin Tone**: To adjust skin tones and get rid of a color cast, use this guided edit.

CORRECT SKIN TONE

Remove a color cast from your photo to get perfect skin tones.

- **Crop Photo**: To achieve the ideal layout of your photograph, crop an image using this guided edit.

CROP PHOTO

Trim the edges of your photo to get the perfect composition.

- **Levels**: You can use this guided edit to make adjustments to your photo's contrast, brightness, and tone range.

LEVELS

Adjust the brightness, contrast, and tonal range of your photo.

- **Lighten And Darken**: Use this guided edit to make adjustments to your photo's highlights, shadows, and midtones.

LIGHTEN AND DARKEN

Independently adjust the shadows, highlights, and mid-tones of your photo to get the perfect exposure.

- **Move & Scale Object**: Selecting an object and adjusting its size, position, and other attributes is now simpler than ever with step-by-step guidance.

MOVE & SCALE OBJECT
Easily select an object and change its position, size, and more.

- **Object Removal**: Unwanted objects can be easily removed from your photos using this edit.

OBJECT REMOVAL
Make unwanted objects vanish.

- **Resize Your Photo**: To quickly produce a version of your photo that satisfies precise size requirements (in pixels, inches, or bytes), use this guided edit.

RESIZE YOUR PHOTO
Easily resize your photo for printing or posting to the web.

- **Rotate & Straighten**: With the help of this guided edit, you can realign an image by drawing a line through it and rotating it by ninety degrees.

ROTATE AND STRAIGHTEN

Easily level out the horizon of your photo.

- **Sharpen**: Make use of this guided edit to enhance an image's clarity.

SHARPEN

Make your photo crisp and crystal clear.

- **Vignette**: Utilize this guided edit to highlight the significance of the subject, group, or object in the center of the picture and to add a vignette effect.

VIGNETTE EFFECT

Darken the corners of your photo to highlight the subject.

- **Color**: With features like enhanced color, Lomo camera effect, cast color removal, saturated film effect, etc., you can use this to alter the color of your photos.

ENHANCE COLOR
Fine-tune and enhance the colors in your photo.

LOMO CAMERA EFFECT
Easily give your photo that high-contrast, heavily saturated Lomo camera look.

REMOVE A COLOR CAST
Remove unwanted color tinting to reveal your photos' true colors.

SATURATED FILM EFFECT
Add a classic saturated slide-film feel to your

- **Black & White**: This edition lets you use features like B&W color pop and B&W selection to convert a portion of the entire photo to black and white.
- **Fun Edits**: You can add intriguing effects to your photos with the Fun edit, like multi-photo text, double exposure, meme creation, and more.
- **Special Edits**: With the use of tools like depth of field, frame creator, Orton effect, perfect landscape, and others, you can add imaginative and artistic effects to your photographs with the Special edit.
- **Photomerge**: You can create a new image by connecting or combining various photographs with the Photomerge Edit. Features like Photomerge compose, Photomerge exposure, Photomerge faces, and Photomerge group are available in the Photomerge edit.

Another part of the Guided Workspace that should not be neglected is the **Search icon**.

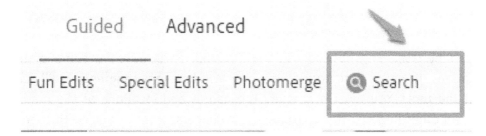

You can search Photoshop Elements for the appropriate Guided Edit using the Guided Edit Search window. Search to find new things to do or quickly and easily find what you want to do.

Basics   Color   Black & White   Fun Edits   Special Edits   Photomerge   🔍 Search

The Advanced Mode

Although it is the most complicated workspace in the Photo Editor, the Advanced Mode (formerly called Expert Mode in prior versions of Photoshop Elements) is nevertheless very user-friendly. Compared to the workspace modes that were previously discussed, it offers a greater selection of tools—and menu options.

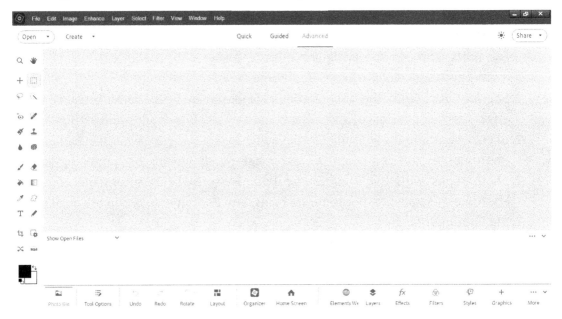

We'll start by discussing how to use the Toolbox. I will describe some of the tool classifications. If you're used to working in a Windows environment, you'll recognize some of the tools. You must first study the names and locations of the many tools, panels, and other items in the surroundings to become comfortable with them. Next, you begin to use the many tools, panels, and objects nearby.

Located on the left side of the workspace is the **Toolbox.** There are several groups or categories into which the tools in the toolbox are organized.

To use the tools in the Toolbox, you can either select them from the Toolbox or use the keyboard shortcuts for the tool (The keyboard shortcut is the letter placed in parentheses() in the tables below).

- The Zoom and Hand tools are part of the **View Group**, which is located at the top.

TOOLS	ICON	USES
The Zoom Tool (Z)		The view of a photograph can be made larger or smaller by using the Zoom tool.
The Hand Tool (H)		This is used for picture movement within the Photoshop Element workspace. You may drag your image with this tool as well.

- The **Select Group** is the next one, and it has several tools to choose from. Although we have already done some selecting, there is still much more to be done in this course.

TOOLS	ICON	USES
The Move Tool (V)		This tool is used to move layers and selections in the Photo Editor.
The Rectangular Marquee Tool (M)		Using this, you may draw a rectangular box around a portion of the image. To make the selection a square, hold down the Shift key.
The Elliptical Marquee Tool (M)		Using this, an elliptical selection is made. To make the selection a

		circle, hold down the Shift key.
The Lasso Tool (L)		You may then use this to create a free-form selection in a specific area of the picture.
The Magnetic Lasso Tool (L)		This tool aids in the creation of a high-contrast outline when a shape inside an image is selected. It works like a magnet.
Polygonal Tool (L)		Straight-edged selection border segments are produced using this tool.
The Quick Selection Tool		Any area of the image that is picked or dragged will yield a color and texture selection when using this tool. This selection tool is hue-sensitive.
The Selection Brush Tool (A)		With this tool, you can select the region you wish to paint with the brush tool.
The Magic Wand Tool (A)		This is used to generate a selection of pixels with similar colors that can be clicked on.
The Refine Selection Brush Tool (Y)		This automatically detects the edges and can be used to add or delete a region from a selection.

Auto Selection Tool (A)		This is used to add or remove an area from a selection by automatically recognizing its margins.

- The **Enhance Group** is next. Many of the tools in the Enhance group are typically used to fix issues like reducing red eye or enhancing an image's illumination.

TOOLS	ICON	USES
The Eye Tool		This fixes closed eyelids and removes the pet-eye and red-eye effects from your images.
The Spot Healing Brush (J)		This is used to choose an area of an image and remove a stain from it.
The Smart Brush Tool (F)		This is the tool used to modify the color balance and tone of specific areas within an image.
The Detail Smart Brush Tool (F)		Similar to the painting tool, this tool lets you make adjustments while painting specific areas of an image.
The Clone Stamp Tool (S)		This tool can be used to duplicate objects, remove objects, or just paint over elements in your image by using an image sample, image imperfections, or paint over objects.

The Pattern Stamp Tool (S)		Using this tool, you can overlay an image with a pattern.
The Blur Tool (R)		This is used to remove some of the edges and smooth the rough areas.
The Sharpen Tool (R)		This tool enhances clarity and focus in images by focusing on the image's soft edges.
The Smudge Tool (R)		The tool helps to stimulate a brush that smears wet paint. Using this tool, you can drag the color to the desired area from the stroke's starting point.
The Sponge Tool (O)		A wet paint-smearing brush is stimulated with the help of this tool. With the help of this tool, you may drag the color to the desired spot from the stroke's beginning.
The Dodge Tool (O)		This is applied to lighter areas of an image. It is also possible to highlight features in shadows with this tool.
The Burn Tool (O)		This tool is used to make certain sections of an image darker. This tool can also be used to highlight specific details in an image.

- This brings us to the **Draw Group**. With these tools, we can sketch over an image or even make an entirely new image. Included in the draw group are text editing tools.

TOOLS	ICON	USES
The Brush Tool (B)		This is used to create strong or delicate color strokes. It can be applied to enhance retouching abilities as well.
The Impressionist Brush Tool (B)		This is used to modify the color and features of the image.
The Color Replacement Tool(B)G		This tool minimizes the number of specific colors in your image.
The Eraser Tool (E)		With this tool, you can reduce the number of pixels in the image as you travel over it. With this tool, you can reduce the number of pixels in the image as you travel over it.
The Background Eraser Tool (E)		This tool allows you to quickly remove an object from its backdrop by changing the color of a pixel to a transparent one.
Magic Eraser Tool (E)		This tool is used to remove a selection with similar-looking pixels in a picture.
Paint Bucket Tool (K)		You can use this tool to fill a space with a color value that is almost identical to the selected pixels.

Pattern Tool (K)		You can use this tool to add a fill or pattern to your image in place of one of the brush tools.
Gradient Tool (G)		This tool is used to apply a gradient to a particular area of an image.
Color Picker Tool (I)		This tool creates a new backdrop or foreground by copying the color of a selected area of an image.
Custom Shape Tool (U)		With this tool, you can draw a variety of forms. When the Custom Shape tool is selected, these forms can be accessed in the Tool Options bar. The shape tools available in the Tool Options bar include rectangle, rounded rectangle, ellipse, polygon, star, line, and selection.
Type Tool (T)		With this tool, you can create and modify a telegraphist on an image. Some other type-related settings in the Tool Options bar include Text on Shape, Text on Custom Path, Vertical Type, Horizontal Mask Type, and Vertical Type Mask.
The Pencil Tool (N)		This is how strong-edged freehand lines are made.

- The **Modify group** is next. We have the means to alter an image's structure within this group. In addition to tools for cropping, this also features tools for removing objects from images.

TOOLS	BUTTONS	USES
The Crop Tool (C)		You can use this tool to crop a specific area of an image.
The Cookie Cutter Tool (C)		You can crop an image to any desired form using this tool.
The Perspective Crop Tool (C)		This tool is used to adjust the image's viewpoint while cropping a photo.
The Recompose Tool (W)		With this, photos may be intelligently resized without losing any of their characteristics.
The Content-Aware Move Tool (Q)		This is how you pick an object and move it to a new place.
The Straighten Tool (P)		This is used to move an image either horizontally or vertically.

- We have a **Color group** below that. The buttons on this page allow us to choose the colors of the background and foreground.

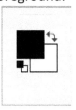

Now that we are done learning about the Toolbox, let us move on to the next- The Tool Bar Options Bar.

At the bottom of the Element window is the **Tool Options bar**. The Tool Options section is an important workspace for the Tools available in Photoshop Elements. It offers several options that can be applied to a selected tool. For example, clicking on the Spot Healing Brush brings up the Tool Options menu below.

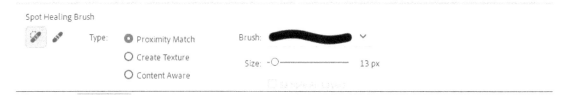

Spot Healing Brush

Type: ● Proximity Match   Brush: ⌄
       ○ Create Texture
                              Size: ─○─────────── 13 px
       ○ Content Aware

Interacting With the Menu Bar and The Workspace Environ

When you launch the Picture Editor in Expert Mode, the following capabilities become available.

- **System Menu Button**: This is available from the menu bar's left side.

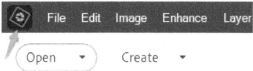

To utilize this feature, just click the button and choose an option from the list that displays.

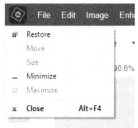

- **Menu Bar**: This section contains commands for executing tasks. *File, Edit, Image, Enhance, Layer, Select, Filter, View*, and *Help* are the commands available on the menu bar.

In the menu bar, to the right of the different subcommands available in each command section, are shortcut keys.

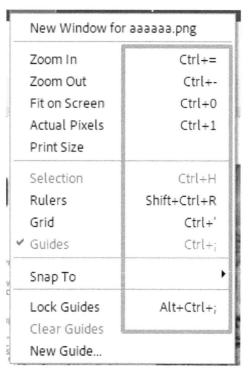

New Window for aaaaaa.png

Zoom In	Ctrl+=
Zoom Out	Ctrl+-
Fit on Screen	Ctrl+0
Actual Pixels	Ctrl+1
Print Size	
Selection	Ctrl+H
Rulers	Shift+Ctrl+R
Grid	Ctrl+'
✓ Guides	Ctrl+;
Snap To	▸
Lock Guides	Alt+Ctrl+;
Clear Guides	
New Guide...	

- **Open Icon**: On the left side of the status bar, beneath the menu bar, is where you can find this button. Open previously accessed photographs by using the Open option located at the far-left end of the shortcuts bar.

- **Create**: As the name implies, it is used to create new documents. when you select the **Create Icon**, ready-made formats are made available for you to work with for your new project.

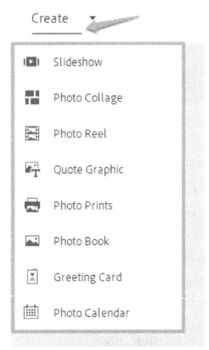

- **Status Bar**: It is the bar that provides you with information about the image you are now working on.

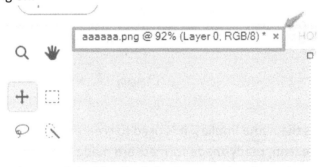

- **Photo Tab**: The Photo Tab holds all of the images that have been opened in the Photo Editor and are by default shown in many tabs at the top of the window, in contrast to the status bar which only shows information about the tab that is now selected.

- **Edit Buttons**: These buttons are located in the middle of the shortcut bar in the Photo Editor. You can select from Quick, Guided, and Advanced modes with these.

39

- **Share:** The Home screen's far right side is where you'll find the Share button. It can be used to create and share collages, calendars, and other things.

- **UI Display Mode**: This is represented by the brightness icon beside the Share button.

When you select it, it opens you up to the Preference Settings that are responsible for the UI display. With this, you can change between the two display modes in Photoshop Elements; *Dark/Light Mode*.

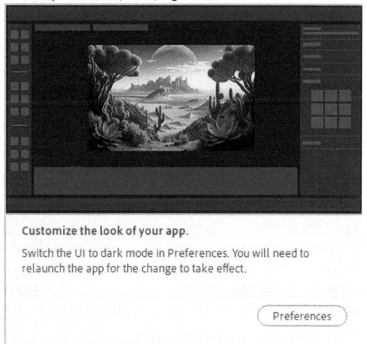

Customize the look of your app.

Switch the UI to dark mode in Preferences. You will need to relaunch the app for the change to take effect.

Preferences

- **The Taskbar**: The most often used panels and operations while editing and modifying photos are shown by buttons on the Photoshop Elements taskbar, which is located at the bottom of the program. The Photo Bin and Tool Choices buttons allow you to switch between showing tool options and thumbnails.

Rotate photos, fast undo and redo actions, and adjust layouts. To launch Photoshop Elements Organizer, you can alternatively click the Organizer button. The home screen is accessible through the Home Screen button. The Element Website icon leads you directly to the software`s webpage. At the right side of the taskbar are arranged panels for easy access.

Working With Panels

In both the Quick and Advanced Edit modes, the panels are located on the right side of the main screen. The Quick Edit mode includes *Adjustments, Effects, Quick Actions, Textures*, and *Frames*. In contrast, there are more panels in the Advanced edit mode, such as *Layers, Effects, Filters, Styles, Graphics*, and *More*.

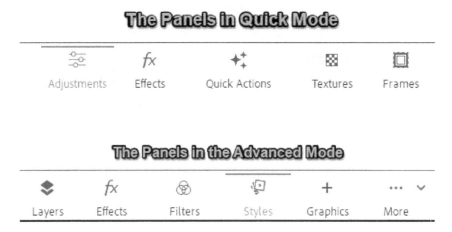

Each of the panels is carefully explained below.

- **Adjustments**: Contained in this panel are commands for editing a photograph/image. *Smart Fix, Exposure, Lightening, Color, Balance*, and *Sharpen* are the adjustment commands contained in this panel. Each of the adjustment commands has its adjustment filter. This is only available in the Quick Mode

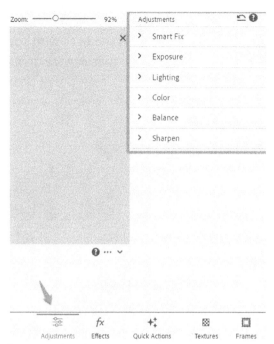

- **Layers**: Out of all the panels, this one is the most crucial. When working on a creative project, the layer panel allows you to add elements to various layers in the document, such as text, multiple pictures, and other features. You can edit any project at any stage of the creation process by using the layer's panel. Several tools are accessible in the top-left corner of the layer panel, while an icon with horizontal lines can be found in the top-right corner.

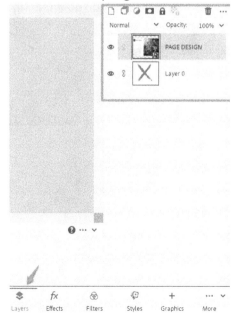

- **Effects**: To choose which effects to apply to photographs, this section offers menus and tabs. This panel provides the user with sophisticated recipes, such as automatic color and special effects, that can be applied to any image with only one click.

- **Quick Actions**: As the name implies, the commands in this panel are AI-generated, with them, you can do more with less but to use these features, you have to download them. For example, using the **Red Eye Fix** instead of using the *Red Eye tool* in the Tool Bar. This is only available in the Quick Mode

- **Textures**: Sunbeams and light leaks are just two of the imaginative elements in this collection that may be used for backdrops, websites, and other projects. You may apply a textured overlay to your image with only one click. You can also get additional overlays and textures by using your Adobe account. This is only available in the Quick Mode

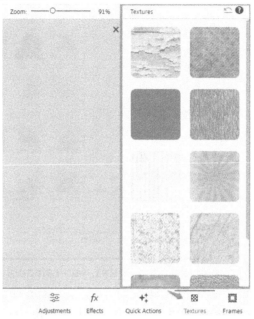

- **Frames**: This contains aesthetic frame elements that can be used to beautify an image/photograph. This is only available in Quick Mode.

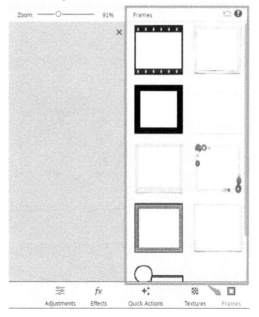

- **Filter**: The operation of each FX filter is depicted in this little thumbnail. To start the effect, just click on the thumbnail. There are billions of combinations imaginable for each of the 98 different filters available.

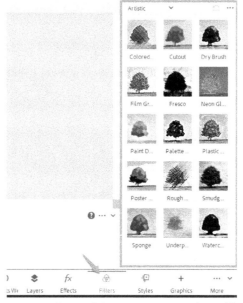

- **Styles**: By using the commands in this, you can apply a filter to the entire layer and change the image. The Styles tab offers drop shadows, glass button effects, glow, bevels, patterns, and glow. Within the Styles section, there are 176 distinct styles.

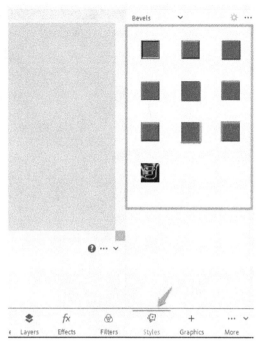

- **More**: Located in the lower right corner of the main window, the More panel is situated to the right of the Graphics panel. When you select the More panel, a pop-up menu opens, giving you access to additional panels not displayed in the Panel bin. A brief description of the other panels is provided below.

  o **Info**: This panel provides or displays the readout for various color values as well as the actual dimensions of your images.

- o **Navigator**: This function allows you to pan and zoom within a picture within the image window.

- o **Favorite**: This panel displays adjustment commands and edits that you have marked as your favorites.

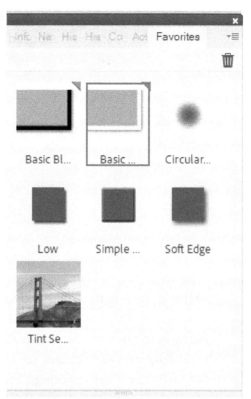

o **History**: A range of previously carried out actions and commands are displayed in this panel.

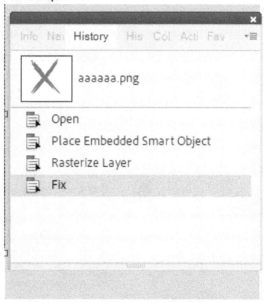

o **Histogram**: A range of tones that can be applied or added to any image in the foreground are seen when this panel is opened.

Among these tones are mid-tone, highlights, whites, blacks, underexposed, and overexposed.

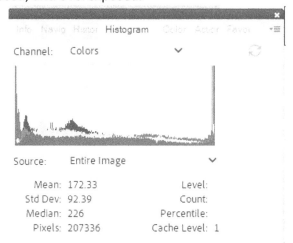

- o **Actions**: This feature was passed down to Element from Adobe Photoshop. You can use this feature to automatically make several changes to your photo. One feature of this technology is the ability to replay certain actions or interactions on the images. Other Actions, such as resizing, cropping, copying, and bordering photographs, can be downloaded from the internet and integrated with the Elements.

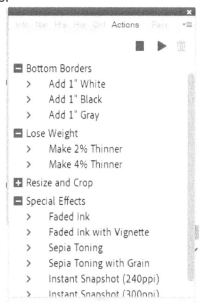

- o **Color Swatches**: Utilize the Color Swatches panels to choose the color type that you want to use. Paintbrushes and pencils can also be used to create this type of backdrop color. With these panels, you can make your unique color swatch to finish a particular project.

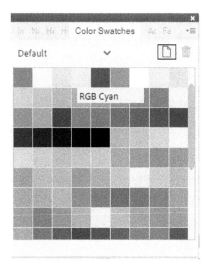

Working Contextual Menus

Like other design programs, Adobe Photoshop, Lightroom, and Illustrator, Photoshop Element also has contextual menus as standard commands, especially in the Photo Editor and Organizer. The contextual menu presents commands that are relevant to the tool, selection, or panel that is presently selected. You may access contextual menus from the *menu bar*.

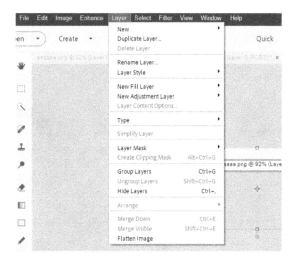

The menu instructions change depending on the features and tools you are using, as well as where you click, while the contextual menu is active. The reason for this is that the contextual menu provides instructions based on the items, tools, and region you are clicking on. You can perform the following to get to the contextual menu:

- Move the cursor over a picture or a panel element (Note: some panels do not have contextual menus), and choose a command from the menu by performing a right-click.
  Below is an instance

Element's Preference Settings

The Preference Dialog Box is the tuning room of Photoshop Elements. This is the workspace that allows you to customize the software program to your taste.

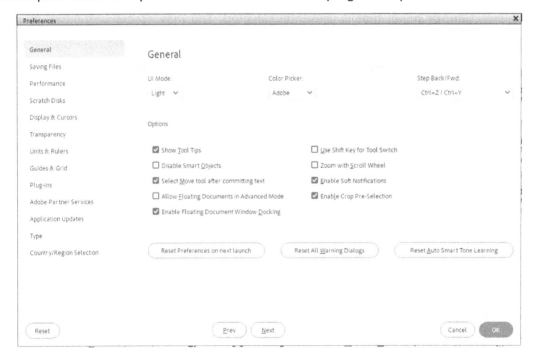

In the General section of the Preferences dialog box, you can customize the UI mode, enable soft notifications, control zoom with the scroll wheel, restore preferences, handle warning dialogs, and more. Preference settings let you customize your work and tailor a program to your preferred way of working. style and give your work a unique touch.

You can use the Organizer or the Photo Editor to open the Preference dialog box. This part will concentrate on using the Photo Editor to reach the preference dialog box.

Interacting With the Preference Dialog Box

To do different operations in Photoshop Element, the Preference dialog box in the Photo Editor divides the options into panes. The General pane is the first to appear when the Preference dialog box is launched. Do either of the following to access the preference dialog box.

- From the **Edit Menu** Select **Preference**, and click on any of the available options to access the Preference Dialog Box.

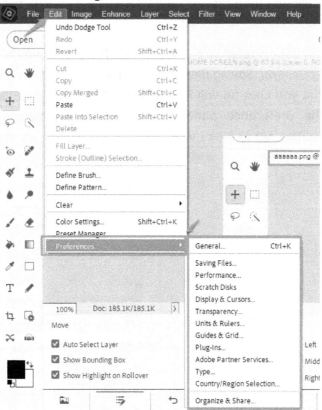

- Another method is to click on the **UI Mode icon** beside the **Share button** and select **Preference**.

Let's quickly review the features and operations of the control buttons in the Preference dialog box.

- **PANE LIST**: The Preference dialog box's Pane list, which shows several panels including *General, Saving files, Scratch drives*, etc., is on the left side. Any of these pages that you click on will instantly bring up more possibilities for you to work with. The preference panes are made up of many panes with different functionalities. Let us look more closely at each pane and its functions.

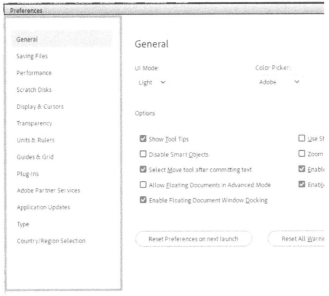

General: This is where you can change the editing environment's general settings.

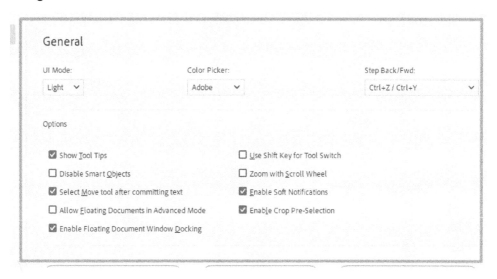

Saving Files: In this part, you can save files with picture previews, layers, and compatibility options, as well as add extensions to filenames.

Performance: This is the window that displays the memory settings, which control how Photoshop Element allocates memory, along with historical information.

Performance

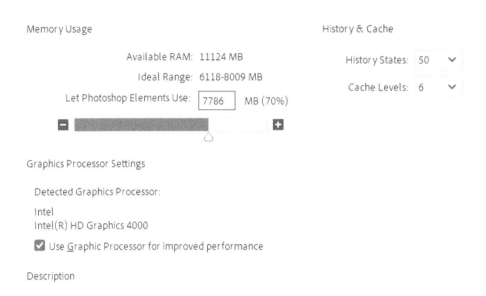

Scratch Disks: This window is in charge of utilizing the hard disk as an extra RAM extension.

Scratch Disks

Display & Cursors: When cropping photos in these panels, you can alter the appearance of the Crop tools and the different tool cursors.

Transparency: With this, you can choose how transparency will be shown in the element in these panes.

Units & Rulers: You can set the default resolutions for the document, the ruler units, and the column guide this way.

Units & Rulers

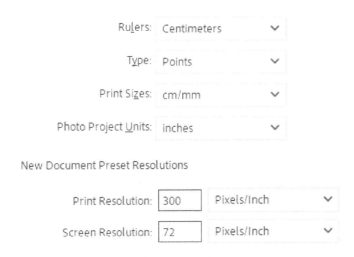

Guides & Grid: Features for gridline color, divisions, and subdivision are provided by this.

Guides & Grid

Plug-Ins: The choice of another Plug-Ins folder is handled by this. Third-party apps known as Plug-Ins help you do things that Element does not cover. It's possible to locate the Photoshop Element Plug-Ins online.

Plug-Ins

Adobe Partner Services: Elements can now search for new services, erase any data that is kept online, and reset all account details. With these, you can set up automatic updates for the Element application and be notified when a new version is available

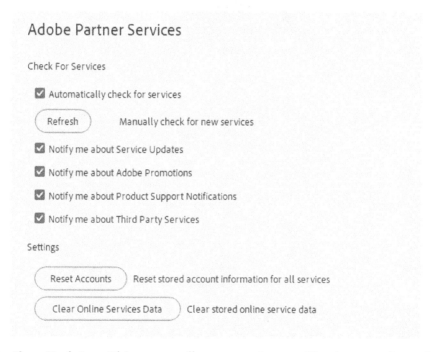

Application Updates: This pane allows you to modify the reaction of your software to new updates from Adobe.

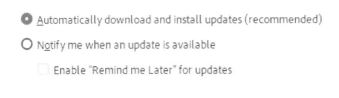

Type: This is the location where you can modify the setting's text properties. In addition to using font kinds like Asian characters that display the font name in English, you can preview font sizes.

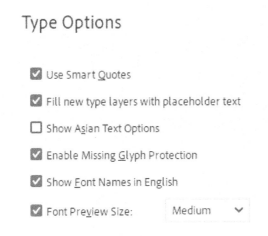

Country/ Region Selection: This lets you choose a nation or area from the list of options.

- **RESET**: By using this option, the Preference dialog box's initial settings are restored. The dialog box where you adjust the new settings remains open after resetting.

- **PREV**: To access the previous pane, use this button.

- **NEXT**: To navigate to the next pane, use this button.

- **CANCEL**: Upon clicking it, the dialog box is ultimately closed and the pane is returned to its initial settings.

- **OK**: This closes the Preference dialog box and verifies any changes made to any of the panes.

BOOK SECTION 2

THE ORGANIZER

CHAPTER THREE- CHAPTER FOUR

❖THE BASICS II; WORKING WITH THE ORGANIZER
❖PERFORMOMG MORE OPERATIONS WITH THE ORGANIZER

CHAPTER THREE

THE BASIC II: WORKING WITH THE ORGANIZER

Knowing The Organizer Intimately

The Photo Editor is not all that there is to Photo Elements, The Organizer is an intricate part of the software. As its name implies, it is used to keep an efficient and well-organized collection of images. It is also used for importing and exploring images in Photoshop Elements.

The Organizer is located at the right side of the Home Screen in the same group as Photo Editor and Premiere.

By carefully going over the workplace overview, organizing files, and adding icons to tasks, we will learn everything about the organizer in this chapter. Before we get into how to organize images using the Organizer workspace, let's have a look at it.

Custom tags, among other things, are displayed when you open an organizer.

- **Menu Bar**: The commands for performing tasks or operations in the Organizer are located in the Menu bar. File. The menu bar has the following commands: File, Edit, Find, View, and Help Menu.

- **Features Button**: The Maximize, Minimize, and Close buttons are located on these buttons. These buttons are located in the upper-right corner of the Organizer on Windows. These buttons are located on the left side for Mac users.

- **Import**: Media files can be imported from scanners, cameras, card readers, and files and folders using the **Import Button**.

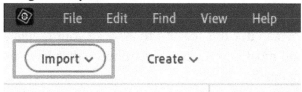

- **Create**: With this command button, you can create several photo projects.

- **Search Bar**: This can be used to locate images and other media assets. Use the Search drop-down menu to enter a term to find photos or media.

- **View Tabs**: There are four categories in this section, namely, *Media, People, Places,* and *Events*. You can locate your images, photographs, and files using these categories.

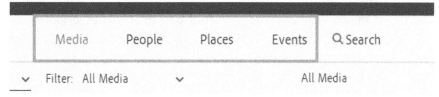

Below is a list of all the view tabs available in the Organizer.

- **Media**: All of the media files are shown or exhibited in this location. Additionally, you can edit your photographs in this window.
- **People**: You can view photographs according to the individuals in them by using the view tab (people). The pictures of the individuals that feature in them can also be arranged.
- **Places**: You can see photos according to the place or places that were taken in this display tab. The photos might also be arranged based on the location or setting in which they were shot.
- **Events**: In this view, you can build an image-based stack of events, each containing an event image. naming the pictures from the occasion and adding an event for a birthday celebration, for example.

- **Sort By**: You can use this feature to arrange your media according to the names, batches, and most current or oldest photos that have been loaded or imported into the organizer.

- **Filter**: This allows you to filter your media files by *Local Media, Synched Media,* or *All Media*.

- **Ratings/Auto Curate**: The rating feature's job is to assign a star rating to your image or media content. Another tool you may use to organize and categorize images and media files is a rating system. The Auto Curator is a tool that allows you to automatically examine an image and search for patterns in it.

- **Share**: The Home screen's far right side is where you'll find this. This button can be used to create and share collages, calendars, and other things.

- **The Sync Icons**: These two icons allow you to synchronize your media files to the cloud storage.

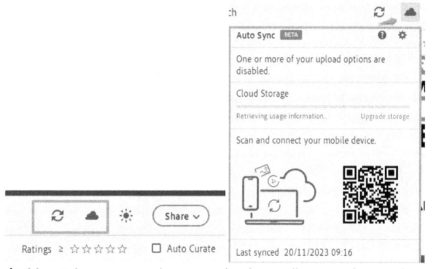

- **Album/Folder Tabs**: You can locate each photo album you've made in your organizer under the Album/Folder Tabs.

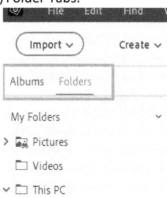

The following features below are located at the base of The Organizer`s workspace:

- **Hide Panel**: When you wish to view all of the photo thumbnails, you can use this option to hide the left panel in the Media Browser.
- **Undo/Rotate**: You can rotate an image both clockwise and counterclockwise with this option. By clicking on a little arrow, you can also undo or redo an action here.
- **Add Location**: This is the area in the Organizer where you can add a new venue. When you choose this option, the new place is added to the Places panel and a window displaying it appears at the top of the Organizer.
- **Add Event**: You can arrange photographs with this additional Organizer tool.
- **Instant Fix**: Using this tool makes it easier to apply Quick Edit edits to your images. With Instant Fix, you may modify lighting, crop, and address red-eye.
- **Editor**: With this symbol, you can go back to the picture editor.
- **Slideshow**: Click the Slideshow button to start a new project named Memory. In the Slideshow, the pictures are shown as videos.
- **Home Screen**: This button returns you to the Home screen when you click on it.
- **Browse Web**: This button leads you to the Beat version of Photoshop Elements.

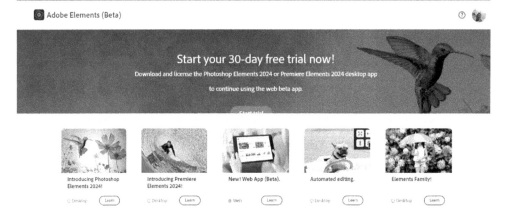

- **Zoom**: The Zoom function is used to enlarge or decrease the size of thumbnails.

The Media Browser in the Organizer

The Media Browser, which is located within the Organizer, displays thumbnails of every image or photo that is imported into the program in the center of the Organizer.

Images from a selected folder in the Media browser can be viewed in the *Import panel*.

On the left side of the Media browser is an Import panel with a list of folders, as seen below.

- **The List View**: The imported folders are all listed in alphabetical order in this view. There is no hierarchical structure to the files in the subdirectory. In the Media Browser, this is the default view by default.

- **The Tree View**: The Media Browser's photo gallery is arranged hierarchically when in this mode. Choose View as Tree from the Menu drop-down menu to switch to this view.

Click on the downward arrow to toggle between the two views.

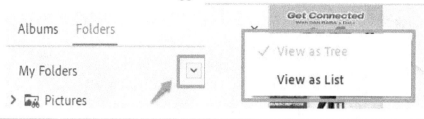

Arranging Pictures and Files on the Hard Disk

The majority of the hard disk is taken up by the media and photographs. For reference, all the photographs would need to be categorized if there were a lot of them. The best course of action is to designate a folder. The folder can have whatever name you like, including times, places, events, and so forth. You can now begin organizing the photos into folders after you're done.

One of the ways to organize your photos/media files on the Organizer is to tag them. Tags are an excellent way to keep your images sorted, and when your photos are categorized, they are usually easier to manage in the organizer. Among other things, an image's time of capture can be used for analysis and classification.

The **Tag/Info command button** can be located at the right-hand side of the workspace's base. Click on it to access the Tag Panels.

The Tag Panel is made up of four custom tags, namely, *Keywords, People Tags, Places Tags*, and *Events Tags*.

Do the following to create tags.

- Click on Your Media Browser and choose the pictures you want to tag.

- To add a new tag, click the drop-down arrow next to the **New button**, which is a plus symbol.

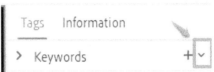

- Select "**New Category**" from the drop-down option.

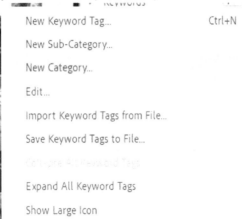

- Type the name of the tag in the **Name text field** and select an icon from the **Category Icon**.

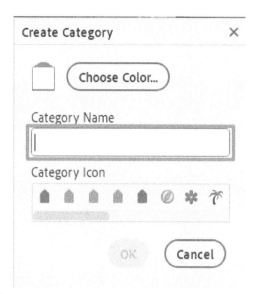

- After that, select **OK**.

Do the following to add icons to a tag.

- Go to the Tags area and click the **New button**.

- Select "**Edit Icon**."

- Click the **Import button** in the **Edit Keyword Tag Icon** dialog box to search through the folder for the image that should be used as the icon.

72

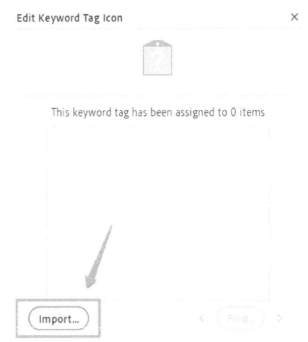

This keyword tag has been assigned to 0 items

Import... ⟨ Find... ⟩

This keyword tag has not been used but you may
import an icon for it

OK Cancel

- Pick the preferred picture, then select **Open**.

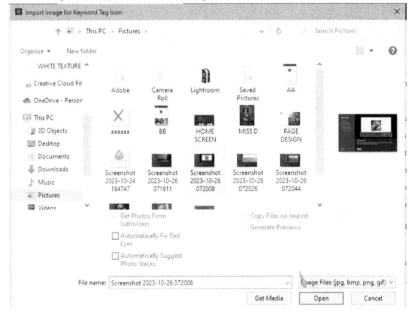

- Next, press the "**OK**" button.

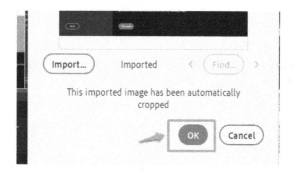

This imported image has been automatically cropped

Before we close this learning section tags, let us quickly explore the command features in the tag panel.

- **New Keyword Tag**: To create a new tag, utilize the New Keyword Tag.
- **New Sub-Category**: This tag is contained inside another tag. Use the procedures listed below to create a subcategory.
    - From the New menu, choose **Create New Sub-Category**.
    - Enter the new subcategory's name in the dialog box.
- **New Category**: You now have the choice to make a brand-new category. To create a new category, click New Category to bring up the dialog box, then enter the new category's name.
- **Edit**: The Edit Keyword dialog box can be accessed by selecting this option. This Edit option allows you to add icons to a tag.
- **Import Keyword Tags from File**: This comes in handy after spending a lot of time and energy organizing files, making a new catalog, importing pictures, and also

importing tags for the pictures. An XML file is linked to every tag, whether it is imported or exported.

- **Save Keywords to File**: This option allows you to save tags in a file and retrieve them at a later time. When you open a different catalog file, you can import the identical collection names that were created in that other catalog file.
- **Collapse All Keyword Tags**: You can use this feature to collapse the list in which the Tags are shown.
- **Expand All Keyword Tags**: This makes the list that contains the tag collapsed and larger.
- **Show Large Icon**: When this option is selected, the tags icon in the Tags panel transforms into a larger icon.

Importing Images to the Organizer

File import is another function of the Organizer. You must first save any picture you wish to add to your organizer to your computer's hard disk. There are two major ways of uploading images to the Organizer. You either use the **Import button** or you use the **Get Photos and Videos** from the **File Menu**.

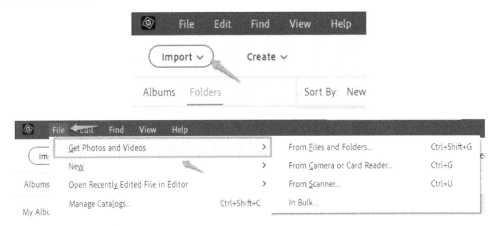

You can use the following methods to upload images from a camera or other device to your computer's hard drive; *From Files and Folders, From Camera/ Card Reader, From Scanner*, and *In Bulk...*

To import From Files and Folders, follow the instructions below.

- Navigate to the **File menu** in the Organizer, pick **Get Photo and Videos**, and then choose From **Files and Folder** on the right-hand side.

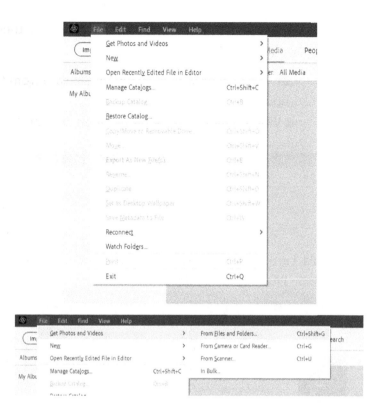

- Navigate your hard drive and choose the picture you want to include in the **Get Photo and Videos** dialog box. Then, press the **Get Media button**.

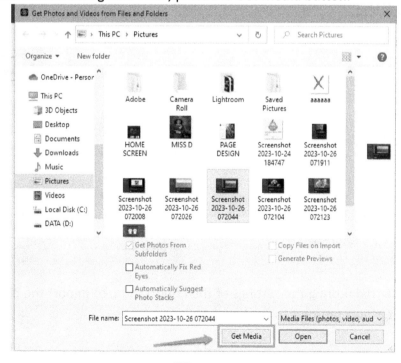

Another method to upload images to your organizer is to upload them from your camera. Carry out the following instructions to do that.

- To access the organizer window, either insert the media card from the camera or connect it to your computer through a USB port.
- Select **Get Photo and Videos** from the **File menu**, then click on **From Camera or Card Reader**.

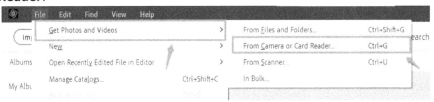

- Choose the media card from the drop-down list under the **Get Photos From section** of the Adobe Photo Downloader dialog box.

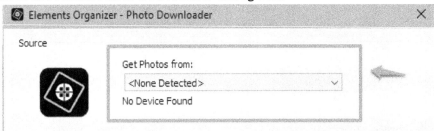

- To copy the image, select the **Browse option** and locate the folder you want to copy it to.

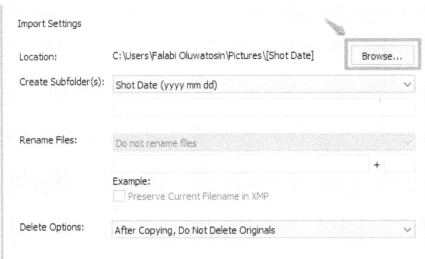

- After monitoring the settings of the importation, to import the pictures, click the **Get Media option**.

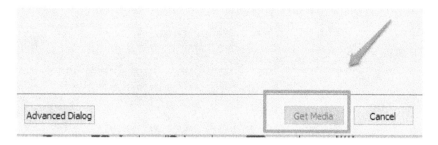

Using Photoshop Element's organizer, you can get scanner scans of your negatives, slides, and pictures. The same USB or FireWire connections can be used to connect the scanner to the card readers and camera.

To import From Scanner, do the following.

- Select **Get Photo and Videos** from the **File menu**, then click on **From Scanner**.

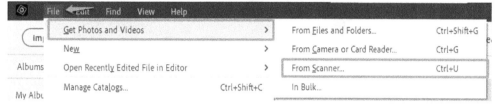

- Select the Scanner you are importing from in the **Get Photos From Scanner** dialog box.

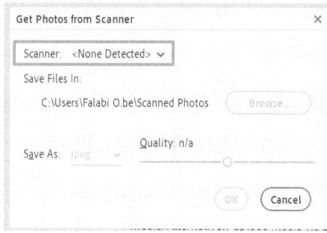

- Click on **Browse** to select the destination of the files you are importing.

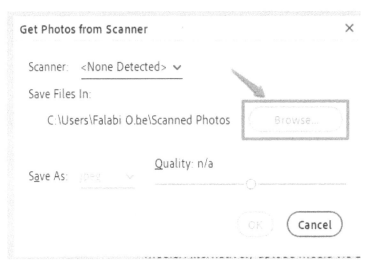

- Select the format you want to save your images in at **Save As**.

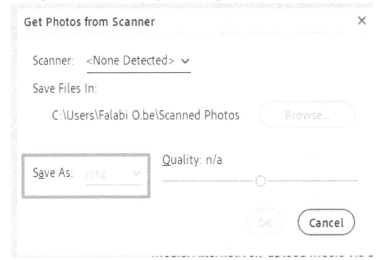

- Use the **Quality Slider** to determine the quality of your images.

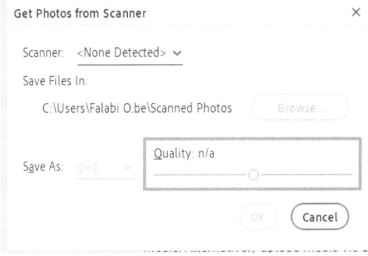

- Select **OK** once you are ready to import the images.

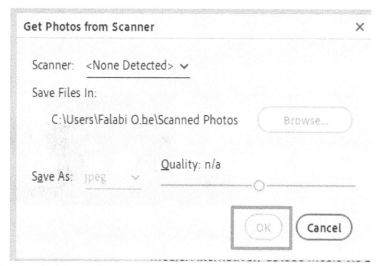

- Once you've made all the necessary changes to the scanned image, click the Scan button in the dialog box that appears.

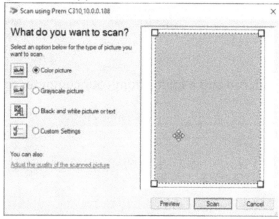

Do the following to import In Bulk.

- Select **Get Photo and Videos** from the **File menu**, then click on **In Bulk**.

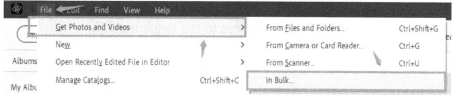

- Make sure the folders you want to import from are ticked/checked.

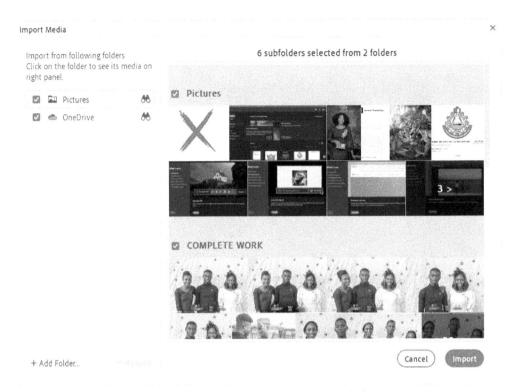

- Select Add Folder to add a folder from your computer to the organizer.

- Select **Import** to upload the images to the Organizer.

Before scanning, you can adjust the resolution and color settings on the scanner device. You have the option to select the resolution you want before scanning a file. To assist you in scanning, consider the following factors.

- **Color**: The most often scanned photographs are those that are colored. For photographs, set the scan resolution to 600 dpi; for the web, set it to 300 dpi. For colorful images, save the file as PNG.
- **Halftone**: These are small dots that make up these images. Tone mapping images need to be scanned at a DPI of 1200 or above for the scanner to properly capture the halftone.
- **Line Art**: This is a kind of picture where there are no colors or gradients—just lines and curves (shadings). Line art includes illustrations such as glyphs, comics, ideographs, and cartoons. It is advised to scan line art at 900 dpi for printing and 300 dpi for the internet.
- **Grayscale Images**: These are graphics that rely on gradients—such as various shades of black—instead of color to produce an image. Therefore, the grayscale image needs to be saved as a PNG file and scanned at 600 dpi or above.

In addition, to uploading images to the organizer with the methods discussed above, you may also transfer media files from several phones, such as iPhones, iPods, and other mobile devices. Use the instructions below to import photos from your phone into your organizer.

- Connect the devices with a USB cord.
- Go to **File,** select **Get Photos and Videos,** and click on **From Files and Folder**

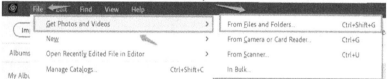

- Proceed to the organizer by first going through the folder where you copied the file on the device.

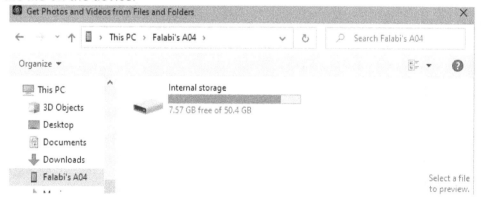

- Select the images you want to import and select **Get Media** to complete the importation into the organizer.

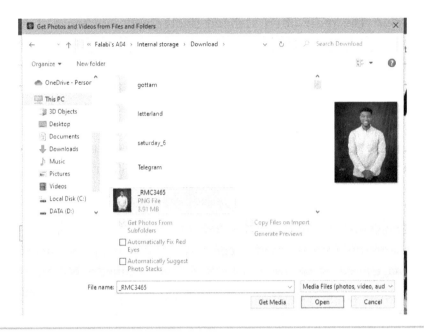

Working with Photo Albums in the Organizer

You can save and organize your photographs in albums similar to traditional albums with the Element Organizer. Your images can be arranged into albums based on several criteria, such as star ratings and tags. The album can include multiple photos, and each photo can be removed.

Do the following to create an album.

- Choose the pictures you want to include in the album. On the Organizer's left-hand side, select **Album**.

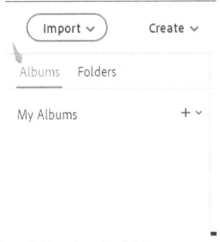

- Select **New Album** after clicking the plus (+) icon.

- In the panel on the right-hand side, type the album's name in the **Name text field** and select the album's category from the drop-down menu.

- Once you're done, click **OK**, and the pictures should show up on the left side of the Media browser.

NOTE: Any of the following actions can be taken to add images to an album:

- *Drag and drop the images from the Media view into the Album panel to create the album.*
- *Drag the album to the picture in the Media view from the Album panel.*
- *Additionally, you can pick the stack and drag it inside the album.*

Do the following to create an album category.

- On the Organizer's left-hand side, select **Album**.

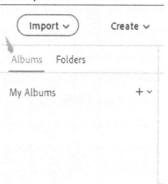

- Pick **New Album Category** after clicking on the downward arrow beside the plus (+) icon.

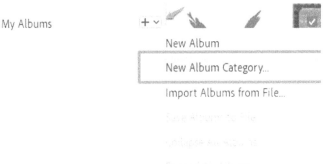

- Enter the name of the album and its category in the **Name text box** and **Category drop-down menu** on the right side of the panel, respectively.

- Then press **OK**.

To organize the pictures in your album, you can use chronological, reverse chronological, or album sorting techniques. The steps listed below can be utilized to arrange the photos within an album.

- From the Album and Folders panel, choose an album.

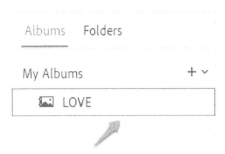

Choose any selection from the following choices in the Media view's **Sort By** drop-down menu.

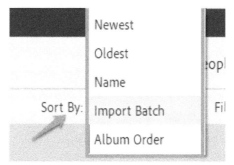

- o **Newest**: In this option, the images are sorted chronologically, starting with the newest.
- o **Oldest**: The pictures in this collection are presented chronologically in order of oldest to newest.
- o **Name**: Using this option, the media is alphabetized by name from A to Z.
- o **Import Batch**: Using this option, the images are arranged according to when they were imported into batches.
- o **Album Order**: This setting sets the photos in a way that best suits the user's tastes.

Double-click an album to see the photographs within an album.

You can use the instructions listed below to take an image out of an album.

- Select the picture with a right-click to remove it from the Album, then select **Remove From Album**

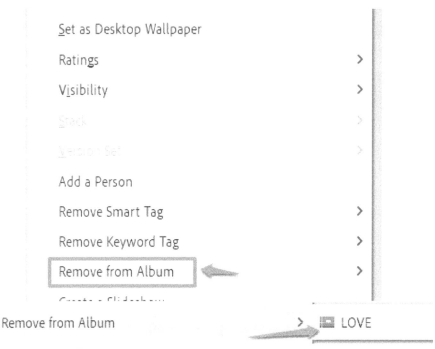

Remove from Album   >   ▢ LOVE

- Then, click "**Remove**."

You can use the instructions listed below to remove an album from the Album panel:

- After doing a right-click on the album, choose **Delete**.

- To delete the album, click **OK** in the Confirm Album Deletion dialog box.

Other Basic Operations in The Organizer

One of the basic operations in the organizer I will be introducing you to in this section is *Auto Curating.*

Visual similarity between photographs is what the Auto Curator searches for. The top photographs appear in the Media Browser after the tests are finished. To carry out this function, you need the least number of ten images.

The Organizer pane's upper-right corner contains the Auto Curator check box.

Next is *Auto Creation.*

To fully grasp the potential of Auto Creation, which you can use to produce a variety of events in your photographs, it is advisable to become acquainted with it.

- To enable Auto Creation, navigate to the **Edit menu**, pick **Preference**, **Media Analysis**, and finally **Generate Auto Creations**.

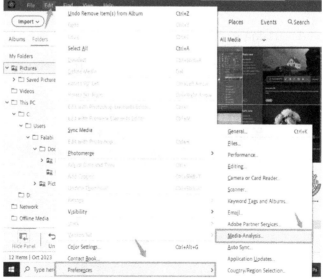

Another is *Ranking.*

Users can assign one to five stars to photographs in the Organizer to rank them. The lowest rating is one star, while the highest rating is five stars. Additionally, you have the option to arrange your photos based on ratings. To assign a star to a picture, do the following.

- Using the Media Browser, pick the image
- To rate something, use the "Ratings" tab on the right side of the screen and select one or two stars.

Lastly, we will be discussing *Adding Events.*

You can add a new event in your Media Browser. To accomplish this, simply do the following.

- Click **Add New Event** in the organizer's lower left corner.

- Once the name, start date, end date, and description have been entered as they appear in the dialogue window, click **Done**.

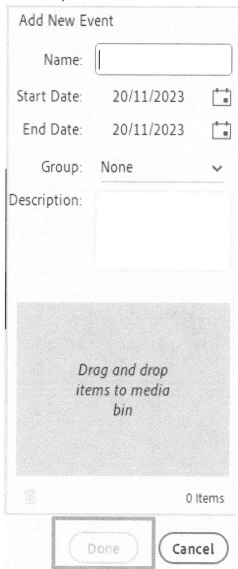

The Organizer`s preference settings

To configure the organizer settings, just follow the steps below.

- Click the **Edit menu**, then choose **Preference**.

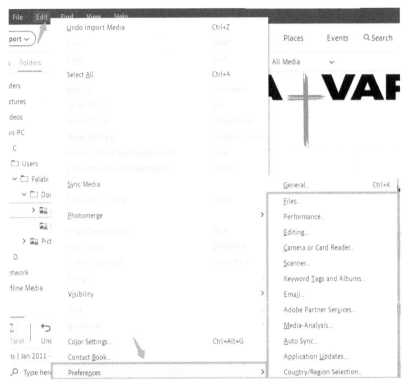

- You can adjust the Organizer Preference in the dialog box. Once finished, select "**Ok.**"

CHAPTER FOUR

PERFORMING MORE OPERATIONS WITH THE ORGANIZER

This chapter will mostly cover the catalog and how to view and organize your photographs in the Organizer.

Working with Catalogs

The organizer names the default catalog My Catalog. A catalog is a file in the Element that has a record of all the imported files. When media is loaded, the catalog immediately updates with basic information about the imported item, like its location and filename.

The Basic information that a catalog carries are:

The address and name of any related audio files, the location of the original, high-resolution file, together with the volume name and filename, the location and file name of the original, unmodified version. The name of the scanner or camera that is attached to the collection of imported media files, and captions being added to the media file. The changes made to the notes in the media file, The media file, which contains projects, photos, videos, and audio files, The time and date of the media file's creation Including the media file with keyword tags, The media file is stored within the album. A media file's background. The pixel count of every picture and video file. The parameters of the project. Pixel dimensions, EXIF, copyright, IPTC data, and file format information are examples of metadata. The changes are applied to the media file. Among the editing techniques employed include cropping, rotating, and red-eye removal.

The catalog manager is where catalogs are added, deleted, and controlled. All you need to do to create a catalog is follow the simple guidelines provided below.

Do the following to create a catalog.

* Locate and select **Manage Catalogs** from the **File menu.**

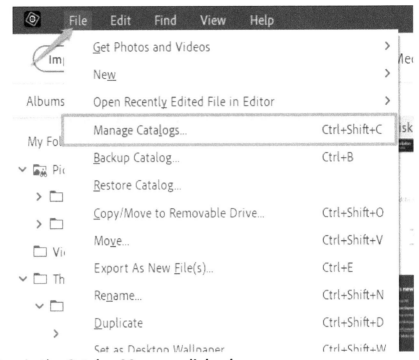

- Click **New** in the **Catalog Manager dialog box**.

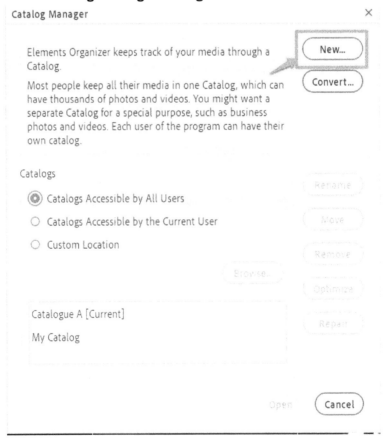

- In the **File Name text box**, provide the name of the new catalog, and then select **OK**.

Do the following to add images/photographs to your newly created catalog.

- From the **File Menu**, select **Get Photos and Videos**.

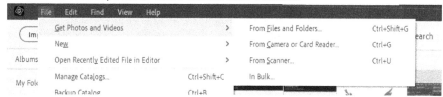

- From the **Get Photo and Videos dialog box**, select the desired images and click on **Get Media** to import the images.

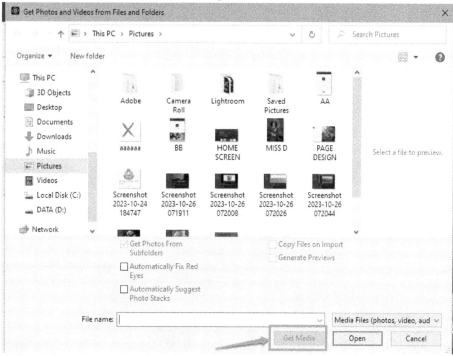

Launching/Opening a catalog is as simple as the breeze, follow the procedures below to open a catalog.

- Locate and select **Manage Catalogs** from the **File menu**.

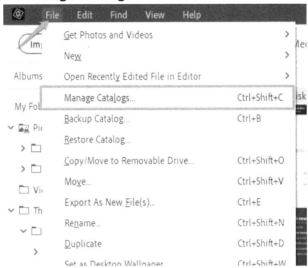

- Click on the catalog you desire to open in the Catalog Manager dialog box.

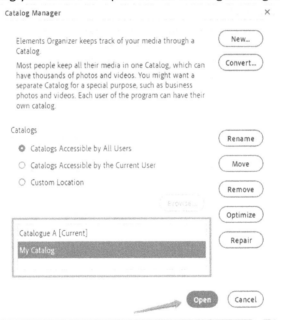

- Next, select **Open**.

Building and maintaining a catalog is not nearly as crucial as backing one up. You can eliminate the worry of data loss due to device damage or error by backing up your catalog. While backing up your library is possible on both Mac and Windows computers, backing up the Elements catalog is limited to Windows computers and requires a CD or DVD.

To back up your catalog, take the steps listed below:

- From the **File Menu**, select **Backup Catalog** or use **Ctrl+B**

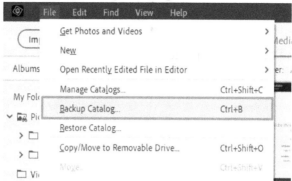

- Select an option from the list below to open the Backup Catalog dialog box, then click the Next button.

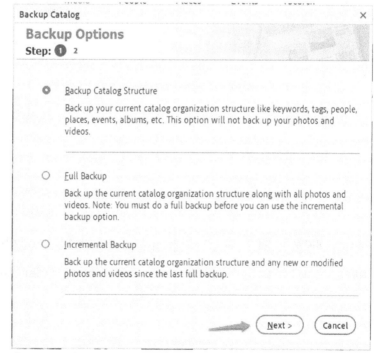

- o **Backup Catalog Structure**: You can back up your catalog's structure, including its tags, users, locations, and events, using this option. In this case, the backup does not contain the pictures and videos.
- o **Full Backup**: This option is selected when you are going to do your first backup or write files to a new media source. This option, to put it

briefly, backs up all of the content in your collection, including the pictures and photos.

- o **Incremental Backup**: This option is selected when you have finished at least one backup and would like to update the files you have backed up.
- Click the desired drive letter to select the **Destination Drive** on the next screen.

  Browse to find the location where the backup catalog should be saved.

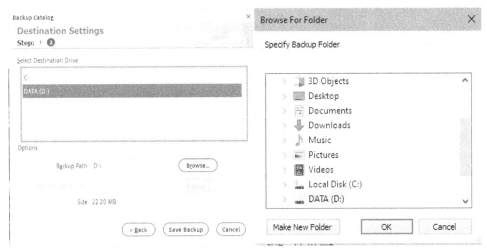

- Ultimately, use the **Save Backup button** to complete the backup by clicking on it.

You can use the following steps to create a backup of your files and photos:

- Navigate to the **Copy/Move to Removable** option under the File menu.

- Select **Yes** in the next dialog box that pops up.

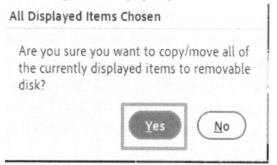

- Click **Copy Files** in the dialog box that appears, then choose **Next**.

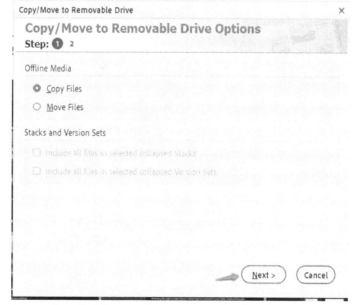

- After choosing a hard drive and entering the backup folder's name, click **Done**.

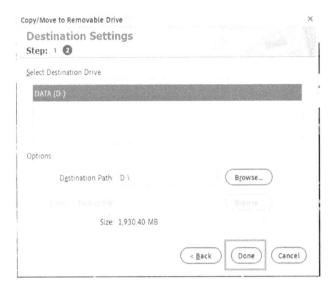

Do the following to restore a backed-up catalog.

- To access the Restore Catalog, navigate to **File** and select **Restore Catalog**.

- From the dialog box that appears, select **CD/DVD**, **Hard Drive/Other Volume**. If you selected a hard drive as your backup location, click **Browse** to locate it.

- Once the backup file has been chosen, click **Browse** in the **Restore Files** and Catalog to specify where the backup file should be restored.

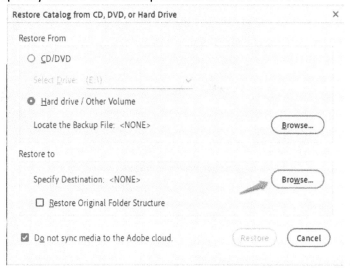

- If you want to keep the files in the catalog, you can select **Restore Original Folder Structure**.

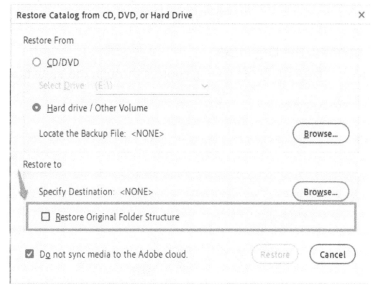

- Next, press the **Restore button**.

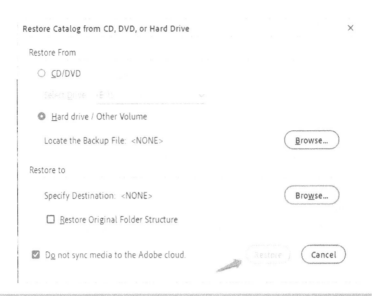

File Handling in the Organizer

Without a doubt, catalogs are composed of files, and we will address additional management and handling of the media file in the organizer in this portion of the chapter.

Viewing Options in the Organizer

You have access to a variety of viewing choices through the View tab on the Organizer.

Go to the View tab and choose any of the following to view various viewing choices.

- **Media Types**: With this option, you can swap out the PDF, audio, and video files in the Media Browser for images and vice versa. Select the Media Brower option from View, then choose the submenu.
- **Hidden Files**: In the View tab, you can now hide your files. Go to View and choose All Files to view every file.
- **Details**: File attributes like star ratings and creation dates are hidden by default. To display a file's details, pick Details from the View menu.
- **File Names**: By selecting Files Names under View in the Media browser, you may see the filenames of your photos. The filenames of photos are not shown by default.
- **Timeline**: You can choose the time the picture was taken by dragging the slider to the left or right on the horizontal bar at the top of the organizer. To utilize this feature, select View and then Timeline.

Hiding and Stacking Images

When working on files straight from the Organizer, you may choose to hide some files, including pictures. To do this, all you have to do is adhere to the guidelines given below;

- After choosing the files you want to keep hidden, navigate to the **Visibility** menu in the **Edit menu**, then choose **Mark as Hidden**.

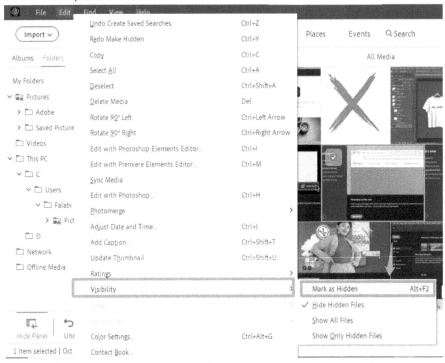

- Use the previously mentioned procedures to reveal the files, then select **Show Hidden**.

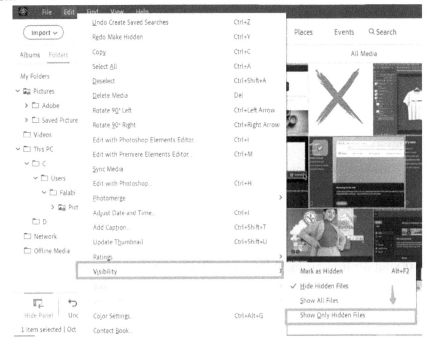

You can stack the photos in the Organizer to arrange them in the order you'd like. Only the first selected image is shown when stacking photographs; the other images are hidden behind it.

Use the instructions listed below to stack your images:

- Select the photographs you want to stack in the Organizer. Then, go to the **Edit menu**, click on **Stack**, and choose **Stack Selected Photos**.

Image Search in the Organizer

You may need to search the Element when searching for your photos in the same location where you saved them.

When browsing through pictures, the Search Icon should be your primary priority. The search bar for the Media Browser is located in the top right corner. The Search symbol has a text field and a magnifying glass on it. To find the image, enter its name into the Search icon.

A window with a list of parameters to conduct your search appears on the left side of the screen when you click the Search icon.

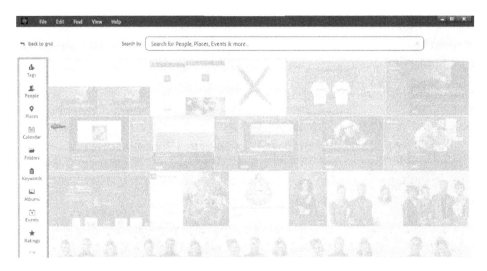

A summary of your most recent searches can be seen in the **Recent Searches section**. To view your past search history, click the search text bar.

Working with the Find Menu

Aside from using the Search icon to locate images, the Find Menu is a crucial set of command options used to search and locate images in the organizer. To access these select **Find** from the **Menu** Bar.

Do the following to search by details.

- From the **Menu Bar** select **Find** and click on **By Details (Metadata).**

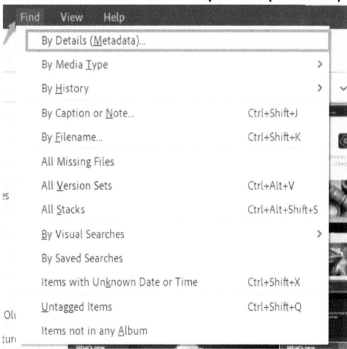

- In the dialog box that appears, input your search criteria and click on **Search**.

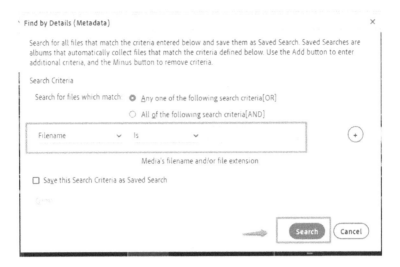

Do the following to search by Media Type.

- After selecting **Media Type** from the **Find Menu,** select the means of search from the options drop-list.

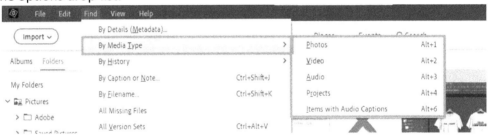

Do the following to search by History.

- After selecting **History** from the **File** Menu, select the means of search and browse through the history list.

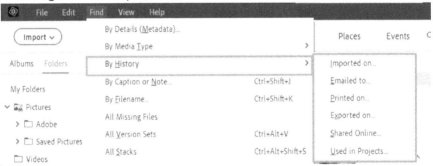

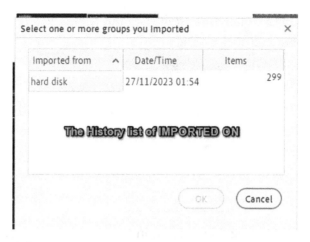

Do the following to search by Captions or Notes.

- After selecting By **Captions or Notes** from the **Find Menu**, insert the caption/note you want to search with into the text box.

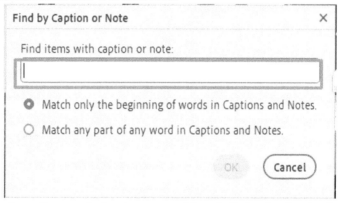

- Select any option of your choice between *Match Only the Beginning of words in Captions and Notes*, and *Match any part of any word in Captions and Notes*. Then click **OK**.

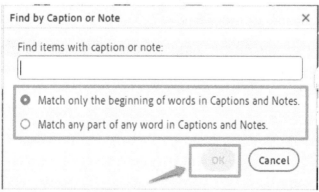

Do the following to search by Filename.

- After selecting By **Filename** from the **Find Menu**, insert the name of the file into the search bar and click on **Ok**.

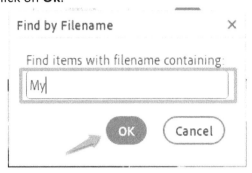

You can use the **All Missing Files** option in the Find Menu to access missing files from the organizer.

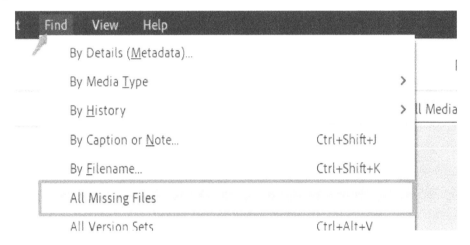

Using the **All Version Sets** option allows you to display the best pictures from each set. This allows you to enlarge each collection to your size. Use the All Version Set by following the guidelines provided below.

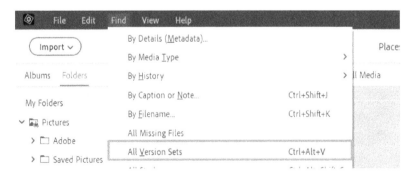

Do the following to search by visual search.

- After selecting By **Visual Search** from the **Find Menu**, select either of the three available options for search.

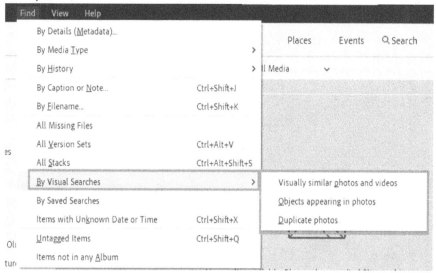

- Select any image (the image you're searching with) and click on the **plus icon (+)** to search.

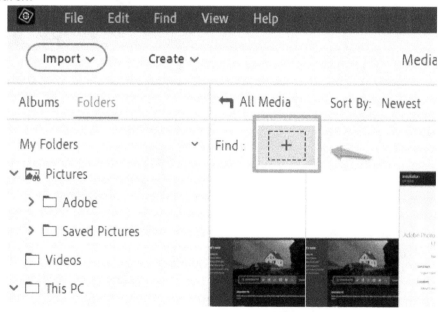

Using By Saved Searches option to search for an image is only possible when you have saved the criteria of your previous searches while using the Metadata mode of search.

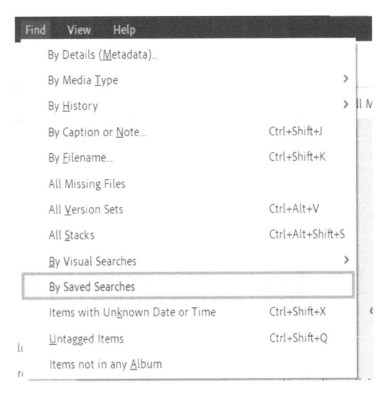

Do the following to search by Saved Searches.

- From the **Find Menu**, select **By Saved Searches**.

- If you don`t have any search saved, select **New Search Query** to input a new one that you can access anytime.

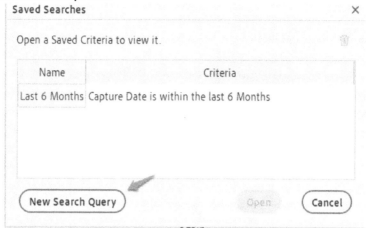

- Select any of the saved searches you have in the **Saved Searches Dialog box** and click **Open** to access the media files there.

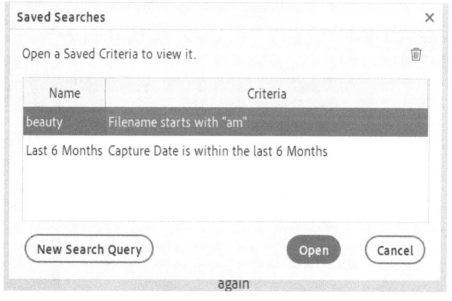

In some cases where some of your files have unknown dates and timelines, select **Items With Unknown Date Or Time** on the **Find Menu** to search for such media files.

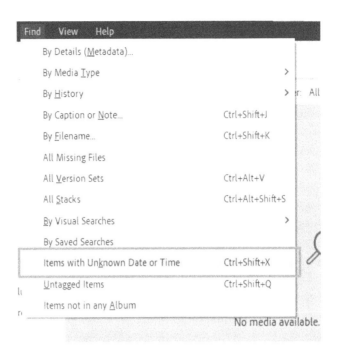

To locate files that are untagged in the organizer, use the *Untagged Items search option* to search for such files. Select **Untagged items** from the **File Menu** to do such.

To find media files that are not categorized into any album, Select **Items not in any Album** from the **Find Menu.**

115

BOOK SECTION 3

THE PHOTO EDITOR

CHAPTER FIVE- CHAPTER TWELVE

- ❖ FUNDAMENTAL TRUTHS ABOUT IMAGE EDITING
- ❖ BASIC OPERATIONS IN PHOTOSHOP ELEMENTS 2024
- ❖ LAYERS IN THE PHOTO EDITOR
- ❖ SELECTION TOOLS AND SELECTIONS
- ❖ BASIC EDITING OPERATIONS
- ❖ WORKING WITH COLORS
- ❖ PAINTING TOOLS IN PHOTOSHOP ELEMENTS
- ❖ TEXTS AND SHAPES

CHAPTER FIVE

FUNDAMENTAL TRUTHS ABOUT IMAGE EDITING

Image Editing Concepts

In this chapter, we will be discussing basic concepts every designer needs to understand regardless of his/her scope of field or level of knowledge in the design industry.

Understanding Pixels

Before you can modify pictures with Photoshop Element, you must understand pixels.

Pixels are the fundamental units of all digital images. All digital images are built upon these tiny building blocks. The term "pixel" is the abbreviated form of "picture element."

The pixels in a photo are usually too small to see when viewed at a regular zoom level (100 percent or less), but when we zoom in closer, we see several tiny squares. Below is a close-up of the image that shows visible pixels.

What Resolution Is

The image resolution of an image controls or affects the size at which the image will be reproduced about its current size.

The amounts of pixels in an image file determines the picture resolution, which is expressed in pixels per inch (PPI). If a 1-inch horizontal line contains 200 pixels, the picture resolution will be 200 PPI.

Printed Images and **Screen Images** are the two major form of images that depends on resolution.

When printing images, a resolution of 300 PPI is advised. An excessively high image resolution causes the printer to take too long to process the data it receives, and an excessively low image resolution results in poor print quality.

When it comes to the images on a screen, the monitor that is being used determines the image resolution.

Resolution on Screens and in Prints

Selecting the right resolution for your photograph is essential before printing or exhibiting it. This is to ensure that the images are of high quality.

Whereas the printer resolution is expressed in ink dots per inch (dpi), the display resolution is expressed in pixels per inch (PPI)

The recommended print and onscreen resolutions for a range of output devices are listed below.

Output Device	Acceptable Resolution	Optimum Resolution
Tablet devices and smartphones	150 PPI	150 + PPI
Screen image (web, slide show, video)	72 PPI	72 PPI
Magazine quality (offset press)	225 PPI	300 PPI
Desktop laser printer (Black and white)	100 PPI	170 PPI
Professional photo lab printer	200 PPI	300 PPI
Large-format inkjet printer	120 PPI	150 PPI
Desktop color inkjet and laser printers	180 PPI	300 PPI

Image Dimensions

The width and height of the image are referred to as the picture dimension. Pixels are the default measurement type for picture dimensions; however, additional units, including Inches, Percentages, Centimeters, Millimeters, Points, and Picas, may also be displayed.

The ideal location to view the image's dimensions and resolution is the Image Size dialog box. You can also adjust an image's size using the Image Size dialog box.

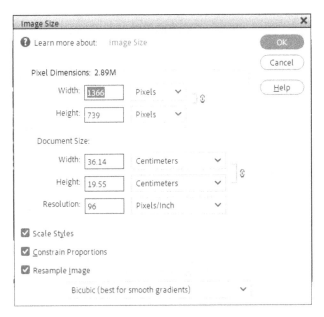

To access the Image Size dialog box, do the following.

- Use the **Image Menu** to select **Resize**.

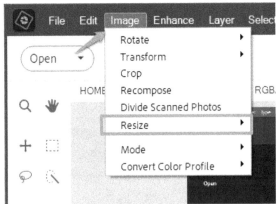

- Next, select **Image Size** from the menu.

- The Image Size dialog box appears on this page with the ability to adjust the parameters.

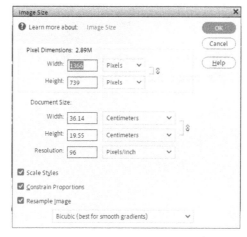

You can modify the image in four different ways using the Image Size dialog box.

- **Pixel Dimensions**: This speaks to the height and width of the image.
- **Image Size**: This is the value that shows the size of the image at the top of the dialog box.
- **Document Size**: This refers to the actual size of the image when printed.
- **Image Resolution**: This is how many pixels there are per inch when the image is printed.

Resampling Images

The technique of adding or removing pixels from a file to change its size is known as resampling. The quantity of pixels is decreased during down-sampling and raised during up-sampling.

Notably, each resample results in a decrease in the shot quality. To avoid resampling, you can create a picture or scan one at a respectably high quality.

Do the following to resample images.

- Select **Image Size** from the **Image Menu**.

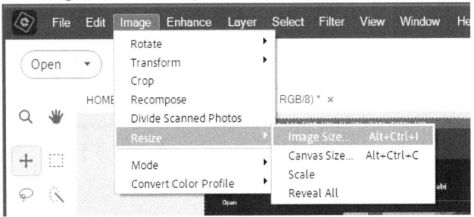

- Click the Resample Image check box and choose any of the **resampling techniques** from the **Image Size** dialog box.

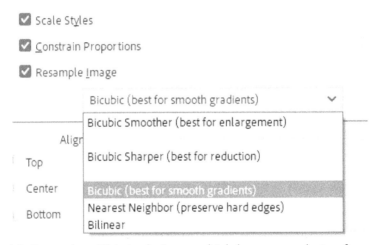

- ○ **Bicubic Smoother**: This technique, which has somewhat softer edges, is an improvement on the Bicubic method. This is the way to use when you want to up-sample a photo.
- ○ **Bicubic Sharper**: This method works best when down-sampling a picture because it produces a high-quality image and result.
- ○ **Bicubic**: This resampling method is the default and yields respectable results. It is the best for smooth gradients.
- ○ **Nearest Neighbor**: This resampling method is used when you wish to merge many files that share the same color into a single, smaller file. The fastest process out there is this one.

- o **Bilinear**: This method works well for line art and grayscale images, producing images of a moderate quality.
- You can use the **Scale Styles** checkbox in the **Image Size** dialog box to apply various style effects to the image.
- Select the **Constraint Proportions** checkbox to preserve the current aspect ratio.

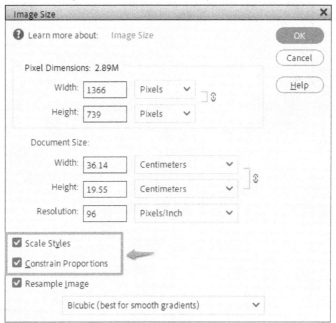

- Lastly, press the **OK** button.

Introduction to Color Usage

It is necessary to understand RGB (Red, Green, and Blue) to apply color in Adobe Photoshop Elements.

The primary or major colors used in Element are the RGB colors, also referred to as the additive primaries. These colors are used in displays, lighting, and video. RGB colors make up the color channels.

A particular channel's color data is stored in its color channels. Information regarding the colors red, green, and blue is stored in the red channel, green is stored in the green channel, and so on a scale from 0 to 255. For instance, the area in the red channel that seems whiter or brighter has more red in it than the darker area.

Follow these steps to view the color channels.

- Select **Adjust Lighting** from the **Enhance Menu**. Then, click on **Levels** to open the **Levels dialog box**.

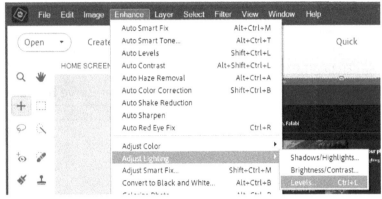

- The Level Dialog box is displayed below with color channels marked out.

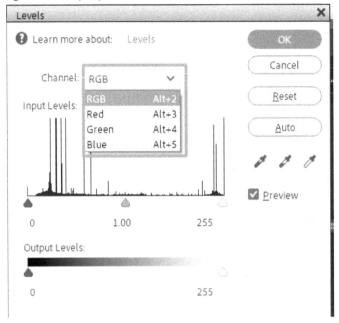

Monitor Calibration

The process of measuring and changing the colors on your computer monitor to match a common standard is called monitor calibration. If your monitor isn't calibrated, you might not be able to see colors on the screen accurately, which could lead to issues with how photos seem when printed or on other devices. A general color cast in your image, which appears flat or washed out on other devices, is one indication that your monitor needs to be calibrated.

You must utilize a Spectrophotometer, which is a device that maintains the color of images through computer software to calibrate your monitor.

Although there are a few ways to calibrate the monitor, a spectrometer is the most precise and efficient option. An ICC (International Color Consortium) profile is created and stored using this screen-hung device, which measures colors, brightness, contrast, and gamma in conjunction with computer software.

When using the spectrometer to calibrate the monitor, all colors and grayscales will appear on the screen. The spectrometer will capture these colors and grayscales and use them to produce an ICC profile that is saved on the computer.

The steps listed below will help you calibrate your monitor.

- Before utilizing the monitor, leave it for a minimum of twenty to thirty minutes to warm up, and make sure that neither ambient light nor daylight is shining directly on it.
- Place the spectrometer on top of the screen after connecting it to the computer via USB.
- Comply with the on-screen instructions provided by the software and wait for it to finish.

The color workspace, which can be either sRGB or Adobe RSG, needs to be specified after the monitor has been calibrated. To go to the color workplace settings, follow the instructions below.

- Select **Color Settings** from the drop-down menu under the **Edit menu.**

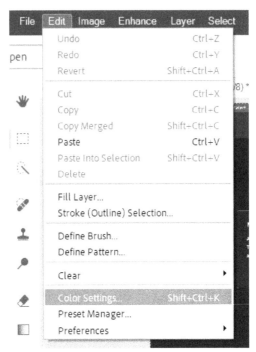

- Select any option from the **Color Settings** dialog box.
    - o **No Color Management**: The display profile is utilized as the working space and all color management is turned off when this option is chosen. This option removes embedded profiles from photos when opening and does not apply tags upon storing.
    - o **Always Optimize Colors for Computer Screens**: When this option is selected, the ratio button is used to set the workspace to sRGB. For printing and viewing photographs on a monitor, the sRGB color space works well.
    - o **Always Optimize for Printing**: You can use this option to change your workspace to Adobe RGB (1998), which when you open untagged files, assigns Adobe RGB and keeps embedded profiles. Because of the color, new monitors and inkjet printers function well in this setting. It is by default configured to this setting.
    - o **Allow Me to Choose**: When opening untagged files, you can choose between sRGB and Adobe RGB with this option.

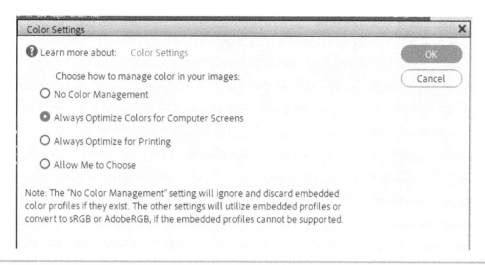

Working With Color Profiles

All color devices in your system need to have precise ICC-compliant profiles to manage color accurately and consistently. For instance, if a specific monitor profile is missing, the image that is seen on the screen may appear differently. This calls for a thorough profile to avoid false depiction, which is time and effort-consuming.

The various profile types that we offer are:

- **Document Profile**: This provides information about the page's exact RGB or CMYK color space. When you tag or assign a profile to a document, the application displays an explanation of the document's true color look. When Color Management is enabled, Adobe applications choose the profile to apply to a new document based on the selections made in the Color Settings dialog box regarding Working Space. Untagged documents are just given a raw color number; no profile has been applied to them. The Adobe application displays and modifies colors based on the current working space profile when working with untagged documents.
- **Monitor Profile**: You should establish the monitor profile first since it allows you to view the color on the display with accuracy. This clarifies why a color is now visible on the monitor.
- **Input Device Profile**: The color that the input device may capture or scan is specified in the input device profile. Adobe recommends utilizing Adobe RGB or sRGB when a digital camera allows for profile selection (the default option).
- **Output Device**: This describes the color space used by output devices, such as printing presses and desktop printers. The output device is used by the color management system to map document colors to the color space of the output

device. It is important to include any specific printing factors, including the kind of paper and ink, in the output profile.

CHAPTER SIX

BASIC OPERATIONS IN PHOTOSHOP ELEMENTS 2024

Learning The Essentials of Image Editing in Photoshop Elements

This chapter will teach you how to use Photoshop Elements to create outstanding designs and the fundamentals of practical operations to create outstanding projects.

This provides information about the page's exact RGB or CMYK color space. When you tag or assign a profile to a document, the application displays an explanation of the document's true color look. When Color Management is enabled, Adobe applications choose the profile to apply to a new document based on the selections made in the Color Settings dialog box regarding Working Space. Untagged documents are just given a raw color number; no profile has been applied to them. The Adobe application displays and modifies colors based on the current working space profile when working with untagged documents.

Creating/Opening Your First Document

To start a new document, you can either open an existing image or photograph in your photo editor, or you can start from scratch and create a blank canvas on which you can draw any design you need.

To open a photograph, do the following.

- Launch the Photo Editor.
- Select the **Open button** or select **Open** from the File Menu.

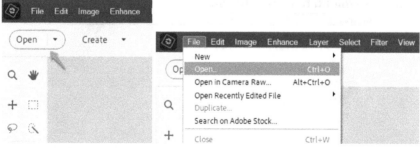

- Select the image of your choice from the Open Dialog box, then click on **Open**.

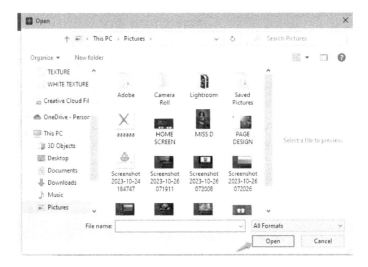

To open photographs in Camera Raw, do the following.

- From the **File Menu**, select **Open in Camera Raw.**

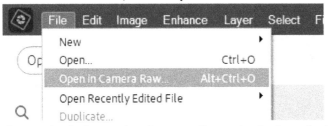

- If you don't have the Camera Raw plugin installed on your PC, Photoshop Elements pops up a dialog box asking you to download the Camera Raw plugin.

  Select **Download** to install the Plugin.

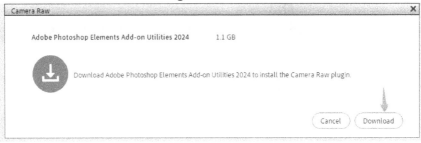

- Follow the subsequent instructions displayed on the screen to install the Camera Raw Plug-in.
- The Camera Raw opens up once it is installed.

Do the following to open recently edited files.

- From the **File Menu**, Select **Recently Edited Files** and click on the file you desire to open again.

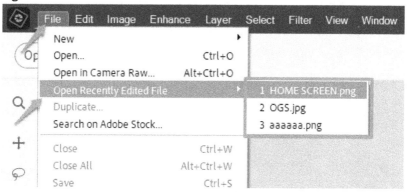

Do the following to create a new document for design in Photoshop Elements.

- From the File Menu, Select **New** and click on **Blank File** or use the shortcut **Ctrl+N**

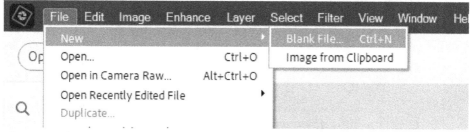

- The New document Dialog box appears

o Insert the name of the new file in the **Name Bar**.

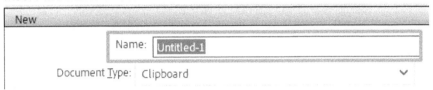

o Specify the document type in **Document Type**.

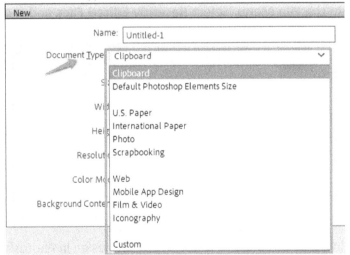

o Adjust the size of the new document by inserting new sizes into the **Width** box and **Height** box.

o Click on the downward arrow beside Pixels to change the unit of measurement.

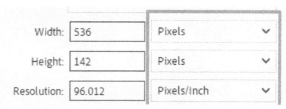

o Adjust the quality of the new document by inserting new figures into the **Resolution** bar.

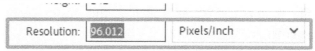

o Adjust the Color mode of the new document by toggling the **Color Mode** bar.

o Use **Background Content** to determine what your canvas will look like.

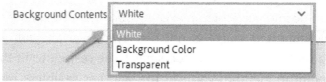

o Use **Save Preset** to save your modified settings on the system so it can be easily accessible next time.

• After adjusting your settings for the new document, select OK to create the new document.

• The New document appears on the Image Window upon creation.

Often, using the drag-and-drop approach is the easiest way to import images into Photoshop Elements.

- Drag a picture from Explorer or your desktop onto the Photoshop Element interface after opening the program.
- To start a new document, release the left mouse button.
  The image's resolution, width, length, and color mode are all the same in the containing document as they were in the source.

Importing Media Files into Existing Documents/Projects

A picture can be imported into an existing document by simply dragging and dropping it. If the newly imported image is not displayed over the full width and height of the document after import, it can be too small to be resized to fit the document. Aside from the drag-and-drop method, you can use another seamless method. To do so, do the following.

- Select the **File Menu** and click on **Place**.
  This will lead you to your File Manager.

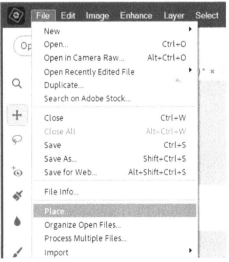

- Select an image and click on **Place**.

133

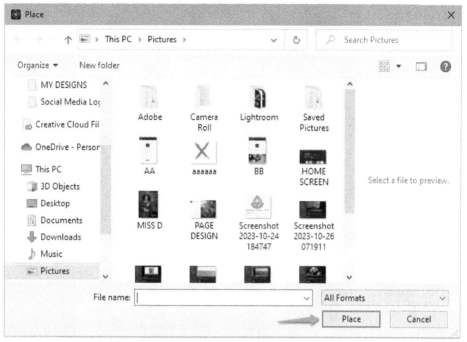

- Resize the imported file to your desired size and click on the done icon to apply the size edit.

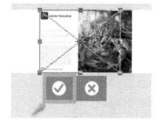

Creating Photo Projects

The Create button allows you to create photo projects by merging two or more images using any format of your choice: *Slideshows, Photo Collage, Photo Reel, Quote Graphic, Photo Prints, Photo Books, Greeting Card*, and *Photo Calendar*.

Photo Projects Format (.pse) is the format in which photo projects are stored. The photo projects can be shared via email, saved to your hard drive, or printed using your home printer.

- After opening the Photo Editor/ Organizer, select **Create** to access Photo Projects.

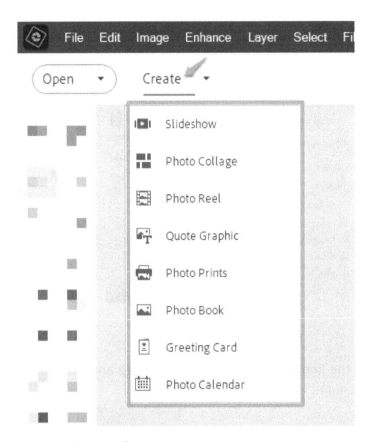

Do the following to create a photo collage.

- Open Photoshop Elements and select two or more images. You can choose up to eight images to make a collage.
- Select **Create** and click on **Photo Collage**

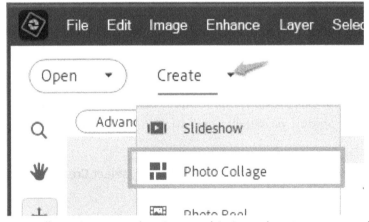

- After a photo collage is created using sophisticated auto-crop, and the most noticeable element of the photo (face) is targeted and placed in the collage

135

frames, which are automatically constructed based on the number of open photos., choose a **Layout** for your collage of photos at the right side of the workspace.

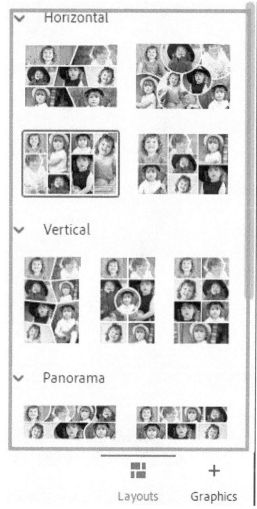

- To select a backdrop or frame, click **Graphics** in the lower-right corner of the screen, and double-click on the background or frame to add it to your collage.

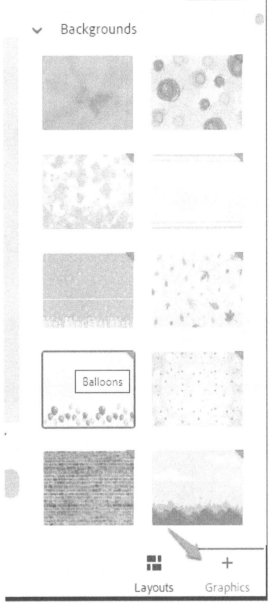

- By selecting **Computer** or **Organizer** on the **Add Photos From** dialog box (located at the right-hand side of the workspace), you can upload more pictures to your photo collage.

- To carry out basic operations, such as **Rotate 90 Right, Rotate 90 Left, Drag to Swap Photo, Change Background, Replace Photo**, and **Remove Photo**, all you have to do is right-click on the image you desire to modify.

Do the following to create a photo reel.

- After selecting two or more images, click on **Create** and select **Photo Reel**.

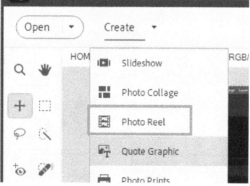

- By selecting **Computer** or **Organizer** on the **Add Media From** dialog box (located at the right-hand side of the workspace), you can upload more pictures and videos to your photo reel.

- The tools available in the Photo Reel workspace are **Zoom Tool, Hand Tool, Move Tool,** and **Text Tool**. You can use either of these to modify your project.

- Click on **Timeline** to view and edit the duration of each photograph during the photo reel.

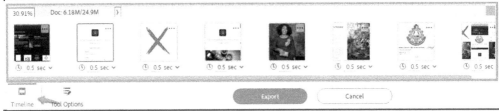

Click on the downward arrow to adjust the duration of each photograph.

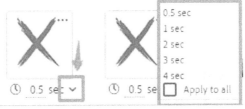

- Select **Layout** from the right side of the workspace to adjust the layout size of your Photo Reel to your taste.

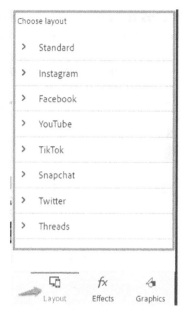

- Select options from **Effects** at the right side of the workspace to apply effects to each media.

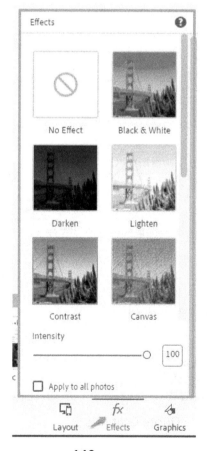

- Select **Apply to All Photos** to apply a single effect to all the images in your Photo Reel and adjust the **Intensity Slider** to modify the intensity of the effects on the photos.

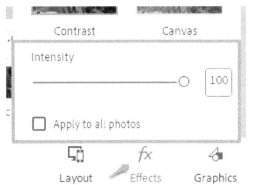

- Add clip art and emojis to your photos by selecting design objects from **Graphics**.

- Click on **Export** to save your photo reel.

Do the following to create a Quote Graphics.

- After selecting **Create**, click on **Quote Graphics.**

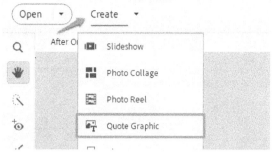

- From the dialog box, you can either **Start from the Scratch**, **Start With a Photo**, or pick from the existing template.

- Set the template size of your project after selecting any of the options mentioned above.

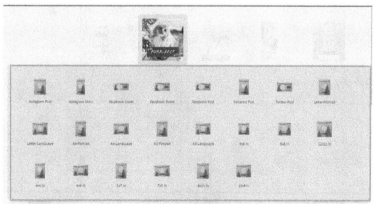

- Located at the right-hand side of the workspace, use the available doorways in **Add Photos From** to add more photographs to your projects.

- Choose any background effect of your choice for, the **Background Panel**.

- Select the **Text Panel** to add test styles, edit texts, add texts, and determine the text size.

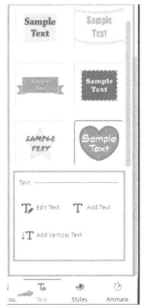

You can also add shapes, styles, and graphics through the **Text Window**, located at the top of the **Text Panel**.

143

- Use the **Styles Panel** to add style effects to your **Quote Graphics**.

- Bring your text to life by using **Animate**. You can select from any of the available presets.

- After you are done with your edits, select **Done** to apply your changes and click on **Save** to save and export your Project.

Do the following to create a photo book.

- From the options that display on your screen after clicking on **Create**, select **Photo Book**.

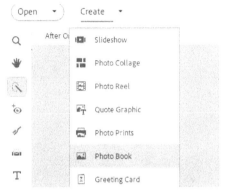

- Fill out the Photo Book dialog box by doing the following, then click OK:

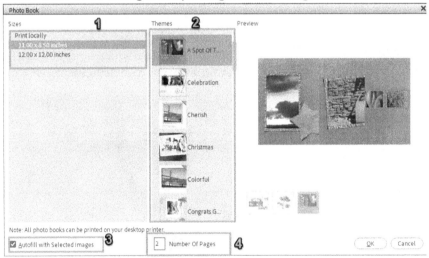

1. Decide on the photo book's size.
2. Decide on a theme.
3. To use the photographs you have selected in the Photo Bin, select Autofill with selected images.
4. Indicate how many pages the picture book will have (between 2 and 78).

- In the lower-right corner of the project, the following options are available: The picture book's pages are displayed by **Pages**.

How the picture book is organized is displayed by **Layout**.

Graphics allow you to alter the photo book's background, frames, and other visual elements. If needed, include graphics.

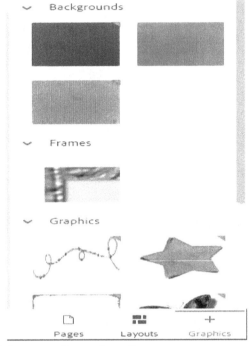

- After you`re done with your edits, select **Save** to save your project.

Do the following to create Greeting Cards.

- Select **Create** and click on **Greeting Card.**

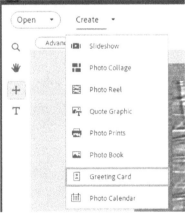

- In the Greeting Card dialog box, complete the following actions and press **OK**:

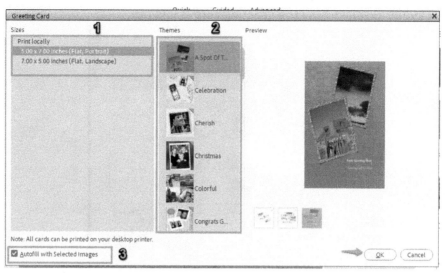

1. Choose the greeting card's size.
2. Decide on a theme.
3. To use the photographs you have selected in the Photo Bin, select Autofill with selected images.

- In the lower-right corner of the project, the following options are available:
  Pages: Displays the greeting card's pages.

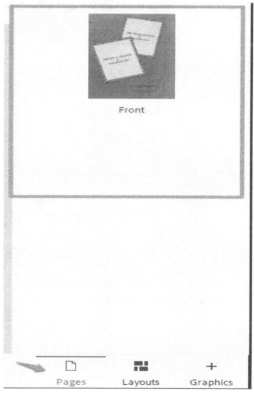

Layout: Displays how the greeting card is laid out.

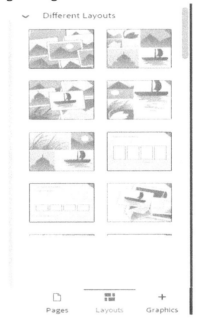

Graphics: This allows you to alter the greeting card's backdrop, frames, and graphics.

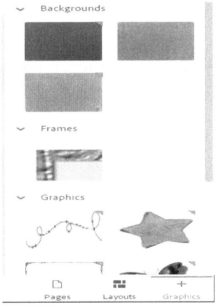

- Click on **Save** to save your greeting card.

Do the following to create a Photo Calendar.

- Select **Create** and click on **Photo Calendar**.

- In the Photo Calendar dialog box, complete the following actions and press **OK**:

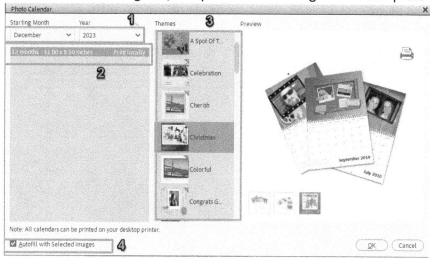

1. Select where you want the date (**Year** and **Month**) of your calendar to start from.
2. Choose the Photo calendar`s size.
3. Decide on a theme.
4. To use the images you have selected in the Photo Bin, select Autofill with selected images.

- The following choices are accessible in the project's lower-right corner:

Pages: displays the pages of the Photo Calendar.

Layout: Shows the arrangement of the photo calendar.

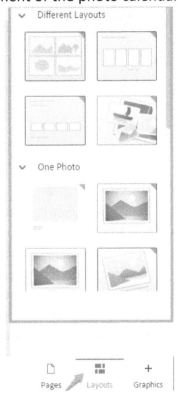

Graphics: This lets you change the background, the frames, and the graphics on the photo calendar.

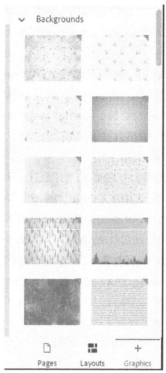

- Click on **Save** to import and save your project.

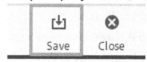

Saving Files/Projects in PhotoShop Elements

Several file kinds can be saved with the Photoshop Element. Below are the file formats that you can save your documents in Photoshop Elements.

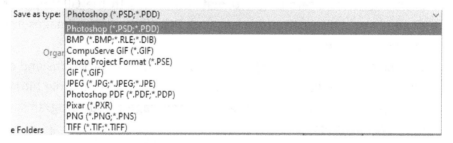

- **Photoshop (PSD)**: This is the default file format used by Photoshop Elements. You can make changes to an image with this file format and yet keep its layers, data, and dimensions.

- **Bitmap (BMP)**: This standard image format was created by Microsoft Corporation for MS Windows and OS/2 to store bitmap digital images across various viewing platforms. Files that are not compressed, such those in as the BMP file format, are easier to view. Furthermore, support for the BMP picture file type has been discontinued.
- **CompuServe GIF (Graphic Interchange Format)**: GIF-formatted images and brief animations are frequently displayed or exhibited on websites. The purpose of developing this compressed file format was to reduce file size and save time. The only supported image format is 8-bit color. To save an image as a GIF file, use the Save As Web command.
- **Joint Photographic Extract Group (JPEG)**: This file format stores data through compression. It is perfect for usage on the web because of this compression, which enables reduced file sizes. Because JPEGs can provide sharp photos with comparatively tiny file sizes, they are also used for printing.:
- **Photo Project Format (PSE)**: This file format is also the standard for producing multiple pages. This file format allows you to save your work and preserves all of your layer and picture data in a multi-page file. This is the format in which all photo projects are saved in.
- **Photoshop PDF**: This cross-platform and cross-application file format shows and maintains the font, page layouts, and bitmap and vector graphics.
- **Pixar (PXR)**: Files in this file format can be exchanged between Pixar image systems. The Pixar workstations were designed and manufactured with advanced graphics applications, like three-dimensional animation and images, in mind. This format also supports RGB and grayscale.
- **Portable Network Graphics (PNG):** This is the most used uncompressed raster picture format online. It is also commonly used to store site designs, digital photos, and images with transparent backgrounds. The PNG file format took the role of the Graphics Interchange Format (GIF). As with the GIF image, the PNG picture can have a transparent background. PNG files contain images in both 24-bit RGB and grayscale color palettes.
- **Tagged Image File Format (TIFF):** File transfers between programs and computer platforms are accomplished via this file format, which is a versatile bitmap image format supported by paint, image editing, and page layout programs. TIFF files can be created by most desktop scanners.

Save, **Save As,** and *Save For Web* are the three commands on Photoshop Elements used for saving projects, designs and images.

Save	Ctrl+S
Save As...	Shift+Ctrl+S
Save for Web...	Alt+Shift+Ctrl+S

The **Save command** is used to save the modifications made to the file that is being worked on. To accomplish this, do either of the following.

- Open the file, select **File Menu** and click on **Save**.

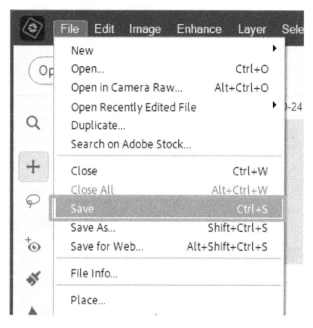

- Or use the keyboard shortcut for saving (**Ctrl+S**).

The **Save As** option allows you to set several parameters when saving photos, including the file name, file type, layers, and more.

To use the Save As Command to save files, do the following.

- Open Photoshop Element and choose the picture you want to save as a file.
- Click on **Save As** when the **File Menu** appears.

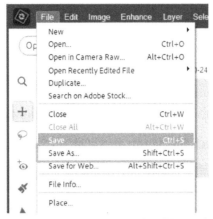

- Choose the location where you want to store the file and type its name in the **File Name text field**.

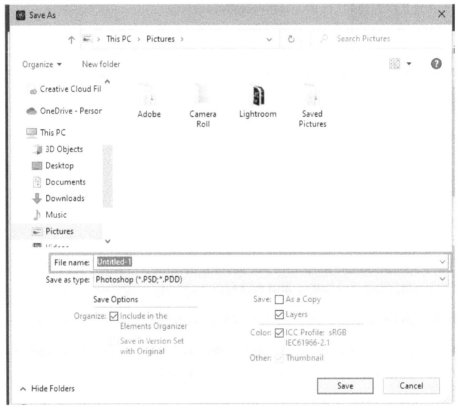

- Choose the format you wish the file to be stored in by clicking on the File Format option (JPEG, GIF, PNG, etc.)

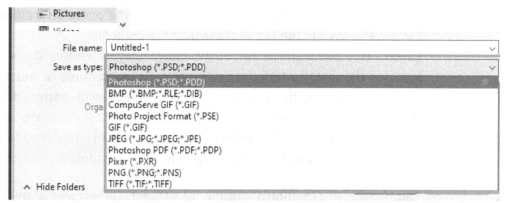

- In the **Save Options**, extra features are provided to utilize while using the Save As command.

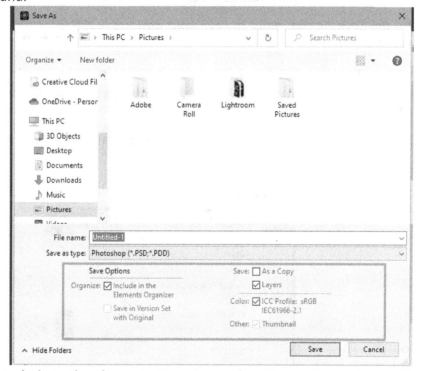

- ○ **Include In the Elements Organizer**: When this option is chosen, the saved file is seen in the Photo Browser and added to the library. The Element organizer is not supported by several file formats, notably the EPS file format.
- ○ **Save In Version Set with Original**: This option saves the file and adds it to a version set in the Photo Browser, keeping the many versions of the image organized. Only after selecting Include In the Organizer will you be able to use this option

o **As a Copy**: When this option is used, a copy of the open file is stored. The file copy is saved in the folder containing the open file.

o **Layers**: This option helps retain the image's layers better. There are no layers in the image when the Layer option is inaccessible or deactivated. When the layer in the image needs to be merged or flattened for the selected format, a warning icon shows up in the Layer check box. If you wish to preserve the layers within an image, select an alternative format.

o **ICC Profile:** For some formats, this means you can apply a color profile to the image.

o **Thumbnails**: Information about the file's thumbnail is stored in this option. This option is available when the Ask When Saving for Image Preview option in the Preferences dialog box is enabled.

NOTE: Use the Save As command to save your projects in different file formats. From JPEG to GIF, PNG, etc.

Using the **Save For Web** command, you may fine-tune photographs for use on web-based media (the Internet), such as blogs and webpages, by compressing them and changing the display characteristics.

However, GIF, JPEG, and PNG are the three main file formats used on the internet.

Take the actions listed below to use **Save For Web**.

- On the **File Menu**, select **Save For Web**.

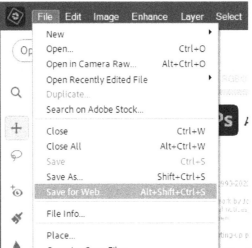

- This opens the **Save For Web** dialog box, which has many options. These are mentioned below.

The Tool Bar at the left side of the dialog box consists of the following.

- o **Hand Tool**: You can use this to navigate around the image in the Preview section when you're zoomed in.
- o **Zoom Tool**: This tool allows you to change the preview image's size.
- o **Eyedropper Tool**: Utilizing this tool allows you to sample a color in a picture precisely as it shows up in the Preview section. This is a sneak peek of the image's appearance.

Located at the right-hand side of the workspace are the following.

- o **The Preview Windows**: After it has been stored. The first image displays the actual image, while the second image displays the preview.
- o **Presets**: With this option, you can select from several presets that are available in the drop-down menu. Pre-configured settings for the dialog box's options are created using the preset.
- o **Image Format**: Here, you can select a file format from the drop-down option (GIF, JPEG, or PNG).
- o **Quality Settings**: Here is where you select the quality of the photograph before saving it. When saving any file as a JPEG, the Quality option shows up; you can set the color number for GIF and PNG.
- o **Image Attributes**: The original width and height are displayed in the Original Size section of this selection. You can adjust the image's width and height in pixels or percentages in the New Size Area.
- o **Animation**: Only animated GIFs can use this option.

158

o **Preview Menu**: A preview of the output can be found here.

Saving Files in Different File Formats

In this section, we will be diving deeper into how to save media files in different file formats like JPEG, TIFF, PNG, etc.

Do the following to save a project in a Photoshop PDF file format.

- After opening your file on Photoshop Elements, select **File Menu** and click on **Save As**.

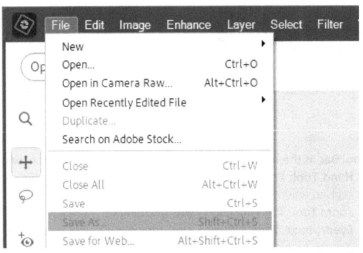

- Choose where you want to store the file and type its name in the **File Name text field**.

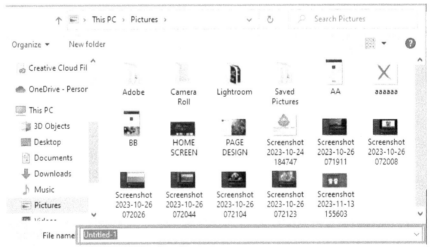

- Select **Photoshop PDF** under **Save As Type**.

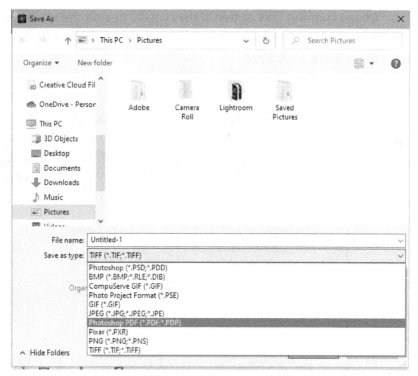

- Select **Save**.

- The PDF Options dialog box appears, allowing you to choose from the options indicated below.

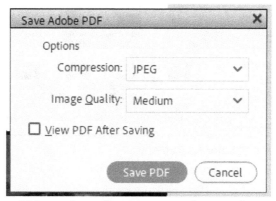

- ○ **Compression**: This option allows you to choose the type of compression you want for the file; **None**, **ZIP** format, or **JPEG**.

- o **Image Quality**: This option allows you to decide the quality of your file.
- o **View PDF After Saving**: This allows you to preview your file after saving.
- After you`re done, click **Save.**

Do the following to save your project in a PNG file format.

- After opening your file on Photoshop Elements, select **File Menu** and click on **Save As**.

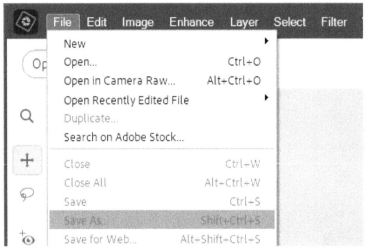

- Choose where you want to store the file and type its name in the **File Name text field**.

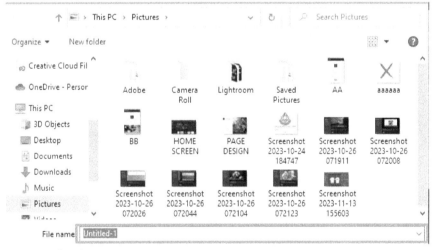

- Select **PNG** under **Save As Type**.

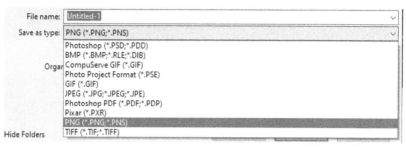

- Click on **Save**.

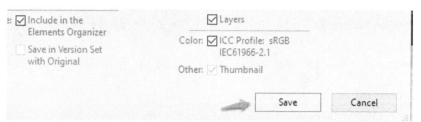

- Subsequently, the PNG Options dialog box appears, allowing you to choose from the options indicated below.

Select the **Interlace** option

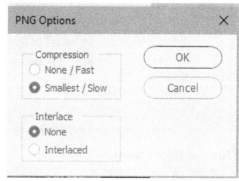

  - o **None:** A browser opens and displays the image after the download is complete.
  - o **Interlaced:** The picture is seen in a browser at a low quality after the download is complete, which expedites the download but expands the file size.
- Once you are done, click **OK**.

Do the following to save your project in a TIFF Format.

- After opening your file on Photoshop Elements, select **File Menu** and click on **Save As**.

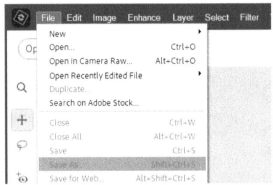

- Choose where you want to store the file and type its name in the **File Name text field**.

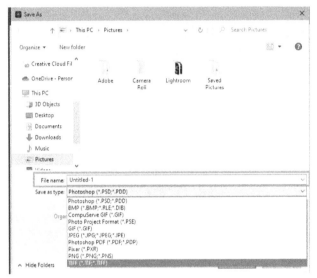

- Choose the **TIFF format** under **Save As Type**.

163

- Click **Save.**

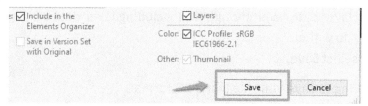

- Subsequently, the TIFF Options dialog box appears, allowing you to choose from the options indicated below.

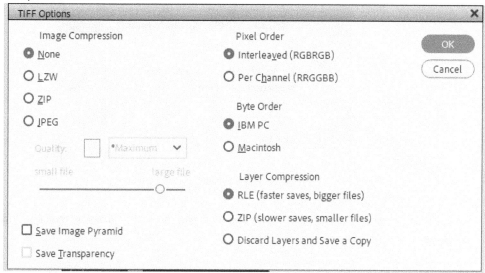

- ○ **Image Compression**: This option is used to specify or choose the compression strategy for the picture data.
- ○ **Pixel Order**: You can select Interleaved from this menu to add the picture to the Element organizer.
- ○ **Byte Order**: This option lets you choose the platform that the file will be read, which is useful if you're not sure which specific program the file may open in.
- ○ **Save Image Pyramid**: This is the Adobe Element feature that allows multiresolution data to be preserved. With this selected, the image will open at the maximum resolution included in the file.
- ○ **Save Transparency:** This option allows a file's transparency to be maintained when it's opened in a different program.
- ○ **Layer Compression:** It describes a technique for data compression for layers' pixels (as opposed to composite data). Many programs skip over layer data when they open a TIFF file because they are unable to interpret it. TIFF files include layer data that Photoshop Elements can read. Layer

164

data can be saved to save and maintain a distinct PSD file containing the layer data, even though files including layer data are larger than those that do without.

- Next, select Save.

Do the following to save your file in a JPEG format.

- After opening your file on Photoshop Elements, select **File Menu** and click on **Save As**.

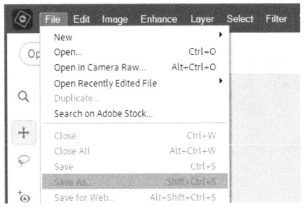

- Choose where you want to store the file and type its name in the **File Name text field**.

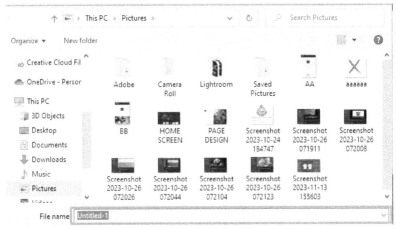

- Select **JPEG** under **Save As Type**.

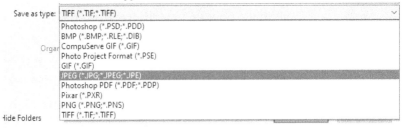

- Click **Save.**

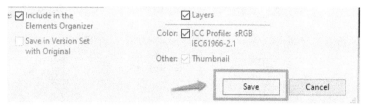

- This page will display the JPEG dialog box, and when it does, do the following.

  o If the image file has transparency, choose a **Matte color** to bring out the background opacity.
  o Identify the resolution and compression of the image by making a selection from the **Quality Option.** You can either slide the **Quality Slider** or input a value between 1 and 12 to select the image quality level.
  o From the **Format Options**, select either **Baseline ("standard")**, **Baseline Optimized**, or **Progressive**. Afterwards, click "OK."

Follow the procedure below to save a media file in GIFF format.

- After opening your file on Photoshop Elements, select **File Menu** and click on **Save As**.

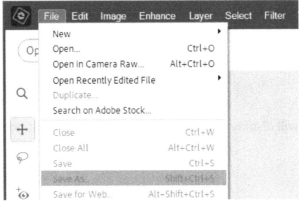

- Choose where you want to store the file and type its name in the **File Name text field**.

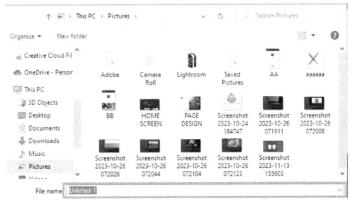

- Select **CompuServe GIF** under **Save As Type**.

167

- The GIF Options dialog box appears, allowing you to choose from the options indicated below.
  - o Use the **Quality Options** or **Quality Slider** to determine the quality of your file.

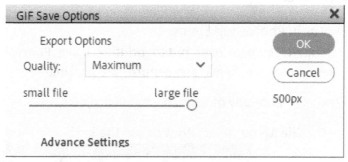

  - o Click on **Advanced Settings** to access more complex options.

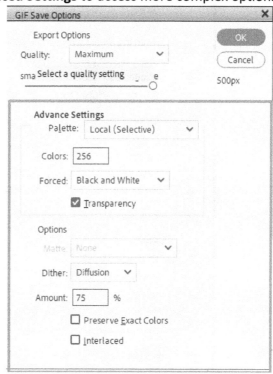

- After modifying your settings, click on **Ok.**

Follow the procedure to save your file in MP4 file format.

Before saving your files, it is important to know that *Moving Overlays, Moving Photos,* and *Quotation Graphics* all allow MP4 export.

- After opening your media files, select **File Menu** and click on **Export**.

- From the format list, select **MP4**.
- To add an image to Elements Organizer, specify its location, file name, and tags. Then, click **Organize**.
- Select "**Save**."

Printing Photos in Photoshop Elements

You have complete control over photo printing using Photoshop Elements. Printing picture packages, contact sheets, and pictures are possible.

Do the following to print any of your concluded projects.

- From the **File Menu**, select **Print** or use the keyboard shortcut **Ctrl/Cmd +P**.

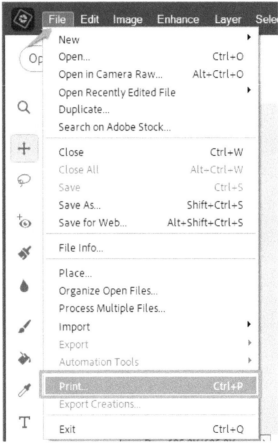

- You can preview the print and adjust the following parameters in the Print dialog box:

Located at the right-hand side of the Dialog box are **Print Options**.

- o **Select Printer**: From the drop-down list, select the type of printing.

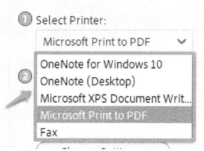

- o **Printer Settings**: show the current settings of the printing process. Select **Change Settings** to adjust the printer settings. To configure the printer, paper type, paper tray, paper size, and print quality, use the Printer Settings.

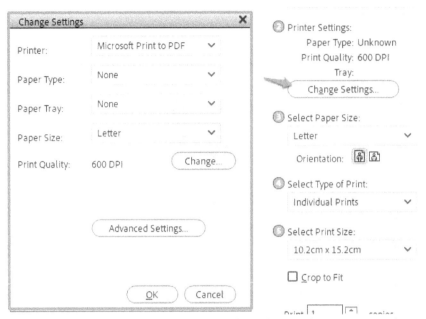

o **Select Paper Size**: From the drop-down list, choose the paper size that you want to print photos on.

o **Orientation**: Indicate if the page should be oriented in portrait or landscape mode.

o **Select Type of Print**: The types of prints available in this option are *Individual Prints*, *Picture Package*, and *Contact Sheet*.

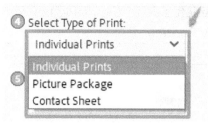

o **Select Print Size**: The photo's print size should be chosen. To set the photo's dimensions, select Custom. See Scale images for further information.

o **Crop To Fit**: To fit a certain image to a given print layout, use this option. To fit the print layout's aspect ratio, the image is cropped and resized as needed. If you wish your photographs to not be cropped, deselect this option.

o **Print Copies**: To indicate how many copies of each page you wish to print, either select the desired number or type it into the text box.

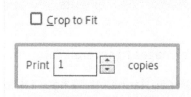

Located at the left side of the dialog box are **Photos Selected for Printing** and **Add Photos for Printing**.

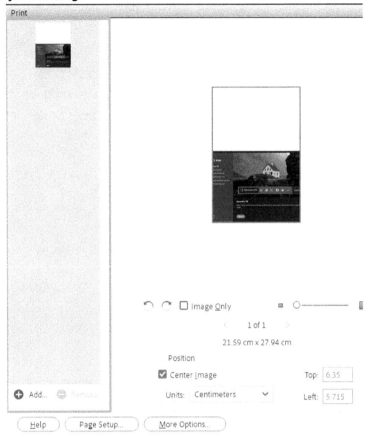

- After modifying the settings, select Print to print out your photos.

Sharing Photographs

In sharing media files in Photoshop Elements, you can use either the **Organizer** or **Photo Editor.**

Do the following to share images to several platforms using Photo Editor.

- From the **Home Screen**, launch the **Photo Editor.**

- Choose the photo you want to share when the Photo Editor opens.
- Choose a choice from the **Share drop-down** choices by clicking on **Share**.

Follow the instructions below to share images using the Organizer.

- Go to the **Home Screen** and open the **Organizer**.

- After choosing your desired picture to share, click on **Media** in the **Organizer**.
- When the **Share drop-down menu** appears, click it and choose an option.

Numerous photo-sharing services allow you to upload and distribute your photos. Photoshop Element is linked to certain picture-sharing services and they are **Behance, DotPhoto, Facebook, Flickr, Google+, Photobucket, Shutterfly, SlicPic, SmugMug, Twitter, Vimeo**, and **YouTube**.

Not only can you share individual photo files online, but you can also share **Video Files, Slideshows**, and **Albums**.

Correcting Mistakes

Sometimes when you are editing your photos, you will make a mistake or decide you don't like the changes you have made. Using the *Undo* and *Redo* commands, you can quickly go back and undo your actions. Do the following to use the aforementioned commands.

- Select the Edit Menu and click on **Undo (Ctrl + Z)** or **Redo (Ctrl + Y)**.

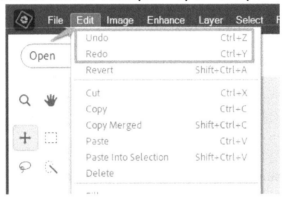

Another way to correct mistakes or adjust the edits of a project in Photoshop Elements is to use the *Revert* command. The image is returned to its original condition and all adjustments and modifications are undone when you use the Revert command. To reverse any

- Select Revert from the Edit Menu.

Aside from using the aforementioned commands, the *History Panel* is also a great tool for correcting errors or reverting the changes made to a project.

The History panel makes it easy to see how an image or project has been edited in the past. The History panel offers an extensive history of all the edits made to the image or photo, and you can move around it to make adjustments during the current work session.

The steps listed below can be used to open the History panel:

- Select **Windows** and click on **History** to open the **History Panel**.

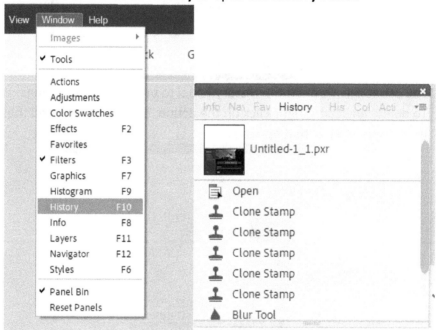

- Another way to access the **History Panel** is to click on **More** on the lower right-hand side of the workspace and click on the **History tab**.

- You can toggle through the History Panel to undo and redo actions.
  To delete an action, right-click on the action, choose **Delete**, and then choose **Yes** from the menu bar that appears.

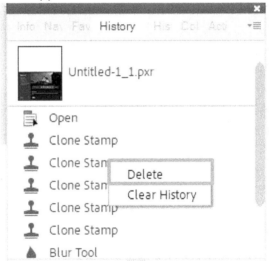

To clear all actions in the history panel, right-click on the action and choose **Clear History,** and select **Yes** to authorize the command.

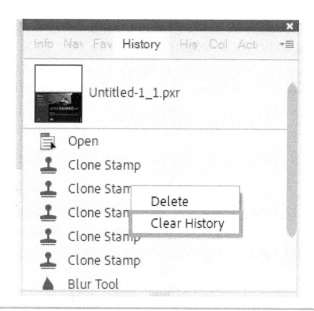

Getting Help in Photoshop Elements

You can run into issues with your Photoshop Element and require assistance. Finding the answers you need is simple when you use the Help Menu

The first place to look is the Help menu, which facilitates access to the Photoshop Help menu. The Help menu is located adjacent to the other menus at the top of the Photo Editor or Organizer interface.

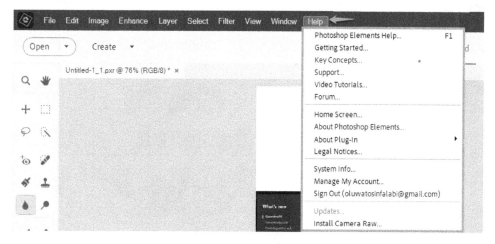

The help commands displayed in the Help Menu are listed below and each command will lead you to Adobe`s Help website.

- **Photoshop Elements Help**: To open the Element Help file, use the shortcut key F1.

- **Getting Started**: This command is helpful if you're looking for tips and information on how to get started with Elements.
- **Key Concepts**: This command can be useful when you see a word or phrase that you don't understand. When you select this option, a web page appears and your default browser opens immediately, displaying multiple web pages that explain the key concepts
- **Support**: ▢ Use this command to open your web browser and go to the Adobe website. On the Adobe website, you may get the most recent information about Elements, problems that users have reported, and some useful tips for utilizing the Adobe Element. The Adobe website has a wealth of materials that will help you make better use of Adobe Elements and provide a ton of remedies for any problems that could come up.
- **Video Tutorials**: This command opens a page on the Adobe website with videos to help you get the most out of the Adobe Element.
- **Forum**: This command leads to a page where you can see questions and comments from users along with answers to common problems that come up when using the Element.

Using the *Tooltips* is another way to get help using the Toolbar. More help resources will show as text beneath your cursor when you hover your mouse over any object in the Photoshop Element. The thing being pointed to is described in the texts that are displayed.

CHAPTER SEVEN

LAYERS IN THE PHOTO EDITOR

After knowing how to create documents, save, print, and share them on Photoshop Elements, knowing how to use layers is important to know how to edit images and photographs and this is what we will be learning in this chapter.

Working With Layers

Using layers—digitally rendered copies of transparent acetate sheets—you may make changes and additions to photos without destroying the original. The actions you can perform on pictures, such as adjusting brightness and color, adding effects, rearranging the contents of a layer, defining opacity, blending values, and so forth, may also be performed on layers.

Layers and The Layer Panel

Every layer in the image is listed in the Layers panel, arranged from top to bottom and foreground to background. Layers can also be moved, hidden, added, and removed. The layers are in the layer panel.

To access the layer panel, go to **Windows** and choose Layers.

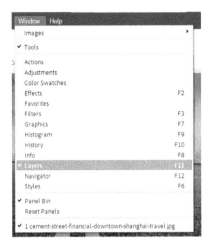

Another way to access the Layer panel is to click on Layers at the lower right-hand side of the workspace.

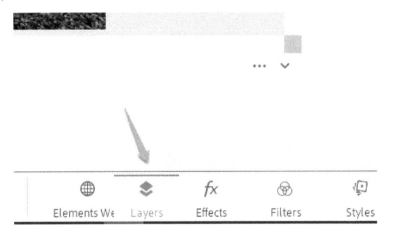

Now let's look at the control buttons in the layer panel.

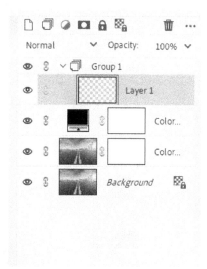

- **Create New Layer**: This is located at the top of the layer panel and can be used to add a new layer to the available stack of layers. You may also select Layer, New from the menu and click Layer to add a new layer to the stack.

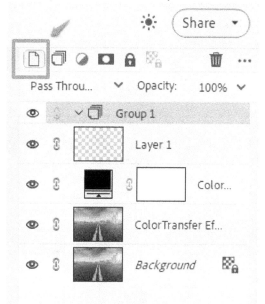

- **Crete New Group**: You can combine a significant number of layers by using this option.

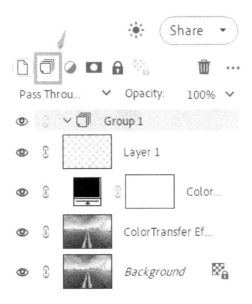

- **Fill/Adjustment Layer**: This enables you to apply colors, gradients, and patterns to a layer. This option also allows you to change the brightness, color, saturation, and levels.

- **Add layer Mask**: Using the layer mask, you can make a certain area of a layer visible or invisible. The visible part of the mask is shown in white, and any section of the mask that is buried within the layer is provided in black. Furthermore, pixels in the thumbnails are visible in white and buried in black.

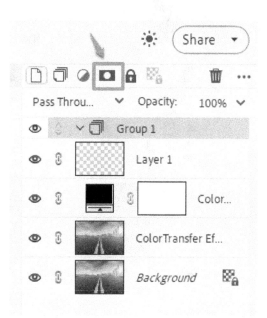

- **Lock All Pixels**: By selecting this button, all layers will be locked to prevent editing.

- **Lock Transparent Pixels**: In this setting, all layers are assumed to be translucent if they have no image pixels in them. Moreover, editing transparent layers is not possible.

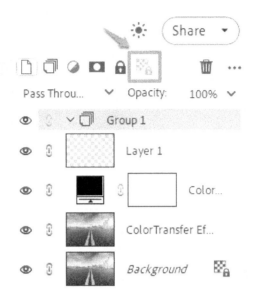

- **Delete Layer**: It lets you remove any chosen layer from the layer stack, as its name suggests.

- **Panel Options**: This setting determines how the layer's image colors interact with the layer underneath.

- **Blend Modes**: This setting determines how the layer's image colors interact with the layer underneath.

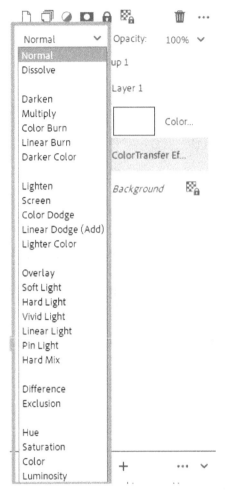

- **Opacity**: This tool allows you to adjust the transparency of a layer.

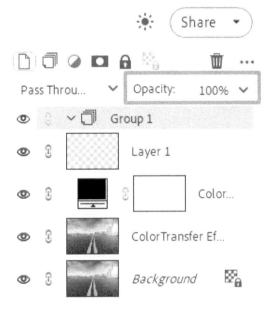

- **Visibility**: The small eye icon that appears on the left side of each layer can be clicked to make a layer invisible. Recall that any changes you make to this layer are similarly hidden until you click on the eye icon.

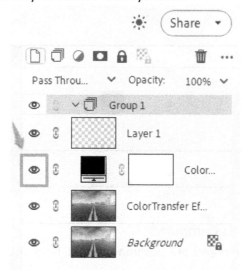

- **Link/ Unlink Layers:** This layer panel option connects multiple layers so that changes made to one will have an impact on all of them.

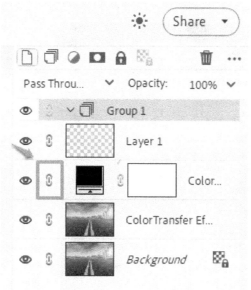

- **Background:** By default, the backdrop layer is the lowest layer. A photo or a new document that you open will always have a partially frozen background.

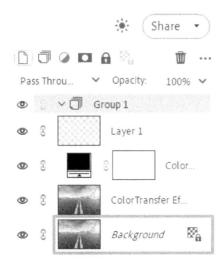

The Layer Menu and its Commands

Contained in the layer menu are commands that help you to use layers and the layer panel effectively.

To access the layer menu, select **Layer** from the **Menu Bar** or right-click on any layer in the layer panel

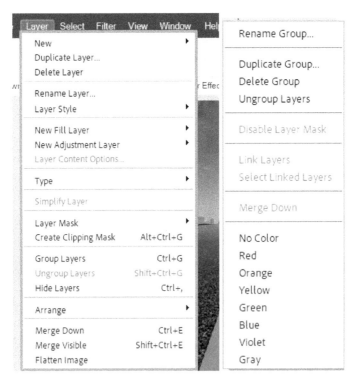

- **New**: This command allows you to create a new layer.
- **Duplicate Layer**: This allows you to make another copy of the selected layer.
- **Rename Layer**: This allows you to give the selected layer another name.
- **Delete Linked Layers and Hidden Layers**: You can remove linked layers or display hidden layers with these instructions.
- **Layer Style**: This command is in charge of managing or overseeing the styles and special effects that are used on the layers.
- **Arrange**: This command allows you to set up your layer stacking order with Send to Back and Back to Front among other possibilities.
- **Type**: This command aids in controlling how type layers are displayed.

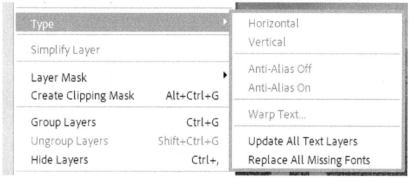

- **Create Clipping Mask**: With the help of this option, you can make a clipping mask in which the layer at the bottom serves as a mask for the layer above it. The best use case for the clipping mask is when you want to fill a shape or text with various image layers.
- **Merage and Flatten**: These commands combine many layers into one layer by joining them together. Additionally, it unites every layer into a single backdrop when flattening.

The Different Layer Types

Image Layers, Adjustment Layers, Fill Layers, Text Layers, and *Shape Layers* are the five types of layers we have in Photoshop Elements.

Original photos and any additional images added to a document in Photoshop Elements are stored as *Image Layers*. See the procedures below to build a new layer.

- Choose **Open** or **Place** from the **File menu** to import any file from your hard drive.

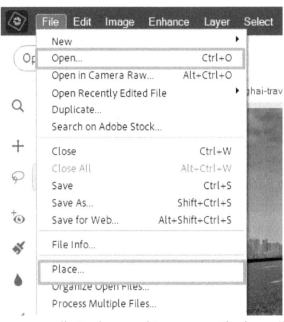

- Double-click the Layer panel's Background to rename the layer if you desire to.

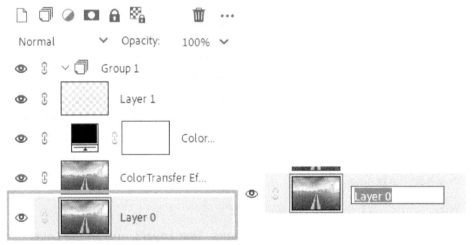

- Next, click OK. Type the layer's name or leave it as is.

Using the **Fill Layers**, you can add a solid color, gradient, or pattern to a picture. Similar to adjustment layers, fill layers also have layer masks.

The steps outlined here will help you create a fill layer.

- Click on **Create New Fill or Adjustment Layers** in the Layers window after launching the Photo Editor.

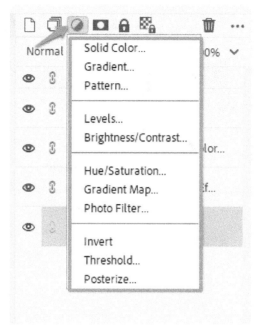

- Select any of the following options from the drop-down list.

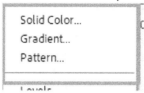

- o **Solid Color**: Here is where you select the color that will be added to the layer.
- o Gradient: This allows you to choose a preset gradient from the drop-down panel and apply it to your layer.
- o **Pattern**: A drop-down menu allows you to choose a pattern. To scale the layer's pattern, you can also enter a value.
- Then click **OK**.

The brightness, contrast, and saturation of an image can be changed using *Adjustment Layers.*

To use the Adjustment layers, follow these steps.

- Choose the desired image to work on by choosing it in the Layer panel.
- Click **Create New Fill or Adjustment Layers** in the **Layers panel**.

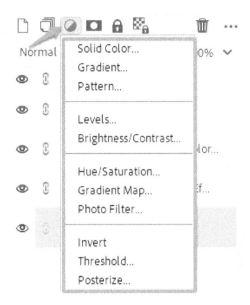

- Select the following settings for the Adjustment layers from the drop-down list.

- o **Level**: This alters the tonal value of the image.
- o **Brightness/Contrast**: Depending on the selection, the image will appear lighter or darker.
- o **Hue/Saturation**: This configuration helps to manage the color deficiency in an image and adds more vibrance to the color tone.
- o **Gradient Map**: In the selected gradient, this setting shows which pixels match which color.

- o **Photo Filter**: This option aids in adjusting the image's color temperature and balance.
- o **Invert**: This is used to produce a photograph that has a negative effect by infusing the image with negativity determined by its brightness levels.
- o **Threshold**: To identify the image's lightest and darkest areas, this is utilized to create a monochromatic image devoid of any gray.
- o **Posterize**: This option gives your picture a flat, poste-like appearance, which lowers the brightness levels in the image. This option reduces the amounts of colors available.
- After selecting the adjustment layer of your choice, click **OK**.

You can apply different forms to an image with the use of the *Shape layers*. It is possible to scale and even smooth the edges of these structures. To use the form layers, take the following actions:

- From the **Toolbar**, choose the **Shape tool**.

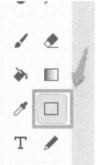

- Select any desired form from the **Tool Option**.

- To design a shape, click and drag the shape on the image.
  The form will be inserted into the layer if one is selected; if not, a new layer will be automatically produced.

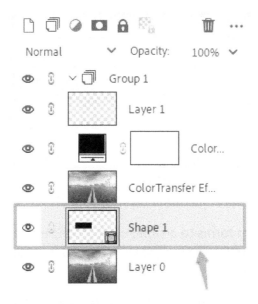

By using *Text layers*, you can add text to your photos. Since text in the Photoshop Element is vector-based by default, you can adjust and resize it as you add it.

- From the **Toolbar**, select the **Text tool**.

- To start typing the desired text, click inside a layer.

- Press the marker symbol once you're finished.

- If you have the blank layer selected, the text will show up on that layer.

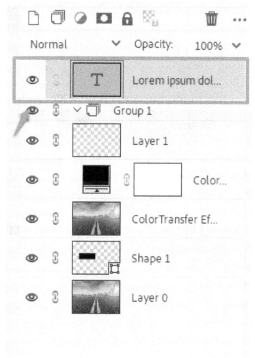

Basic Operations with Layers

To properly and efficiently complete a design project, there are a few operations that one has to be able to do with the layers in Photoshop Elements, some of which will be covered in this section.

Create, Duplicate and Transform

Do either of the following to create a new blank layer in the Photo Editor.

- On the **Layers panel**, click **Create a new layer**. A new layer with the default name **layer 1** will be generated automatically.

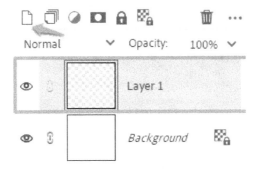

- Select **Layer** from the menu bar and choose **New**, then click **Layer**.

- Set the options shown below in the **New Layer dialog box**.

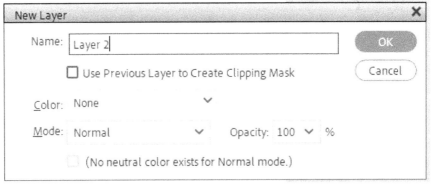

- Name: Put the new layer's name here.
- Color: Decide which color you want to use.
- Mode: Using the Mode drop-down list, select the mode.
- Opacity: To adjust the layer's opacity, use the Opacity slider.

- After that, select **OK**. The new layer will then appear in the layer panel on the left as a thumbnail.

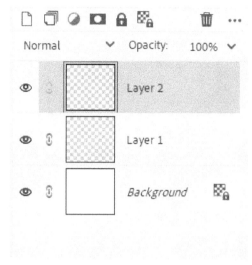

You can make several copies of your layers and duplicate them as often as you like. To duplicate layers, follow the guidelines below.

- Click the **Duplicate layer** after choosing **Layer** from the **Menu Bar**.

- Set the available choices in the **Duplicate layer dialog box**, then click **OK**.

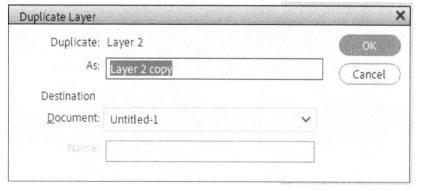

Instead of using the copy-and-paste approach, you can duplicate a layer by using the drag-and-drop command. To achieve this, adhere to the following steps.

- In the **Layer panel**, choose the layer you wish to move.
- Select the **Move tool** from the **Toolbar**.

- Drag and drag the object to the desired location

You can make a fresh copy of another layer by using the Layer via copy and Layer via cut commands in the Layer menu.

- From the **Menu bar**, select **Layer**. Then, choose **Layer Via Copy or Layer Via Cut** and the new layer is created.

Your photographs can be scaled or rotated as part of layer adjustments using the Transform and Free Transform commands. Follow the procedure listed below to do such.

- The layer you want to change should be selected.
- After choosing **Transform** from Image, click **Free Transform**.

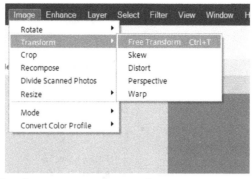

- In this case, a bounding box surrounds your layer.

- Use the following settings to modify the bounding box:
    - **Size the Layer**: Drag the corner handle to perform this.
    - **Limit the dimensions**: While dragging, press the Shift key.
    - **Rotate the Layer**: Move the mouse pointer outside the corner handle, wait for it to turn into a curved arrow, and then drag to rotate the content.
    - **Apply Distort, Perspective, Skew**: Right-click and choose the desired command from the context menu to use these options. In the Tools Option, you can also find the scale and skew icons, even if you enter the transform values numerically.

Free Transform	
Scale	
Free Rotate Layer	
Skew	
Distort	
Perspective	
Warp	
Rotate Layer 180°	
Rotate Layer 90° Right	
Rotate Layer 90° Left	
Flip Layer Horizontal	
Flip Layer Vertical	

- After transforming the layer to your desired appearance, double-click inside the bounding box.

Flattening and Merging

In Photoshop Elements, flattening layers is the process of combining all visible layers into one background layer. This helps to minimize file size and streamline the editing procedure.

To flatten layers, all visible zone needs to be covered with white and hidden layers removed to flatten the layers, which require the removal of concealed layers.

Take the following actions to use the Flatten option:

- Make sure layers that need to be flattened are visible.

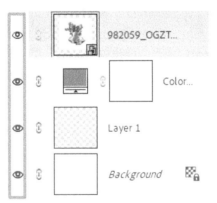

- Select the **Layer Menu** and then select **Flatten Image**.

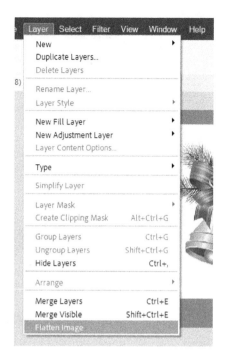

File merging can be used to combine all of the layers into a single Background. This helps save memory and storage space by combining visible, linked, or nearby levels into a single layer.

What distinguishes flattening an image from merging layers? The distinction is that if you flatten a picture in Photoshop, all of the layers will be combined into one layer, but if you merge layers, you can choose to merge all of the layers, just the visible layers, or just the selected layers.

Follow these steps to combine layers:

- Choose every layer to combine.
- Select **Layer** from the **Menu bar**, then click **Merge Layers**.

202

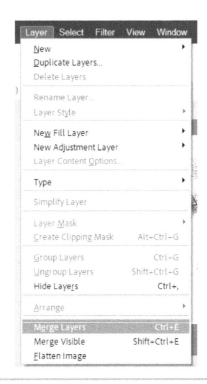

Applying Layer Mask

The layer mask, a resolution-dependent bitmap image, governs and controls the visibility of the layer that it is applied to. The layer mask allows you to show or hide specific areas of an image. The visible part of the mask is shown in white, and any section of the mask that is buried within the layer is provided in black.

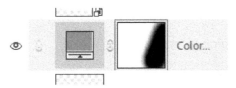

The layer mask can be changed without removing any layer pixels by raising or decreasing the masked area.

Do the following to add a layer mask to a layer.

- To apply the layer mask, choose the desired area of the image
- From the **Layer Panel** click on the **Add Layer Mask** button.

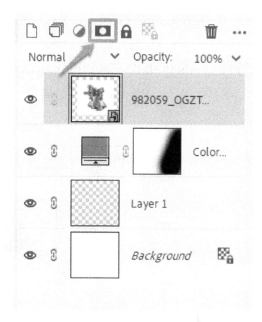

Layer masks can be used for the following tasks.

- To make a layer mask thumbnail in the Layers panel invisible, shift-click on it.

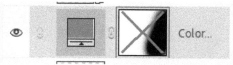

- To see the mask without showing the image, alt-click the Layers panel thumbnail for the layer mask.

- To remove a layer's relationship to a layer mask, click the link symbol in the Layer panel.

- To remove a layer mask, drag its thumbnail to the Layers panel's trash icon.

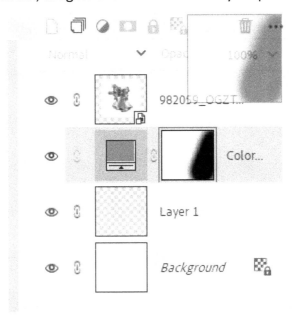

CHAPTER EIGHT

SELECTION TOOLS AND SELECTIONS

Introduction to Selections and Selection Tools

Making the most of Photoshop Element's Selections is one of the fundamental skills you can't afford to ignore.

A selection is an area of a digital image that is marked for edits or you wish to modify. Once a selection is made, the selected region can be edited. To create a selection, you can use the selection commands or the selection tools. Each time you make a selection, the selection border—a dotted outline—appears. You can modify, copy, or erase certain pixels from the image using the selection boundary. Remember that nothing can be done outside of the selected area until it is deselected. Contained in Photoshop Elements are not only **Selection Tools** but also **Selection Commands** which will be treated in this part of the book.

Working with Selection Tools

The selection tools in the toolbar are **Rectangular Marquee Tool, Elliptical Marquee Tool, Lasso Tool, Magnetic Lasso Tool, Polygonal Lasso Tool, Quick Selection Tool, Selection Brush Tool, Magic Wand Tool, Refine Selection Brush Tool**, and **Auto Selection Tool**.

The following discussions will be on how to effectively use these tools.

Rectangular Marquee Tool

This selection tool allows you to create selections using a rectangular boundary line.

Do the following to use the Rectangular Marquee Tool.

- From the **Toolbar**, select the **Rectangular Marquee Tool**.

- The additional marquee tool options are available at the footer panel's **Tool Options.** In the Tool Panel, select the marquee tool options.

- o Choose the type of selections you want to make:

  New An object can be expanded to create a new selection, or it can be moved by dragging your cursor over it.

  Add: Every decision you make will be combined with the previous one.

  Subtract: When a newly formed selection is placed on top of a previously made selection, the overlapping area of the two selections is removed.

  Intersect: Only the shared space between two selections remains selected when you create a new selection on top of an existing one.

- o To soften the selection border so that it blends into the area outside the selection, enter a **Feather value.**

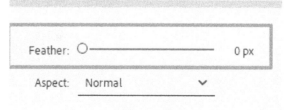

- o In the **Aspect** section, select **Normal** to visually adjust the selection border's size and proportions; **Fixed Ratio** to establish the selection border's width-to-height ratio; or **Fixed Size** to set the height and width of the marquee from the Mode pop-up menu.

- o Use **Refine Edges** to adjust how the edges of your selection will turn out by toggling through the options in its dialog box.

- Move the mouse pointer to the point where you want to make a selection in the image drag the mouse from the desired area to the opposite corner and then let go of the mouse to make a rectangle selection appear on the image.

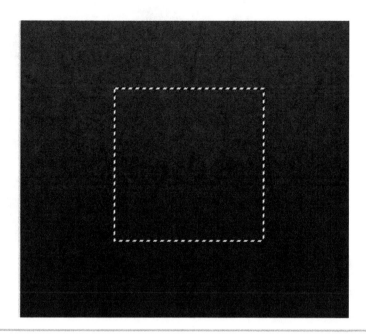

Elliptical Marquee Tool

This selection tool allows you to make selections with an elliptical boundary. Follow the instructions below to use the elliptical selection tool.

- From the **Toolbar**, select the **Rectangular Marquee Tool…**

and select the **Elliptical Marquee Tool** from the **Tool Options** panel.

- The Elliptical Marquee Tool also uses all options available in the Tool Panel as the Rectangular Marquee Tool including **Anti-aliasing** (which is not included in the options for the Rectangular Marquee Tool).
    - ○ **Anti-aliasing**: This option allows you to soften the edges of your selections.
- Once you are done adjusting the tool options, then you can make your selections.

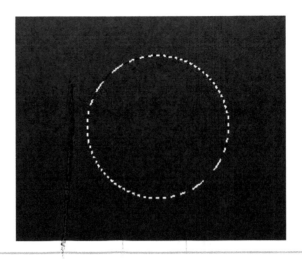

Lasso Tool

To create freehand selection borders on a picture or object, use the Lasso tool. To make a freehand selection, adhere to the steps listed below.

- From the **Toolbar**, select the **Lasso Tool**.

- Set the options in the **Tool Options** panel to your desired settings, then make your selections.

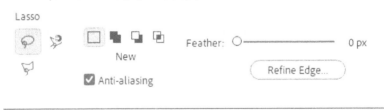

Magnetic Lasso Tool

When you drag over objects in the picture, the Magnetic Lasso tool creates a selection boundary that immediately attaches to their edges. Drawing accurate selection borders is made easier as a result. You may swiftly choose objects with intricate edges placed against high-contrast backgrounds by using the Magnetic Lasso tool. Do the following to use this section tools.

- From the Toolbar, select Lasso Tool...

...and select the **Magnetic Lasso Tool** from the **Tool Options** panel.

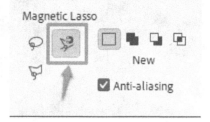

- In the Tool Options panel, give the **Frequency** of the Magnetic Lasso tool a number between 0 and 100 to define the pace at which it establishes fastening spots. The selection border is swiftly fixed in place by a greater value.

- Use the **Contrast Slider** to adjust the Magnetic Lasso tool's sensitivity to photo edges, and set the Edge Contrast parameter to a value between 1 and 100 percent. Only edges with a strong contrast to their surroundings are detected by a higher value; edges with a lower contrast are detected by a lower value.

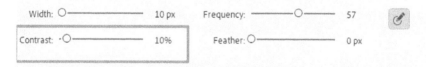

- Make your selections after you're done with adjusting the tool options to your taste.

Polygonal Lasso Tool

Segments of a selection border with straight edges are drawn using the Polygonal Lasso tool. To construct a selection boundary, you can create as many segments as necessary. Do the following to use this selection tool.

- From the Toolbar, select Lasso Tool...

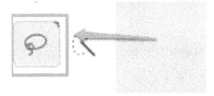

...and select the **Polygonal Lasso Tool** from the **Tool Options** panel.

- Adjust the tool options to your satisfaction and make your selections.

Quick Selection Tool

When you click or click-drag the desired region, the Quick Selection tool selects it based on similarities in color and texture. The Quick Selection tool produces a border quickly and logically, so you don't need to draw an exact mark. Do the following to use this selection tool.

- From the **Toolbar**, select the **Quick Selection Tool**.

- In the **Tool Options Panel**, set the following
    - You can draw a new selection with **New Selection**. The Default selection is made for this option. You can add to an already-existing selection by using the **Add To Selection** function. You can deduct from an existing selection by using the **Subtract From Selection** command. You cannot access this option until you have made a selection.

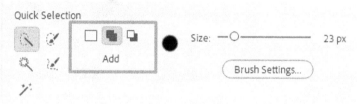

    - Adjust the **Size Slider** to determine the size of your brush for selection and click on **Brush Settings** to access advanced options for the brush.

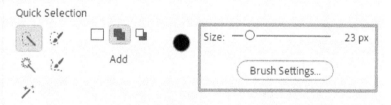

    - **Sample All Layers**: Mark this option to allow your selection to affect all layers when you have multiple layers and if not, uncheck it.

- Check the **Auto-Enhance** checkbox to have the pixel selections you make automatically enhanced. The "auto" results can be disabled by unchecking this checkbox if you'd rather not have them.

Refine Edge

☐ Sample All Layers
☐ Auto-Enhance

- After the options have been adjusted to your satisfaction, make your selection(s).

Selection Brush

With the Selection Brush tool, selections can be made in two ways: either by painting over the desired area in Selection mode or by utilizing a semi-transparent overlay in Mask mode to paint over selected areas. Also, you can use this selection tool to modify and refine the selections made by other selection tools. Do the following to use the selection brush.

- Select **Quick Selection Tool** from the **Toolbar**...

... and select the **Selection Tool** from the **Tool Options panel**.

- In the **Tool Options panel**, set the following
  - o Determine the mode of selection either **Selection** or **Mask**.

  - o Use the **Size Slider** to adjust the size of the brush and the **Hardness Slider** should be used to the intensity of the brush`s tip.

  - o Select the type of brush you want to use in the **Brush Presets**.

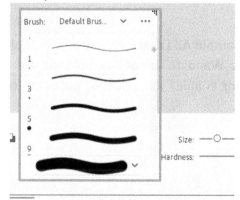

- After you are done setting the options to your satisfaction, make your selections.

Magic Wand Tool

With a single click, the Magic Wand tool selects pixels that fall within a similar color spectrum. You can choose the tolerance, or color range, for the Magic Wand tool. When you have an area with similar colors, such as a blue sky, use the Magic Wand tool. Do the following to use this selection tool.

- Select the **Quick Selection Tool** from the **Toolbar**...

... and select the **Magic Wand Tool** from the **Tool Options** panel.

Magic Wand Tool (A)

- In the **Tool Options** panel, set the following.
  - Use the **Tolerance Slider** to choose from a wider variety of colors. With a number between 0 and 225, the region will select a single color at range 0, and all of the colors in the image will be selected at range 255.

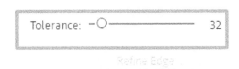

  - Use **Sample All Layers** when using multiple layers, **Contiguous** enables the Magic Wand to choose pixels that are adjacent to one another. **Anti-aliasing** enables you to loosen the selection's border by one-pixel column.

- After you are done making the necessary settings, make your selection(s).

Auto Selection Tool

You can use the Auto Selection tool to automatically choose an object by drawing a shape around it. All you need to do is sketch the outline of the thing you wish to choose; it doesn't have to be exact. Do the following to use this section tool.

- Select **Quick Selection Tool** from the **Toolbar**...

... and select the **Auto Selection Tool** from the **Tool Options panel**.

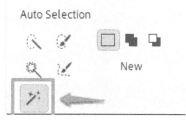

- Adjust the settings of the tool in the **Tool Options** panel.
    - ○ **Rectangle** allows you to make selections with a rectangular boundary, **Ellipse** with an elliptical boundary, **Lasso** allows you to make a freehand selection and **Polygon Lasso** allows you to make your selection with straight-edged segments.

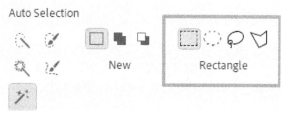

    - ○ Check the **Constrain Selection** checkbox to limit the selection to the inside of the area that you are clicking and dragging across.

        By now you know the purpose of **Sample All Layers**

        ☐ Sample All Layers
        ☐ Constrain Selection

- Make your selection after modifying your options to your satisfaction.

Refine Selection Brush Tool

With the Refine Edge, you can fine-tune your selections. You can add or remove any section of your selection with the Refine Selection Brush Tool, which detects borders in the image automatically. Do the following to use this selection tool.

- Select **Quick Selection Tool** from the **Toolbar**...

... and select the **Refine Selection Brush Tool** from the **Tool Options panel.**

Refine Selection Brush

Add

- In the **Tool Options panel**, set the following.
    - ○ Let you manually add to the current selection by clicking "Add to Selection."
    - ○ **Add to selection,** let you manually add to the current selection. **Subtract From Selection**, lets you manually subtract the current selection. **Push Selection** allows youadjust the size of your selections (When the cursor is inside a selection, the selection expands inside the outer circle and snaps to the first edge of the image that is detected. The selection inside the outer circle is contracted when the cursor is moved outside of it, causing it to snap to the first edge of the image that is detected).
    Smooth Selection, let you smoothen the current selection.

Add

    - ○ Use **Size Slider** to modify the size of your brush and **Snap Strength** to adjust the snapping edges of the selection boundary. **Selection Edges** allows you to set the selection edge radius.
    You can toggle all these sliders towards the **Soft** or **Hard** side.

Add or make a new selection

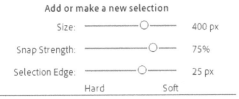

Size:	400 px
Snap Strength:	75%
Selection Edge:	25 px
Hard	Soft

    - ○ **View** provides options for viewing the choice that is being made. Choose between hard black or white, or an overlay color with adjustable opacity.

o Adjust the overlay's opacity using the **Opacity Slider.**

- After adjusting the settings, you can refine your selections.

Working with Selection Commands

After that we have learned how to use the selection tools in the toolbar, let's move to how to learn selection commands to make selections. These selection commands are found in the **Select Menu.**

Selecting a Subject, Sky or Background

With only one click, you may instantly choose the Subject, Sky, or Background in your picture. Photoshop Elements recognizes the Subject, Sky, or Background in your shot using Adobe Sensei AI technology*. You can either access these selection features from the Select Menu or from selection tools.

Subject enables you to select the most prominent and noticeable element in an image...

Sky enables you to select the sky in an image....

enables you to select the background in an image...

To access these selection features, use either of these methods.

Method 1

- After opening the image you want to work on, select any selection tools from the toolbar.
- From the right-hand side of the Tool Options Panel, select either of the three to carry out your operation.

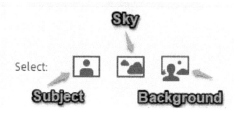

Method 2

- After opening the image you want to modify, select **Subject/Sky/Background** from the Select Menu.

All, Deselect. Reselect, Inverse

These four commands are the first set of commands in the Select Menu.

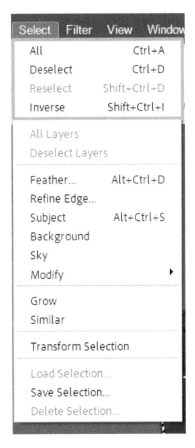

- From the Menu Bar, select the **Select Menu**, click on **All**, or use the keyboard shortcut command; **Ctrl + A** to select every object in the picture.

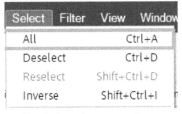

- **Select > Deselect** to remove all of the elements from your image.

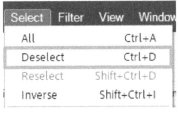

- Navigate to **Select** and select **Reselect** to bring back your previous selection.

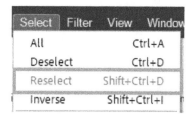

- Select your image, then click Inverse to use the Inverse selection.

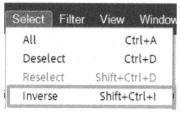

Feather and Modify

The next selection commands we will be discussing in this section are **Feather** and **Modify**.

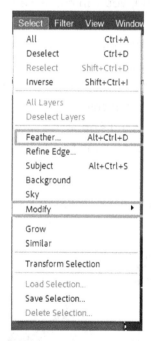

To add feathering to a selection, select it and enter the desired number between 0.2 and 250 pixels.

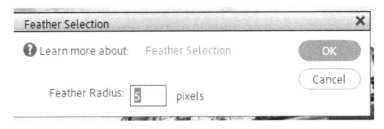

The feather command only functions when a selection has been made.

Although the Modify commands might not be necessary, you never know when they might come in handy. Let's just quickly review the updated commands.

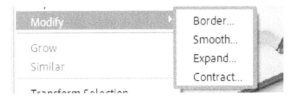

- **Border**: With this command, you can choose a region inside the selection border that is between 1 and 200 pixels in size.
- **Smooth**: With this command, you can enter a number between 1 and 100 pixels to smooth off any rough edges.
- **Expand**: By using this command, you can provide a value between 1 and 100 pixels to expand the size of your selection.
- **Contract**: The Expand command's opposite is this one. You can use this command to reduce the selected border by one to one hundred pixels.

Saving and Loading Selections

Saving a selection can allow you to have access to it later when you need it, and all you have to do to bring it back is load it. Do the following to save and load selections.

- Open and make a selection or selections.

- Click **Save Selection** from the **Select Menu**.

- Set the selection to **New Selection** in the Save Selection dialog box that appears, then enter the name of your selection in the **Name box**.

- Once you've completed this, click **OK**.
- Afterward, you can load the previously saved selection by selecting it from the Selection drop-down box by going to **Select** and clicking on **Load Selection**.

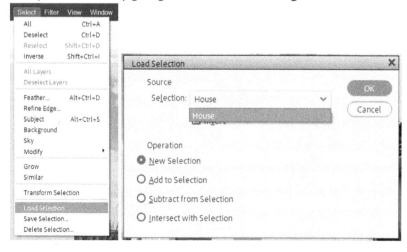

CHAPTER NINE

BASIC IMAGE EDITING OPERATIONS

Fixing and Enhancing Photographs

After knowing how to use basic tools in Photoshop Elements, knowing how to edit images and photographs is what we will be learning in this chapter.

Cropping Photograph

One of the most crucial editing techniques you should master is cropping photos. Cropping a picture can assist in creating a strong focal point and get rid of distracting backgrounds. One of the easiest and fastest ways to crop an image is to use the Crop tool.

Use the Crop tool by following the instructions below.

- Select the **Crop tool** from the **Toolbar**.

- Select the aspect ratio and resolution choices from the available Tool Options.

- o **No Restriction**: You can now resize your image to any size thanks to this.

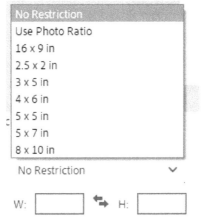

- ○ **Use Photo Ratio**: When cropping, this aids in maintaining the original aspect of the picture.

- ○ **Preset Sizes**: This provides you with multiple choices for standard photography sizes.

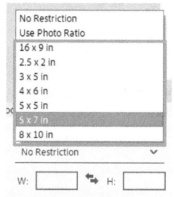

- ○ **Width (W) and Height (H)**: This gives you the option to crop an image to the desired width and height.

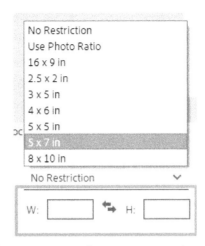

- o **Crop Suggestion**: This gives you four automated suggestions on how to crop your image/photograph.

- o **Resolution**: This lets you select the resolution for your cropped picture that you'd like.

- o **Pixels/ins** and **Pixel/cm**: This is where you select the desired unit measurement.

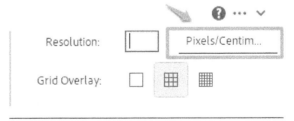

- o **Grid Overlay**: Before cropping, this aids in framing your photo. There are three components to this option: Rule of Thirds, Grid, and None.

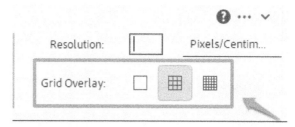

- When the crop marquee appears as a bounding box with handles at the corners and size, drag over the area of the image you want to maintain, and then let go of the mouse.

- Next, press the **Marker** button to commit the operation.

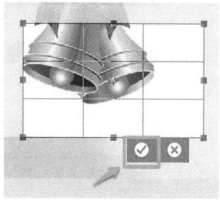

Another way to crop images is to use the selection tools.

You may also crop an image using the selected tool. When an image is cropped with a selection border, the area outside the border is removed. You can use the methods below to crop an image with a selected boundary.

Do the following to crop out a selection.

- To choose the area of the image you want to save, use any selection tool, like the **Rectangular Marquee tool** (you can also use the elliptical tool).

- Click on the **Image Menu** and choose **Crop**.

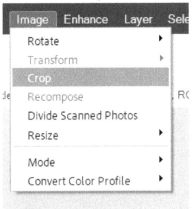

Housed in the Crop Tool is another cropping tool known as *Perspective Crop Tool*.

Select the **Crop Tool** from the **Toolbar...**

...and click on the **Perspective Crop Tool** in the **Tool Options Panel.**

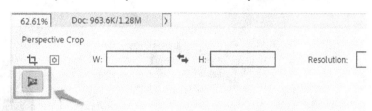

When cropping an image, you can adjust its perspective with the use of the Perspective Crop tool. When you have a distorted image, this is helpful. When an object is photographed at an angle other than straight on or when a wide-angle lens is utilized to capture a significant portion of an object, distortion results. So, using the perspective crop tool is the best bet.

Do the following to use the Perspective Crop Tool to adjust a distorted image.

- Open the distorted image you want to straighten and select the **Perspective Crop Tool.**

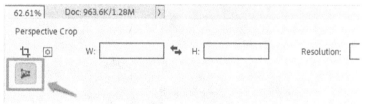

- To adjust the perspective of an object, draw a marquee or boundary around it, then crop the image to fit within that area.

- To change the marquee's shape, use the selection's corners. When the pointer turns white when you hover over a corner, click to move it.

- In the Tools Options panel, you may also enter settings for the **Width (W), Height (H)**, and **Resolution Fields**. The finished image is resized to fit the given resolution, width, and height.

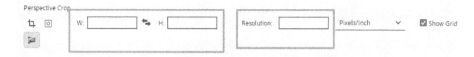

- Next, press the **Marker** button to commit the operation.

Aside from the Perspective Crop Tool, *Cookie Cutter Tool* is another tool in the Crop Tool.

A photo can be cropped into any desired shape with the Cookie Cutter tool. To crop your photo into a certain form, select a shape and drag it over the image. To obtain the region you wish to crop, you can alternatively resize and shift the bounding box. Do the following to carry it out.

- Select the **Crop Tool** from the **Toolbar.**

- Click on the **Cookie Cutter Tool** in the **Tool Options Panel.**

- Click on the alternative library and select a shape from the **Shapes drop-down menu** to view additional libraries.

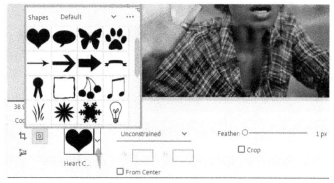

234

- To build the shape border and transfer it to the desired spot inside the image, drag within the image.

- For the cropping to be completed, click the **Marker** button or hit Enter. Press **Esc** or click the **Cancel** button to stop the cropping process.

Content-Aware Move Tool

You can use the Content-Aware Move tool to select an object in your photo and either move or enlarge the selection. After the image is recomposed, the void is filled in with complementary picture parts. It is not necessary for you to perform laborious modifications with numerous layers and intricate selections.

Do the following to use the Content-Aware Move Tool.

- Choose the Content-Aware Move Tool from the toolbar.

- To indicate whether you wish to transfer or duplicate an object, select a mode from the Tool Options panel.

- o **Move**: Provides the ability to reposition things within the image.
- o **Extend**: Permits you to duplicate the item more than once.
- Decide what kind of selection you wish to make:
  - o **New** You can move an object by dragging your mouse around it, or you can expand it to make a new selection.

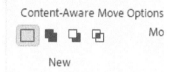

New

  - o **Add**: Any choice you make will be added to the one before it.

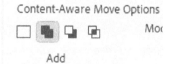

Add

  - o **Subtract**: The overlapping area of a newly made selection is eliminated when it is placed on top of an already-made selection.

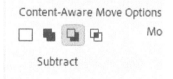

Subtract

  - o **Intersect**: When you make a new selection on top of an already-made one, just the shared space between the two selections stays selected.

Intersect

- To move or enlarge an object, drag the mouse pointer over it in the image and move the object to a new location after making a selection. Click and drag the object to a new spot to accomplish this.

The region from which the selection is moved is automatically filled in, taking into account the surrounding image content.

- Change your choice to the new address. Select one of the subsequent menu items:

   - **Rotate** gives you the option to move your selection to a new location inside the picture.
   - You can change the size of your selection using **Scale**.
   - You can adjust the perspective of your selection in the image using **Skew**.
- Choose the **Sample All Layers** check box and move the **Healing slider** if the automatically-filled area does not appear to be the correct size.

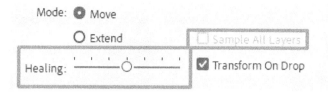

Straightening and Recomposing Images

A misaligned image can be the result of a camera shake. The image can be realigned vertically or horizontally in Photoshop Elements using the Straighten Tool. The straighten tool can be used both in the Quick and Advanced Mode.

Do the following to use Straighten tool in the **Quick Mode.**

- In the **Quick Mode**, select the **Straighten Tool** from the **toolbar.**

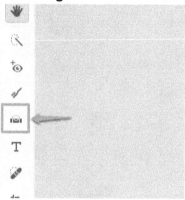

- Select either of the following.

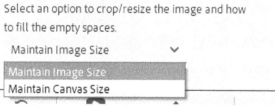

- o **Maintain Image Size**: In order to eliminate any white background that shows up after straightening, this resizes the image. There are some clipped pixels.
- o **Maintain Canvas Size**: This fits the rotated image on the canvas by resizing it. Corners of the image fall outside the current canvas when straightening. There are vacant background patches in the straightened image, but no pixels have been cropped.
- o **Autofill Edges**: Select this if you want the edges of the image to be filled after straightening.

238

Select an option to crop/resize the image and how to fill the empty spaces.

Maintain Image Size ⌄

☑ Autofill edges

- Draw a horizontal line along an edge to align it horizontally, then a vertical line to align it vertically, to straighten the image.

Do the following to straighten an image in the **Advanced Mode**.

- Select the **Straighten Tool** from the **Toolbar**.

- Select either of the following.

- **Grow or Shrink**: With this, the canvas is resized to accommodate the rotated image. Image corners that are straightened out of the current canvas will fall outside of it. Although there are areas of white space in the straightened image, no pixels have been cropped.

- **Remove Background**: This removes any white background from the photograph by cropping it after it has been straightened. There are some clipped pixels.

239

- **Original Size**: This maintains the original image's dimensions on the canvas. The image has been straightened, however, some pixels have been cropped and there are blank background patches.

- **Rotate All Layers**: In cases where your project image has more than one layer. Having this option ticked makes all the layers rotate during the process of straightening if required.

- **Autofill Edges**: If you wish the image's edges to be filled in after it has been straightened, choose this.

- Once your settings are established, To straighten the image, draw a horizontal line along an edge to align it horizontally, then a vertical line to correct it vertically.

The Recompose Tool allows you to safeguard content intelligently during resizing, which is useful if you wish to keep or eliminate specific sections when scaling an image. You can upscale or downscale photographs with Recompose to adjust the orientation, fit a layout, or improve composition.

The Recompose tool makes it easier to resize images intelligently without affecting key visual elements like people, buildings, animals, and more. You can recompose a photograph in the Guided Mode and Advanced Mode.

Do the following to use the recompose tool in the **Guided Mode**.

- Open an image in the **Photo Bin** and choose the **Guided Mode**.

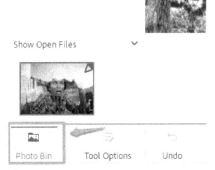

- From the **Special Edits**, select **Recompose**.

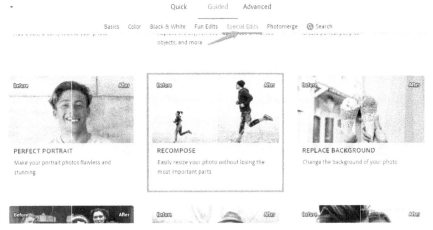

- Located at the right-hand side of the workspace are two Recompose options; *Recompose-Simple* and *Recompose with Finer Details*.

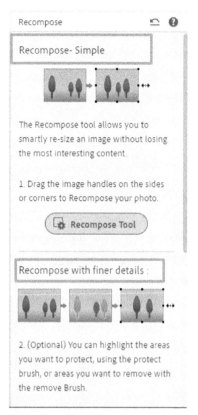

- In the **Recompose with finer details** option, use the Protect brush to mark the areas that need to be protected and the Remove brush to mark the areas you want removed.

- When you right-click on the image, you can choose from the following modes.

242

- o **Use Quick Highlight**: It is possible to rapidly identify the areas that need to be protected. around the topic to draw attention to the necessary areas. Trace the circle's perimeter, for instance, to emphasize the region inside the circle. The Quick Highlight feature makes sure that the circle's contents are designated as protected.
- o **Use Normal Highlight**: Painting and this mode are comparable. List all the areas that need to be protected. For instance, painting or outlining the complete circle is necessary when using Normal Highlight to safeguard it.
- o **Clear Protect Highlights**: Select Clear Protect Highlights from the menu when you right-click the image to remove portions of the undesired marked areas (green). The Protected are marked in Green color.

- o **Clear Remove Highlights**: Select Clear Remove Highlights from the menu when you right-click the image to remove portions of the undesired marked areas (red). The region of removal is indicated by Red Color.

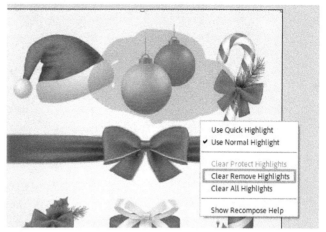

- o **Clear All Highlights**: This allows you to clear all highlights.

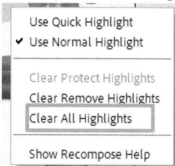

- Click **Next** after you`re done with your modifications.

- Then, click on Done after selecting your **Savings** options.

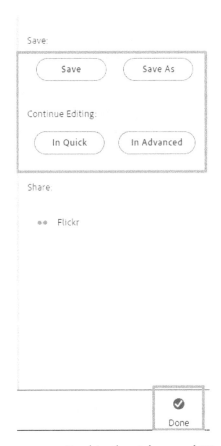

Do the following to use the Recompose Tool in the **Advanced Mode**.

- Select the **Recompose Tool** from the **Toolbar** in advanced mode after opening the image you want to edit.

- Use the **Remove brush** to designate areas you want deleted and the **Protect brush** to mark regions that need to be protected from the tool panel.

You can also adjust the **Size slider** to determine the size of your brush and the **Threshold slider** to determine the intensity of the brush effect.

- When you right-click on the image, you can choose from the following modes.

- ○ **Use Quick Highlight**: It is possible to rapidly identify the areas that need to be protected. around the topic to draw attention to the necessary areas. Trace the circle's perimeter, for instance, to emphasize the region inside the circle. The Quick Highlight feature makes sure that the circle's contents are designated as protected.
- ○ **Use Normal Highlight**: Painting and this mode are comparable. List all the areas that need to be protected. For instance, painting or outlining the complete circle is necessary when using Normal Highlight to safeguard it.
- ○ **Clear Protect Highlights**: Select Clear Protect Highlights from the menu when you right-click the image to remove portions of the undesired marked areas (green). The Protected are marked in Green color.

- ○ **Clear Remove Highlights**: Select Clear Remove Highlights from the menu when you right-click the image to remove portions of the undesired marked areas (red). The region of removal is indicated by Red Color.

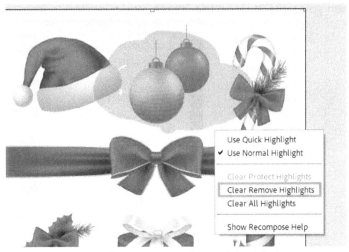

- o **Clear All Highlights**: This allows you to clear all highlights.

- Use the resizing options in the **Tool panel** to determine the size of the image. Then click on the **Marker icon** to apply your changes.

Enhancing Photographs with Auto Fixes

With a single menu command, you may enhance a photo's appearance by rapidly modifying its lighting, contrast, and color with the help of the Auto Fixes. These commands can be found on the Enhance menu in both Quick and Advanced mode.

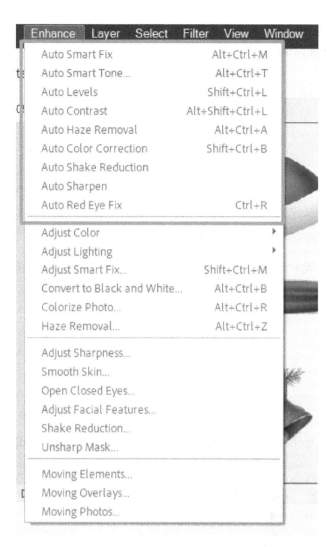

The **Auto Smart Fix** is a powerful tool for quickly addressing common problems with saturation, contrast, and color balance. The shortcut command for Auto Smart Fix is **Alt+Ctrl+M**.

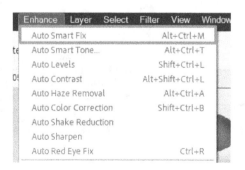

The **Auto Smart Tone** was created to change the tonal values in your photo. The shortcut command is **Alt+Ctrl+T**.

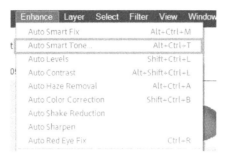

Do the following to use this automated tool effectively.

- Select **Enhance** and then click **Auto Smart Tone** once your image has opened.

- Place the controller in the middle of the image for the best adjustment.

- You can use the **Three Dotted icons** to adjust the Auto Smart Tone.

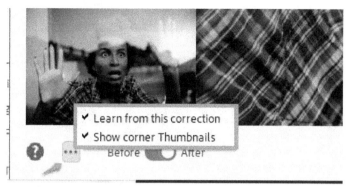

- Toggle the **Before/After** icon for previews.

- Select **Reset** to all clear edits, **Ok** to apply edits and **Cancel** to stop editing.

- Click the Learn from This Correction option located in the lower-left corner of the dialog box to learn about the tool.

- Once the required adjustments have been made, click **OK**.

Both the hue and overall contrast of an image can be adjusted using the *Auto Level*. By turning the image's lightest and darkest pixels to black and white, this function makes the darkest part of the image darker and the lightest area lighter. Its shortcut is **Shift+Ctrl+L**.

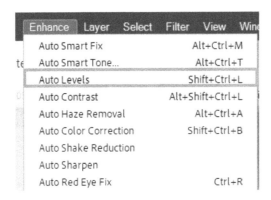

You may change the contrast of an image without changing its color by using the *Auto Contrast tool*. This works best with blurry photographs. The shortcut is **Alt+Shift+Ctrl+L**.

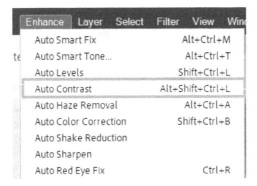

With *Auto Haze Removal*, you can remove haze and fog from your images. Should this command not meet your needs, you might wish to check out the Tools panel's Haze Removal tool. The shortcut is **Alt+Ctrl+A**.

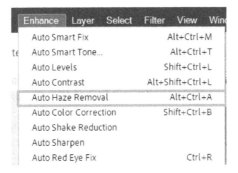

Auto Color Correction can enhance an image's color and contrast by concentrating on the shadows, highlights, and mid-tones. You can also use this command to remove a color cast or balance the colors in your image. The Shortcut is **Shift+Ctrl+B**.

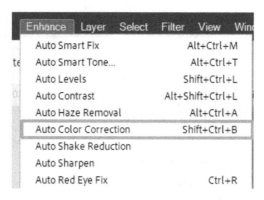

Auto Shake Reduction was created to reduce the blur brought on by camera movement. This command is helpful when needed. For even more Shake Reduction fun, go to Enhance and choose Shake Reduction.

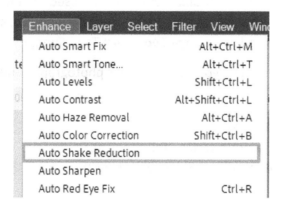

The focus of the image is sharpened by improving pixel contrast with the help of the **Auto Sharpen** command. An overly sharpened image has a grainy, noisy appearance.

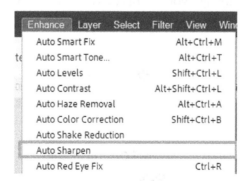

The **Auto Red Fix** command can be used to identify and remove red-eye from an image. A crimson eye occurs when an animal or person looks directly into the flash. If the Auto Red Eye function does not work, you can use the Red Eye tool found in the Tools menu. The Shortcut command is **Ctrl+R**.

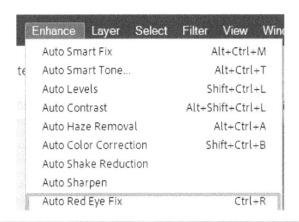

Enhance	Layer	Select	Filter	View	Wind
Auto Smart Fix				Alt+Ctrl+M	
Auto Smart Tone...				Alt+Ctrl+T	
Auto Levels				Shift+Ctrl+L	
Auto Contrast				Alt+Shift+Ctrl+L	
Auto Haze Removal				Alt+Ctrl+A	
Auto Color Correction				Shift+Ctrl+B	
Auto Shake Reduction					
Auto Sharpen					
Auto Red Eye Fix				Ctrl+R	

Retouching Photographs and Images

There are a few tools in the toolbar that can be used to enhance and retouch a photograph. Some of which are **Healing Brush, Spot Healing Brush, Smart Brush, Detail Smart Brush, Clone Stamp Tool, Dodge Tool, Burn Tool, Sponge Tool** etc.

All aforementioned tools allow you to tweak your photographs and retouch them better for your use.

Healing Brush and Spot Healing Brush

Distinctive flaws, irregular skin tones, and other abnormalities can be eliminated with the **Healing Brush tool**. It does this by combining them with the surrounding image's pixels.

Do the following to use the Healing Brush.

- After opening the image you want to retouch, from the **Toolbar**, Select the **Healing Brush**.

- Adjust the brush settings in the **Tool Options** Panel.
  - Use the **Size Slider** to determine the brush size and click on the **Brush Settings** to access other options like **Spacing, Roundness**, and **Hardness**. When you complete a stroke, the **Aligned checkbox** makes the beginning point continue to follow your cursor. As opposed to leaving it out, which results in each stroke's sample point starting at its initial position.

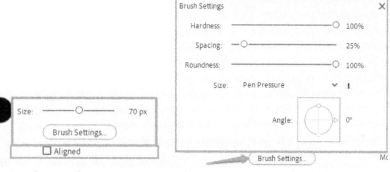

o The region from whence your sampling portion is picked is determined by **Source** which is of two types, **Sampled** and **Pattern**. On the other hand, **Sampled** lets you select any area of your picture to use as a healing sample source. You can use **Pattern** to select the pre-set patterns in Photoshop Elements as a source for healing samples.

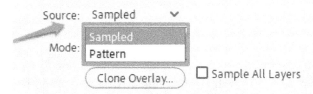

o *Overlay Clipped, Auto Hide*, and *Invert Overlay* are the three options in the **Clone Overlay**. Mark **Show Overlay** to display clone source overlay, **Clipped** to clip the overlay effect to the current brush, **Auto Hide** hides the overlay painting and **Invert Overlay** as the name implies produces an inverted overlay.

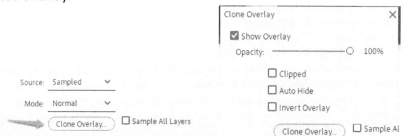

- After adjusting the Tool's setting Alt-click a portion of the image to sample it and drag it over the part of the photograph you want to retouch.

Dust spots and other little flaws can be fixed with the **Spot Healing Brush**. The greater the size of the thing you remove, the more likely it is that the Spot Healing Brush will do so seamlessly.

Do the following to use the spot healing Brush.

- Select the **Healing Brush** from the **Toolbar** and select the **Spot Healing Brush** from the **Tool Options** Panel.

- Adjust the brush settings in the **Tool Options** panel.
  - ○ **Type**: For spot healing, ***Content-Aware*** will be your best option. Use the Spot Healing Brush in this version. When you use the ***Create Texture*** tool in Photoshop Elements, a pattern made of the pixels close to the image you want to replace will be created. ***Proximity Match*** examines the pixels directly surrounding the damaged area.

  - ○ Use **Size Slider** to determine brush size and the **Brush Preset Menu** to determine the kind of brush to use.

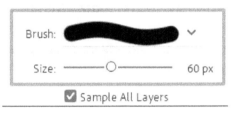

- After tweaking the tool to your satisfaction, you can now make edits with it.

Smart Brush and Detail Smart Brush

With the Smart Brush tool, you may apply several effects to your image selectively by brushing over it. There are fifty pre-made effects to choose from. With the help of these effects, one can create and enhance details, modify color and tone, and more.

Do the following to use the Smart Brush

- Locate and choose the **Smart Brush tool** from the **Toolbar**.

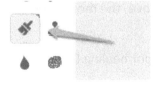

- To apply effects, such as photographic and natural effects, go to the **Preset menu**.

Blue Skies

- To modify the bush properties, navigate to the **Brush Settings drop-down box**.

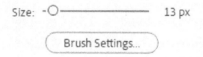

- To create, add, and subtract selections, respectively, use the **New**, **Add**, and **Subtract** Selection icons.

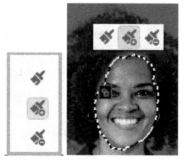

- To refine the region of your image that you have picked, use the **Refine Edge** and **Inverse** to make your selection edit and apply to the unselected portion of the image leaving the selected part unattended to.

Inverse

Refine Edge...

- To fine-tune the image adjustment, use the Adjustment layer automatically created in the Layer panel.

- Click OK once you've finished making the necessary changes.

The Detail Smart Brush tool is comparable to the Smart Brush tool. The only tool that differs is the Detail Smart Brush tool, which gives you additional options and allows you to paint changes straight into the image.

The process of using the Smart Brush Tool also applies to the Detail Smart Brush.

Sponge, Dodge and Burn Tool

Color saturation is impacted by the **Sponge Tool**. It can increase or decrease a hue's saturation. This means that we can either increase or decrease the intensity of the colors of particular pixels by utilizing the sponge tool.

Do the following to use the sponge tool.

- Select the **Sponge Tool** from the **Toolbar.**

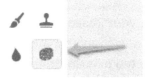

- From **Mode**, select **Saturate** to increase color intensity and **Desaturate** to decrease color intensity.

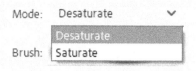

- Select brush type from the **Brush Preset Menu.**

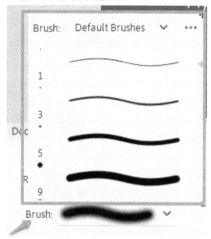

- The **Size Slider** defines the brush size, while **Flow** determines the amount of saturation or desaturation that will happen when we use the sponge tool.

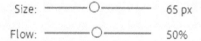

- After adjusting the aforementioned options in the Tool Options panel, you can now paint over your photograph. You may also adjust the tool's options as you work.

In essence, you can paint the pixels of a selection or image by using the **Burn tool.** Eventually, if you use it for long enough, it will turn entirely black, just like if you had burned it. Burn can be applied to produce thick shadows.

Do the following to use the Burn Tool.

- Select the **Sponge tool** from the **Toolbar** and select the **Burn Tool** from the **Tool Options** panel.

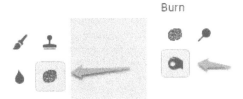

Burn

- From the Tool Options panel, adjust the settings of the tool.
  - ○ When you select the **Range** option, a drop-down menu with the following three alternatives will appear:

The grayscale image's middle tonal range is changed by **Mid-tones**. It is the range's default setting. **Shadows** modify the image's shadows. The image's bright parts are altered by **Highlights**.

  - ○ Select brush type from the **Brush Preset Menu.**

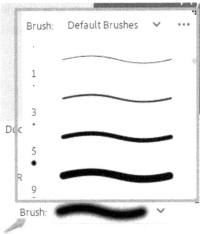

  - ○ The **Size Slider** helps to determine the size of the Brush, and **Exposure** influences the intensity of the tool's impact.

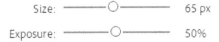

- Apply the brush to your image after making the necessary edits.

Use the **Dodge tool** in Element to lighten the affected area of the image without altering the hue or saturation. It can also be employed to highlight particular picture features.

The process of using the Burn Tool also applies to the Dodge Tool, except its result lightens the image`s hue or saturation.

Blur and Sharpen Tool
By omitting details, the **Blur tool** softens sharp edges or portions of an image. Adding some blur to a cluttered background will help focus your subject more. It can also add a creative element to the image, but how it does so will depend entirely on how you utilize the tool.

Do the following to use the Blur Tool.

- From the **Toolbar**, select the **Blur Tool**.

- Determine the type of brush to apply the blur effect from the **Brush Preset Menu** while **Mode** determines how the blurry effect applies to the pixels of the image.

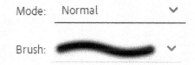

- The Size Slider determines the size of the brush while the Strength Slider can be used to adjust the intensity of the blurry effect.

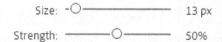

- Drag the mouse cursor over the desired area of the image to be blurred. You can also tweak the tool`s options as you work on your photograph till the desired result is produced.

The **Sharpen Tool** highlights the image and increases pixel contrast. When utilizing this tool, you have to exercise extreme caution because any area of the image that is "sharpened" will become more pronounced. Thus, take care not to sharpen it excessively.

Do the following to use the Sharpen tool.

- From the toolbar, select the **Blur Tool** and click on the **Sharpen Tool** in the **Tool Options** panel.

Sharpen

- The **Brush Preset Menu** lets you choose the kind of brush to use to produce the blur effect, and **Mode** controls how the effect is applied to the image's pixels.

Mode: Normal

Brush:

- While the **Strength Slider** can be used to change the degree of blurriness, the **Size Slider** sets the brush's size.

Size: 13 px
Strength: 50%

- **Protect Detail** employs controlled localized sharpening.

Size: 13 px
Strength: 50%
☐ Sample All Layers   ☑ Protect Detail

Cloning in Photoshop Elements

Using the Clone Stamp Tool enables the cloning of individual images or portions of an image. You can paint over items in your photo, duplicate things, and fix image flaws with the Clone Stamp tool. It uses an image sample as paint. Parts of an image can also be copied to create new images.

Do the following to use the Clone Stamp Tool.

- From the toolbar, select the **Clone Stamp Tool**.

- To fix the brush's tip. Click the arrow next to the brush sample to select a brush thumbnail, then use the Brush drop-down menu to choose a brush category.

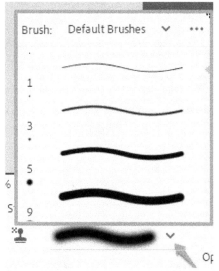

- **Size**: Modifies the pixel size of the brush. You can either move the Size slider or type a size in the text box.

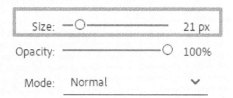

- **Opacity**: Defines the degree of opacity of the pattern you use. When the opacity is low, the underlying pixels of a pattern stroke are visible. You can either drag the slider or enter an opacity value.

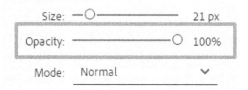

- **Mode**: Shows how the paint you apply will blend in with the pixels that already make up the image.

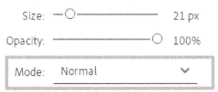

- If you select the **Aligned option**, you can stop sketching on the freshly cloned image in the middle of it without losing your position. The clone will begin drawing at the sampling point if you remove the mouse button and pick up the painting again after it is deselected.

- In Clone Overlay, to make the overlay visible inside the brush size, select **Show Overlay**. Enter a percentage in the **Opacity** text box to adjust the overlay's opacity. Turn on the **Clipped** option to clip overlay to the brush size. Choose **Auto Hide** to conceal the overlay while you apply the paint strokes. Choose **Invert** to flip the overlay's color scheme.

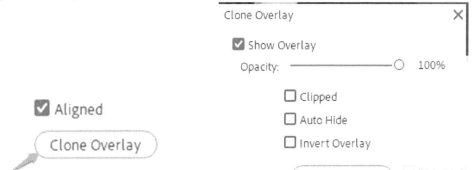

- Place the mouse pointer where you wish to sample an image by selecting it with the mouse, then click or press the **Alt Key** (**Option Key** on Mac OS). As you paint, the tool replicates the pixels in your image at this sample location.
- To clone the sampled region, do one of the following methods.
  - To apply the tool's paint to the same image, drag or click.
  - Use the tool to paint on the other targeted image by dragging or clicking.

Animating Images

There are three commands in the Enhance menu that allow you animate images or part of a photograph in different ways and they are namely **Moving Elements, Moving Overlay,** and **Moving Photos**.

Moving Elements

This function, which allows you to add motion to components in a static image, was introduced in the software's previous edition, specifically the 2023 version.

Do the following to apply Moving Elements

- After opening your image, select **Moving Elements** from the **Enhance Menu**.
- In the dialog box, use the selection tools in *Sky, Background*, or **Manual** to select the area you wish to add motion to.

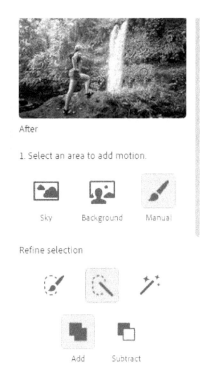

After

1. Select an area to add motion.

Sky Background Manual

Refine selection

Add Subtract

- In the area you have selected for editing, click the **Arrow Cursor** and move your mouse pointer in the direction you want the motion to travel.

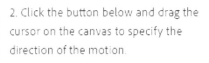

2. Click the button below and drag the cursor on the canvas to specify the direction of the motion.

- By adjusting the speed slider, you can adjust the element's motion speed until you are happy with it.

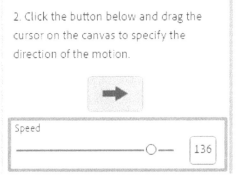

2. Click the button below and drag the cursor on the canvas to specify the direction of the motion.

Speed ─────────────────○─ 136

- Select the "play" button to view your sneak peek.

- When you are happy with your changes, click **Export** to export your work.

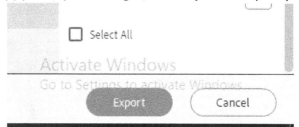

- Your file can be exported as an **MP4** video file or as a **GIFF**.

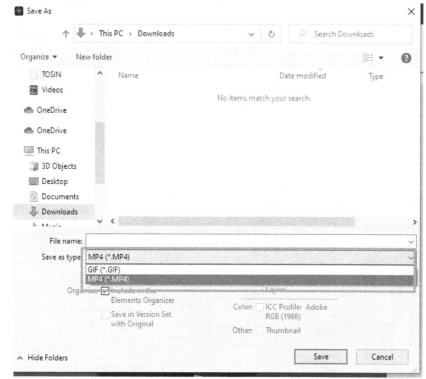

- Select **Save** to finally export your work.

Moving Overlay

You can add overlay animations to your photo with the Moving Overlay Command. The Moving Overlay Command Center's animated elements fall into three categories: overlays, graphics, and frames.

Use the steps below to apply the moving overlays to your photo:

- After opening the image you want to alter, select **Moving Overlays** from **Enhance Menu**.

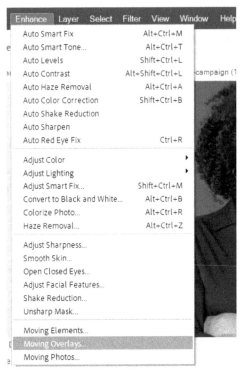

- Choose from **Overlays**, **Graphics**, and **Frames**—the three types of Overlay Animations you'll love to apply to your photo—on the right-hand side of the dialog box.

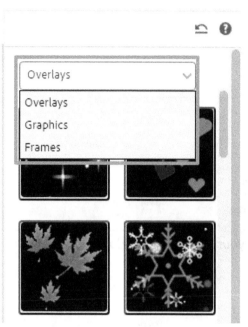

- By selecting **Protect Subject**, you can shield your photo's subject from overlay modifications.

- To change the additional animations' opacity, use the **Opacity Slider**.

- To reposition your animation overlay, click the Refine **Overlay option**.

- Press the **Play** button to view a preview of your changes.

- Click **Export** and follow the prompts to export the picture as an animated gif. Next, select **Save**.

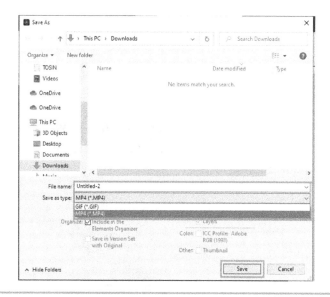

Moving Photos

You can take a photo and apply a simple pan, zoom, or rotate effect at the same time by using the Moving Photos command. To make the image move, you can export it as an animated gif. An animated image can be created by following the methods shown below.

- After opening the photo you want to animate, From the **Enhance Menu** select **Moving Photo**.

- In the dialog box, Use the **Zoom** and **Hand tools** on the left to adjust the zoom and pan of the preview image as desired.

- To see a preview of the effect emerge on the image, double-click the options in the **Motion Effect** to apply them. On the right side of the display, in the scrollable pane, are the **Motion Effects**.

Double-click to apply effect

Zoom In-Out

Zoom In

- Click the 3D Effect toggle button at the bottom to turn the **3D Effect** on or off.

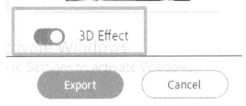

3D Effect

Export   Cancel

- After an effect has been played, click the **Play** button that appears below the previous image to replay the effect preview.

- Click on **Export** and follow the steps to export the image as an animated gif.

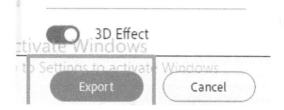

CHAPTER TEN

WORKING WITH COLORS

The Concept of Colors

It is impossible to know how the graphic world works without understanding the concept of colors.

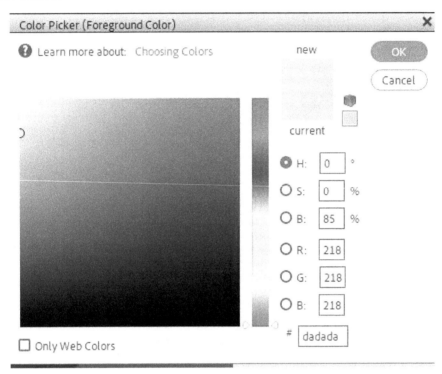

Color theory describes how colors interact with one another and how combinations of colors can elicit particular emotions, moods, and behaviors. It is a concept used in visual arts and design.

Element's Color Models and Color Wheel

Color Models are systems used to describe colors, some of which are CMYK, RGB, BITMAP, etc. To work with color in Photoshop Elements, you need two color models. Hue, saturation, and brightness (HSB) and Red, Green, and Blue (RGB).

HSB Color Model

The HSB model explains three basic properties of color based on how humans perceive color. Photoshop Elements does not allow you to generate or modify photos in the HSB mode, but you can use the HSB model to define a color in the Color Picker dialog box.:

- **Hue**: It is the color that an item transmits or reflects. It is measured as a point on the conventional color wheel and given as a degree that ranges from 0 to 360. In common language, hue is denoted by the color name, such as red, blue, or green.
- **Saturation**: It is a color's intensity or purity. Saturation is a percentage ranging from 0 (gray) to 100 that indicates the amount of gray relative to the hue (fully saturated)
- **Brightness**: It is the proportion of a color's lightness or darkness, typically expressed as a percentage ranging from 0 (black) to 100. (white).

RGB Color Model

The RGB (red, green, and blue) light can be mixed in different ratios and intensities to represent a wide section of the visible spectrum. Monitors, video, and lighting all use the additive primary colors. Red, green, and blue phosphors, for instance, allow light to be emitted, which produces color on your monitor.

The Color Wheel

An additional tool for understanding the relationships between colors is the **color wheel**. Four image modes—RGB, bitmap, grayscale, and indexed color—that control how many colors are displayed in a picture are offered by Photoshop Elements.

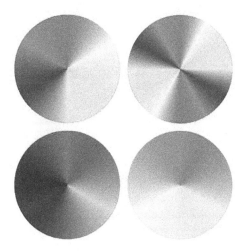

RGB stands for red, green, and blue as the additive primaries. The subtractive primaries are CMY, or cyan, magenta, and yellow. The complement of each additive primary, which is red-cyan, green-magenta, and blue-yellow, is located just across from it.

To choose and work with color, you use the HSB and RGB color models. You can better comprehend the relationships between colors by using the color wheel.

Fixing Color, Clarity, And Contrast

When quick and easy fixes don't live up to your standards, you may need to use manual fixes to improve contrast, color, and clarity in your photographs. All these will be treated in this section. Most of these manual fixes are found in the Enhance Menu.

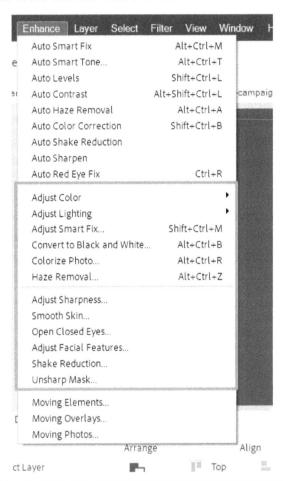

Using Adjust Color

The primary purpose of this enhancement feature is to correct Color problems in an image and increase the color expression of a photograph or image. It is located in the

Enhance Menu and houses other features sharing the same enhancement properties which include; *Remove Color Cast, Adjust Hue/Saturation, Remove Color, Replace Color, Adjust Color Curves, Adjust Color for Skin Tone*, and *Defringe Layer*.

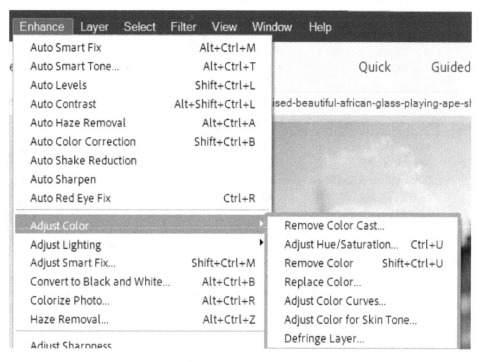

A color cast occurs when an image's color channels are out of balance. The unwanted appearance is often the result of the image's bad lighting, and it usually manifests as an unusual color tint. Fluorescence light is one of the main factors that contribute to the color cast in pictures. To remove the cast and balance the color in your photos use the **Remove Color Cast** command.

To use the Remove Color Cast, adhere to the following instructions.

- Select **Adjust Color** from the **Enhance Menu**, then click on **Remove Color Cast** after choosing Enhance.

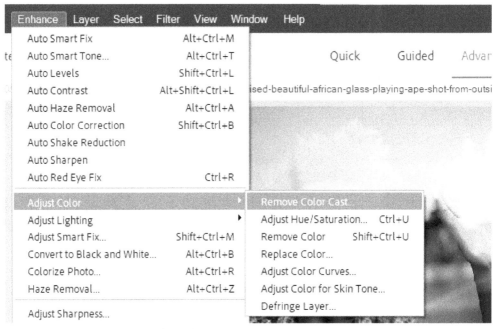

- Click **Ok** on the next dialog box that pops up.

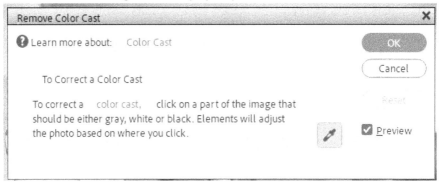

- Then, select the portion of the image with color cast.

In a situation where there is color or vibrance deficiency in an image, use **Adjust Hue/Saturation** to change or enhance the color of an image. Do the following to do such.

- Select **Adjust Hue/Saturation** from **Adjust Color**.

- Select **Master** to apply your effect to all colors or select the color of your choice from the drop-down menu.

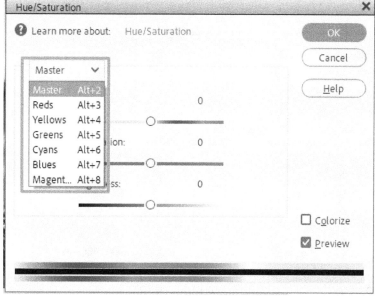

- Use the **Hue Slider** to change the colors in the image/selection, use the **Saturation Slider** to adjust the intensity of the colors and the **Lightness Slider** to determine the degree of light in the image.

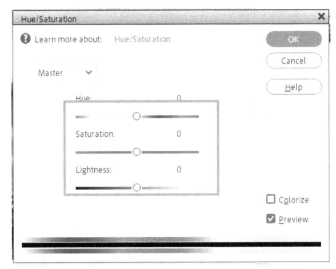

- Click **OK** once you are done with your edits.

To remove color from a photograph or image. Select **Remove Color** from the **Adjust Color drop-down menu**.

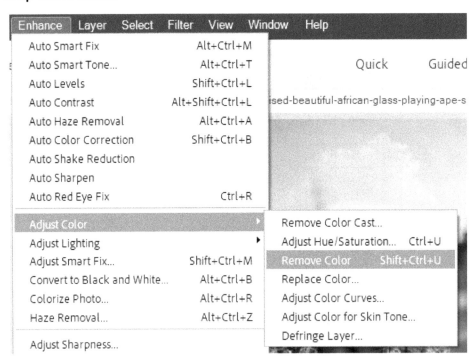

Do the following to replace colors in a photograph.

- From the **Adjust Color drop-down menu**, select **Replace Color**.

279

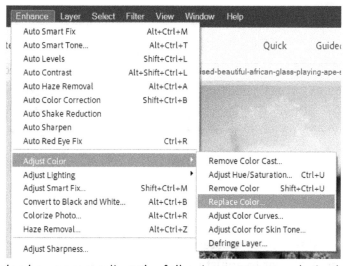

- When the dialog box opens, adjust the following to get your desired result.

- Use the **Color Picker Tool** to select the color you want to replace, **Add Sample** to add more than one color and **Remove Sample** to remove colors from your selection

280

- Select **Localized Color Clusters** to limit the influence of your selection and move the Fuzziness Slider to adjust the softness of the selection.

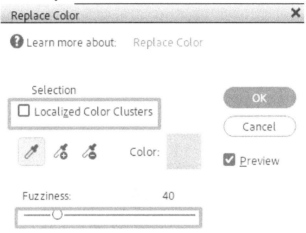

- Choose either **Selection** or **Image** from the menu; Selection displays the mask in the Preview area, while Image displays the actual image.

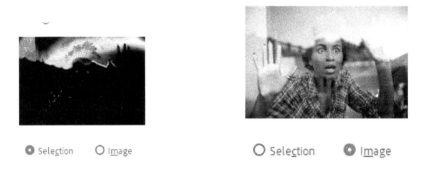

- Select **Color** to determine the color you want to change your selections to.

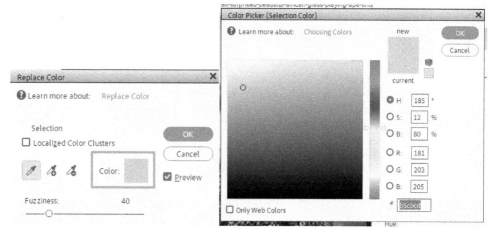

- To alter the hues of the image or selection, use the **Hue slider**; to modify the color intensity, use the **Saturation slider**; and to ascertain the amount of light present in the image, use the **Lightness slider**.

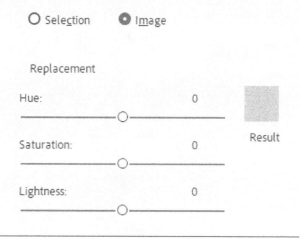

- After you are done with making your changes, select **OK**.

The **Adjust Color Curves** command attempts to expand the overall tonal range in color photos by modifying the highlights, shadows, and mid-tones in each color channel. The best images for this command are those with a dark backlight or those that are overexposed. Do the following to use the **Adjust Color Curves** command.

- Click on **Adjust Color Curves** after choosing **Adjust Color** from the **Enhance menu** bar.

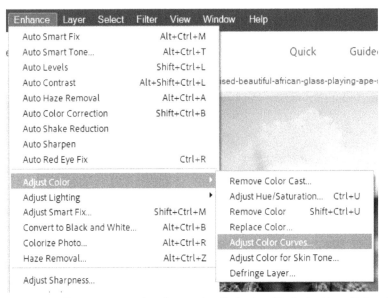

- Choose the curve adjustment styles from the **Select a Style** in the dialog box.

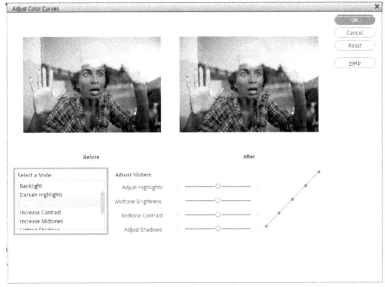

- For more precise adjustments, use the sliders for highlights, brightness, contrast, and shadow modification.

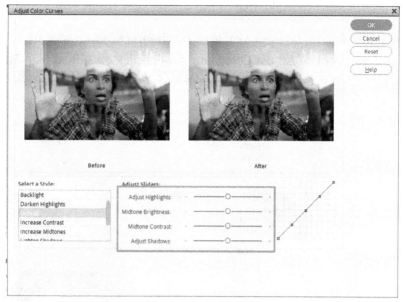

- Once you're satisfied with the adjustment, click OK.

There are many different factors in your images or persons that can contribute to unflattering skin tones. The **Adjust Skin Tones** command is provided by Elements to help the skin tone return to a more natural appearance. With this command, you can change a selection or an entire layer. The part of your image that you do not want to change should be changed by using the selection tool to choose the area of the tool that you want to update.

Use these instructions to make use of the Adjust Skin Tones command.

- Once the desired layer or skin area has been chosen, navigate to Enhance in the menu bar, choose Adjust Color, and finally click on Adjust Skin Tone.

- Select the area of skin that requires adjusting by clicking on it.
- Configure the subsequent settings:

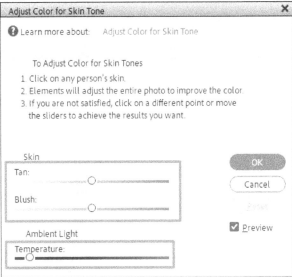

- ○ **Tan**: To reduce or increase the amount of brown in the skin
- ○ **Brush**: To increase or decrease the skin's level of redness
- ○ **Temperature**: To change the skin's general tone, making it more red (hot) or less cool (left toward blue)

- Click OK once you've finished making the necessary changes.

The region that is usually encountered when a selection is made, moved, or copied is referred to as the "fringe." The fringe is the collection of background pixels that encircles your selection. These unnecessary additional pixels have their colors changed to match neighboring non-background pixels when the **Defringed Layer** command is applied. Do the following to do this.

- You can copy and paste a selection onto a new or existing layer, or you can drag and drop a selection into a new project.
- Click on **Defringing Layers** after choosing **Adjust Color** under **Enhance** on the menu bar.

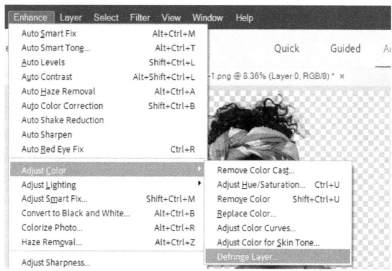

- Enter the amount representing the number of pixels you want to convert.

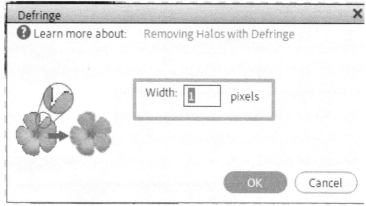

- Once the required changes have been made, click OK.

Using Adjust Lighting

Instead of doing auto repairs, several simple strategies can be utilized to improve the lighting in images. Most importantly, these manual corrections are included in the Expert and Quick modes. The Adjust Lighting Command contains **Shadows/Highlights**, **Brightness/Contrast**, and **Levels**. Now let's look at them.

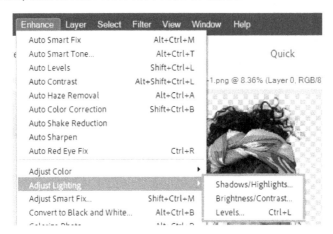

You may quickly and simply correct overexposed and underexposed areas in your photos by using the **Shadows/Highlights** commands. This feature performs well on images captured in strong lighting or from above. To use this feature, adhere to the following instructions.

- From the **Enhance menu**, select **Adjust Lighting**, and then select **Shadows/Highlight**.

- On the dialog box, use the **Lighten Shadows Slider** to correct shadows, **Darken Highlights** to correct backlights, and the **Midtone Contrast** to adjust midtones (Mid-tone is a kind of light in between the Light and Dark spectrum).

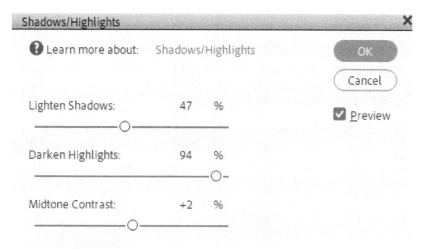

- After you are done with your edits, you can click **OK**.

Do the following to use the Brightness/Contrast feature.

- From the **Enhance menu**, select **Adjust Lighting**, and then select **Brightness/Contrast**.

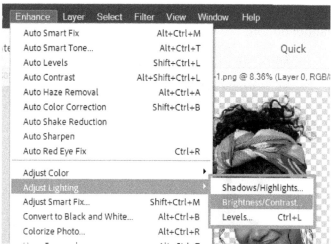

- Check the Preview check box, drag the sliders, or input a value in the **Brightness** and **Contrast** dialog box to adjust the brightness and contrast adjustment level.

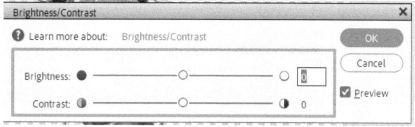

- When you're finished making the adjustment, click **OK**.

With the Level command, the result of edits is precisely under your control. Levels provide you with much greater control over tone variation—up to 256—and result in a much more natural-looking final output than the Brightness/Contrast command.

Use Levels by following these guidelines.

- From the **Enhance menu**, select **Adjust Lighting**, then **Levels**.

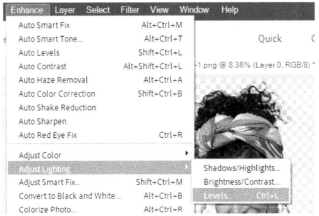

- In the dialog box, click the **Preview check bo**x for preview and choose **RGB** from the **Channel** option.

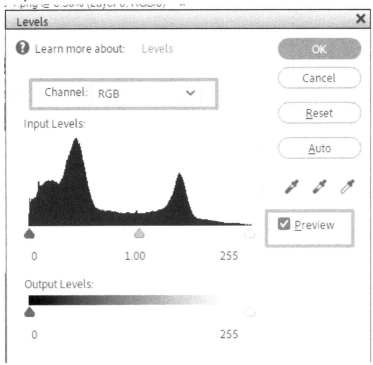

- Use the **black and white Input Levels sliders** to adjust the shadow and highlight values, or enter the values into the first and third Input Levels text boxes.

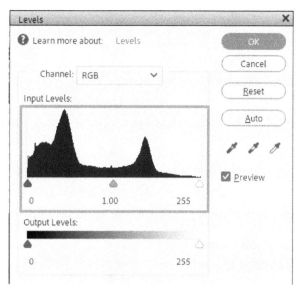

- After that, select **OK**.

Using Adjust Smart Fix

Adjust Smart Fix is a manual way of applying Smart Fix. Do the following to use the Adjust Smart Fix.

- From the **Enhance Menu**, select **Adjust Smart Fix or** use the keyboard shortcut **Shift+Ctrl+M**.

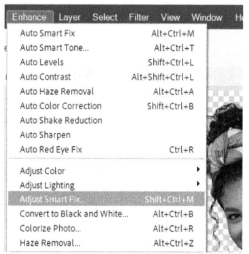

- On the dialog box, adjust the **Slider** or input a digit into the text field until you are satisfied and click on **OK**.

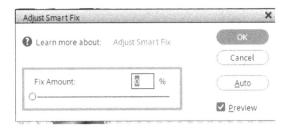

Using Convert to Black & White

Why is this feature different from the normal Black & White command? Because it allows you to determine how the Black & White effect will be applied to your pictures. Do the following to use the Convert Black & White command.

- From the **Enhance Menu**, select **Convert to Black & white or** use the keyboard shortcut **Alt+Ctrl+B**.

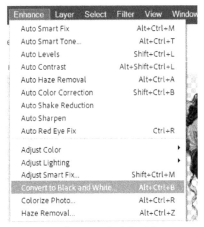

- In the dialog box, the preview window is divided into two; **Below** and **After.**

Before   After

Tip

- Select how you want the effect to be applied to your image from the **Select A Style**.

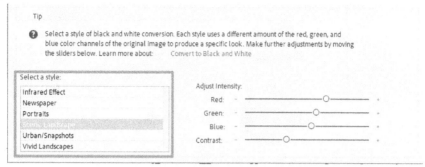

- Use the sliders in **Adjust Intensity** to determine the Black & White effect that will be applied on the colors and its intensity on them.

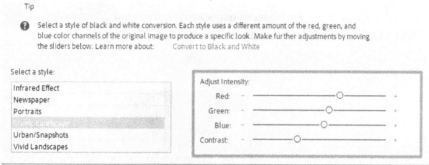

- Click on **OK** when you are done.

Using Colorize Photo

This feature allows you to apply color effects to your images. Do the following to use Colorize Photo.

- From the Enhance Menu, select Colorize Photo

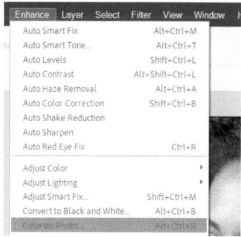

- You will be asked to download the feature if you don`t have it installed on your Elements. Click **Download** to download and install Colorize Photo.

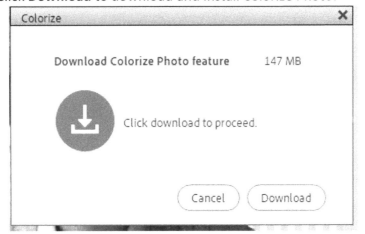

- After downloading, the dialog box opens.

- Toggle the **Auto/Manual** button at the right-hand side of the workspace to switch between the Auto and Manual settings.

Auto gives you access to already colorized preset options to apply to your picture.

while **Manual** allows you to do the edits by yourself from the start by following the given instructions in the dialog box.

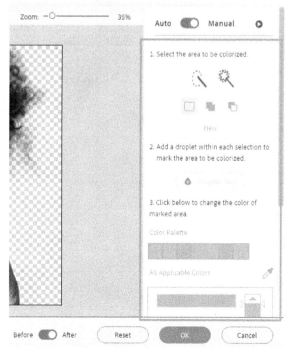

- Use the Zoom Slider to zoom in and out of your image.

- Use the **Before/After** button to see the before and after effects of your editing.

- Select **Reset** to cancel all changes made to the image, **OK** to apply all edits, and **Cancel** to remove all edits and exit the Colorize Photo dialog box.

Using Haze Removal

Use the Haze Removal tool to manually remove fog and haze from your image. Haze or fog can be created when light interacts with dust, dirt, or other particles in the air. To utilize the Haze Removal Tools, adhere to the guidelines provided below.

- Once the desired image has been chosen, pick **Enhance** from the menu bar and then choose **Haze Removal**.

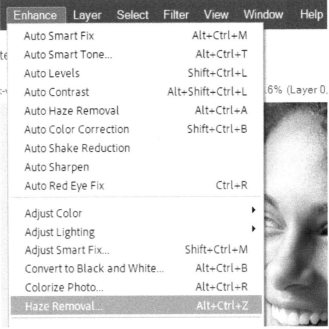

- Set these choices in the **Haze Removal** dialog box.

- o **Haze Reduction**: You can change the amount of haze in the image with this slider.

- o **Sensitivity**: The sensitivity of the photos to the Haze Removal can be changed with this slider.

- o **Before/After Button**: Using this, you may go between your image's before and after views.

296

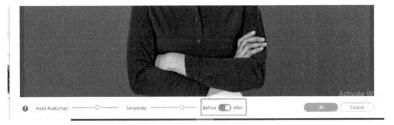

- Once the changes are complete, select **OK**.

Using Adjust Sharpness

This command on Photoshop Elements allows you to manually add sharpness to your images and reduce the blurriness in them. Do the following to apply this feature.

- From the **Enhance Menu**, select **Adjust Sharpness**.

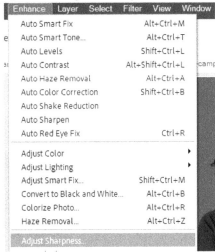

- In the dialog box that appears, set the following options.

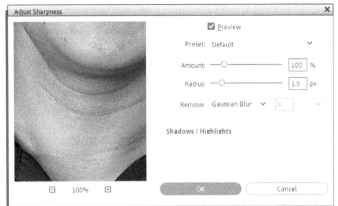

  - Use the **Amount Slider** to determine the rate of sharpness and the **Radius Slider** to determine the intensity of sharpness.

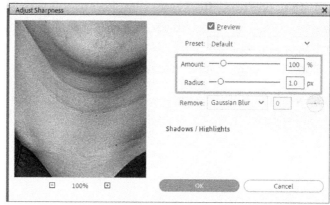

- o In the **Remove** drop-down menu, select the kind of blur you want removed from the image.

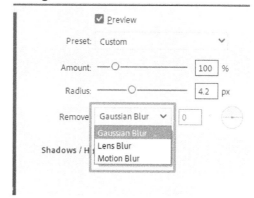

- o In the **Preset** section, you can save and load effects into your photographs.

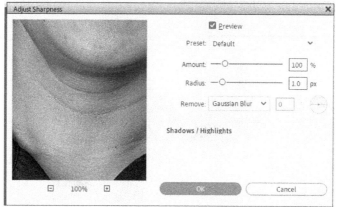

- o After you are done click on **OK**.

Using Smooth Skin

With the Smooth Skin command, you may quickly and efficiently reduce the visibility of wrinkles in a face's skin within the Photoshop Element by softening the lines that make

298

up the skin. A small blurring effect is also applied to the face to accomplish this, even if doing so helps to make the chosen face's skin appear smoother. This command only applies to the face and will not work effectively if the face is not properly visible. To use the Smooth Skin command, follow these steps:

- To begin working on an image, open it and choose **Smooth Skin** from the **Enhance menu**.

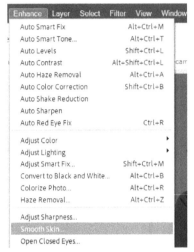

- In the dialog box, do the following.

- o Adjust the **Smoothness Slider** to determine the intensity of the face smoothness, use **Before/After** to see the effect preview and select **Ok** once you are satisfied with your result.

Using Open Closed Eyes

The open-closed eyes command allows you to apply a set of selected eyes to a face inside an image if the Element can detect the presence of eyes in a face. This makes it easy to copy a matching pair of eyes from one photo to another and alter closed eyes inside a photo. To use the Open Closed Eyes command, follow the steps outlined below.

- After opening the image you want to work on, select **Open Closed Eyes** from the **Enhance Menu**.

- The affected area is surrounded by a circle in the Open Closed Eyes dialog box.

- Select one image from your computer, organizer or photo bin to use as the eyes source image.

Eye Source

Open a photo that can be used as the
Source of replacement eyes for this photo.

Open from

Computer   Organizer   Photo Bin

Or try the given samples.

Try sample eyes:

- Click on Ok after you are satisfied with your result.

Using Adjust Facial Features

The Adjust Facial Features command in Photoshop Element allows you to change an individual's lips, eyes, nose, and face in an image. If the face of this image is partially hidden, the command will not work. Like the smooth skin command, this feature only applies to the face.

Do the following to access these features.

- After opening the image you want to modify, select **Adjust Facial Features** from the **Enhance Menu**.

301

- At the right-hand side of the dialog box are facial features to adjust manually which include *Lips, Eyes, Nose, Face Shape*, and *Face Tilt*. Adjust the slider in each section to apply effects to the face.

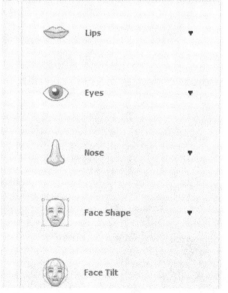

- Click **Ok** once you are satisfied with your result.

Using Shake Reduction

To manually remove the blur or shake that occurs when holding your phone or camera while taking a picture, use the Wobble Reduction feature. The steps listed below can be used to use the Shake Reduction command.

- Once you have chosen the image you want to modify, select **Shake Reduction** from the **Enhance menu**.

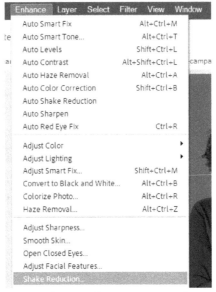

- In the Shake Reduction dialog box will pop up, a selection box will appear over your image. To adjust the size of the selection box, click and drag its resizing handles

- The **Sensitivity slider** can be used to change how much sharpness is applied to the image.

- To add another region, utilize the **Add Another Shake Region tool**.

- To see what happens before and after applying the Shake Reduction effect, use the **Before and After toggle button**.

- Once all the changes have been made, select **Ok**.

Using Unsharp Mask

In a photograph, the Unsharp Mask enhances the contrast of the image around the borders of objects. Although the effect can't really detect edges, it can recognize pixel values that differ by a specific amount from those of their nearby pixels. Next, the mask will make the adjacent pixels more contrasted, lightening the light and darkening the dark pixels. Do the following to apply this feature to an image.

- After opening the image you want to edit, select **Unsharp Mask** from **Enhance Menu**.

- In the dialog box, adjust the following.

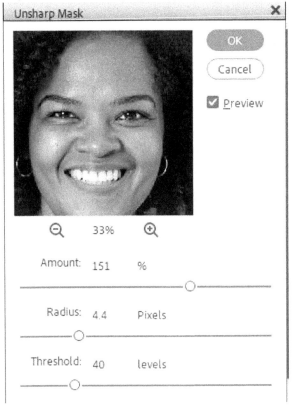

- o **Amount**: To enhance the contrast in the pixels, move the Amount slider. The appearance of increased sharpness is produced by this contrast augmentation.

305

- o **Radius**: To specify how distinct the sharpened pixels must be from the surrounding pixels to be regarded as edge pixels, use the Threshold parameter.
- o **Threshold**: To find out how many pixels next to the edge pixels will influence the sharpening, move the Radius slider. The sharpness will be more noticeable and have a wider effect the larger the radius.
- After you are satisfied with your result, click **Ok**.

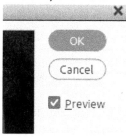

CHAPTER ELEVEN

PAINTING TOOLS IN PHOTOSHOP ELEMENTS

Painting in Photoshop Elements

The color of an image's pixels can be altered using painting tools. Similar to conventional drawing tools, the *Brush and Pencil tools* apply color using brush strokes. Color is applied over huge regions using the *Gradient tool, Paint Bucket tool*, and *Fill command*. The colors already present in an image can be altered with tools like the *Smudge, Blur, and Eraser tools*.

The Foreground and Background Color

The Foreground and Background Color Plates can be found directly below the Toolbar. The color of the background is represented by the bottom box, and the foreground by the top box.

In the image above, the Foreground Color Plate is represented with Red and the plate with the White color is the Background Color Plate.

When filling selections with the Paint Bucket tool and painting with the Brush or Pencil tools, you apply the foreground color. The background color is the color that you apply using the Eraser tool to the Background layer.

Working with Blending Modes

The way a painting or editing tool affects individual pixels in an image can be adjusted using blending modes.

The blend modes regulate how colors interact with one another in pictures, layers, and even when you paint over a layer. Without affecting the pixel quality of your image, you may easily add, modify, and remove blend modes. There are twenty-five blending modes in all. The Blending Mode section is located in the Layer Panel.

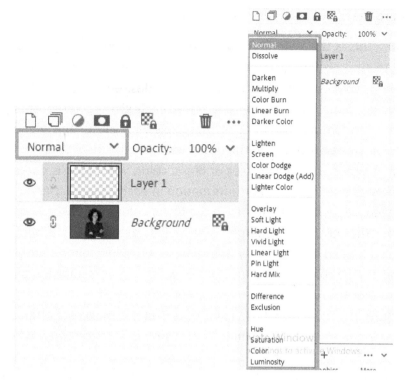

All 25 blending modes are categorized into six categories. Normal and Dissolve into *General Blend Mode*. Darken, Multiply, Color Burn Linear Burn, and Darken Color into *Darken Blend Mode*. Lighten, Screen, Color Dodge, Linear Dodge, Lighten Dodge, and Lighter Color into *Lighten Blend Mode*. Overlay, Soft Light, Hard Light, Vivid Light, Linear Light, Pin Light, and Hard Mix into *Contrast Blend Mode*. Difference and Exclusion into *Inversion Blend Mode*. Hue, Saturation, Color and Luminosity into *Component Blend Mode*.

The purpose of the **Darken Blend Modes** is to add effects that make your photographs darker.

Using **Lighten Blend Modes** can help you add brightening effects to your photographs.

The **Contrast Blend Modes** combine elements of both the Lighten and Darken categories.

To produce the blend, **Inversion Blend Modes** search for differences between the base and blend layers.

Component Mix Modes combine hue, saturation, and brightness—the three fundamental color components—to produce the desired blend.

Listed below are the blending modes available in Photoshop Elements.

- **Normal**: This is the default mode of two layers overlapping. It applies paint or editing to each pixel to give it the desired color. This is how things normally work.
- **Dissolve**: It applies each pixel to achieve the desired color by editing or painting it. However, depending on the opacity at each given pixel location, the output color is a random replacement of the pixels with either the blend color or the base color. Large brushes and the brush tools are the ideal tools for this setting.
- **Darken**: It chooses the base color or blend color, whichever is darker, as the final color after examining the color information in each channel. Darker pixels remain unchanged, while those lighter than the blend color are substituted.
- **Multiply**: The color that emerges is always darker. Black is produced when any color is multiplied by black. Any hue remains the same when multiplied by white. Painting using a color other than black or white requires applying painting strokes after another to create increasingly darker colors.
- **Color Burn**: It darkens the base color to reflect the mix color after examining the color information in each channel. There is no difference when white is blended in.
- **Linear Burn**: It darkens the base color to reflect the blend color by lowering the brightness after examining the color information in each channel. Adding white to blend yields no results.
- **Darker Color**: Because Darker Color selects the lowest channel values from both the base and the blend color to form the result color, it does not produce a third color, which can arise from the Darken mix.
- **Lighten**: It chooses the base color or blend color, whichever is lighter, as the final color after examining the color information in each channel. Lighter pixels remain unchanged, while those darker than the blend color are substituted.
- **Screen**: There is always a lighter color as a result when you use this blending mode. Black screening preserves color integrity. White is produced by screening with white.
- **Color Dodge:** It brightens the base color to reflect the mix color after examining the color information in each channel. Adding black to a blend yields no results.
- **Linear Dodge (Add):** It examines each channel's color data and increases the brightness of the base color to reflect the mix color. Adding black to a blend yields no results.
- **Lighter Color**: It displays the color with the higher value after comparing the total of all channel values for the base and blend colors. selects the highest channel

values from the base and blend colors to create the result color, so it doesn't make a third color, which could come from the Lighten blend.

- **Overlay:** Depending on the base color, it either multiplies or screens the colors. Colors or patterns cover the original pixels, keeping the base color's highlights and shadows intact. To reflect the original color's lightness or darkness, the base color and blend color are combined.

- **Soft Light:** depending on the mix color, it either lightens or darkens the hues. It looks like a diffused spotlight was beaming on the picture. The image is lightened if the blend color is less than 50% gray. The image is darkened if the blend color is less than 50% gray. Pure black or white paint does not generate pure black or white; instead, it creates a noticeably darker or lighter area.

- **Hard Light:** Depending on the blend color, it either screens or multiplies the colors. The effect is similar to shining a harsh spotlight on the image. The image is lightened if the blend color is less than 50% gray. This is excellent for adding highlights to an image. The image is darkened if the blend color is less than 50% gray. This helps enhance an image's shadows. Pure black or white paint produces pure black or white.

- **Vivid Light:** Depending on the blend color, it either burns or dodges the colors by raising or lowering the contrast. The image is brightened by reducing the contrast if the blend color (light source) is lighter than 50% gray. The image is made darker by raising the contrast if the blend color is less than 50% gray.

- **Linear Light:** Depending on the blend color, this blending mode burns or dodges the colors by adjusting the brightness. Brightness is increased to lighten the image if the blend color (light source) is lighter than 50% gray. The image is made darker by lowering the brightness if the blend color is more than 50% gray.

- **Pin Light:** Depending on the hue of the under-blend, it replaces the colors. Pixels darker than the blend color are replaced; pixels lighter than the blend color remain unchanged if the blend color (light source) is lighter than 50% gray. Pixels lighter than the blend color are replaced; pixels darker than the blend color remain unchanged if the blend color is more than 50% gray.

- **Hard Mix:** Depending on the base and mix colors, it reduces colors to white, black, red, green, blue, yellow, cyan, and magenta.

- **Difference:** It subtracts the base color from the blend color or the blend color from the base color based on which channel's color information has a higher brightness value. Blending with black yields no change, while blending with white inverts the base color values.

- **Exclusion**: It produces a similar impression to the Difference mode, but with less contrast. The base color values are inverted when blending with white. Adding black to a blend yields no results.
- **Hue**: Using the hue of the blend color and the brightness and saturation of the base color, produces a result color.
- **Saturation**: Using the saturation of the blend color and the brightness and hue of the base color, produces a result color. There is no difference when painting in a neutral gray area (zero saturation area) with this mode.
- **Color**: Using the hue and saturation of the blend color and the brightness of the base color, produces a result color. This is helpful for coloring monochrome photos and tinting color images while maintaining the image's gray levels.
- **Luminosity**: It combines the luminance of the blend color with the hue, saturation, and brightness of the base color to create the resultant color. The effect produced by this mode is opposite to that of the Color mode.

Making Edits with Painting Tools

Right in the segment of this chapter, we will be extensively discussing the operation of each painting tools and how to effectively use them.

Brush Tools and Pencil Tools

Color can be applied in delicate or strong strokes with the Brush tool. It can be used to mimic retouching methods. Additionally, it can be used to paint over a blank layer or image. There are two other types of brushes housed by the brush tool in the Toolbar, namely **Impressionist Brush Tool** and **Color Replacement Brush Tool**.

Brush

Do the following to use the brush tool.

- To paint, choose a color by setting the foreground color.

- Choose the **Brush tool** from the **toolbox**.

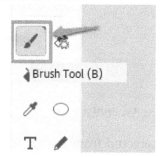

- To paint, drag the Brush tool within the image after setting up the tool's parameters as needed in the **Tool Options** panel.
  - While **Airbrush** simulates conventional airbrush techniques by adding progressive tones to an image, **Brush** is the default mode.

  - Select a brush thumbnail after setting the brush tip and clicking the arrow next to the brush sample in the **Brush section**. Next, pick a brush category from the Brush drop-down menu. To ascertain the brush size and transparency, utilize the **Size Slider** and **Opacity sliders**.

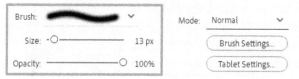

  - Select the type of blending mode you want to use from **Mode** and the **Brush Settings** for advanced brush settings. Use **Tablet Settings** to determine how an external tablet device can be used to influence your brush application.

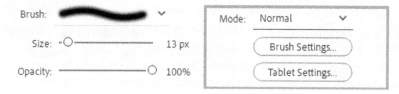

The Impressionist Brush tool is a type of brush tool that modifies the colors and details in your picture to make it appear as though it was painted with stylized brushstrokes.

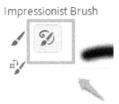

Impressionist Brush

Do the following to use the impressionist brush tool.

- With the **Brush Tool** selected from the toolbar, select **Impressionist Brush Tool** from the Tool Options panel.

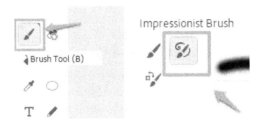

Impressionist Brush

Brush Tool (B)

- To use this brush tool effectively, adjust the settings of the brush in the Tool Options panel to your satisfaction.
    - Select the type of brush from the **Brush Preset Picker**.

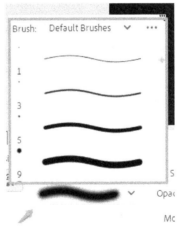

- Determine brush size with the **Size Slider**, the transparency of the brush with the **Opacity Slider** and the blending mode of your painting from **Mode**.

- Select **Advanced** to access **Tolerance**, **Area** and **Style**.

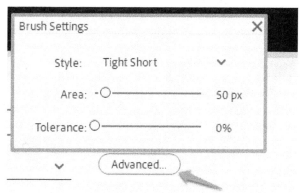

The brush stroke's shape is influenced by **Style**. The brush stroke's size is controlled by **Area**. There are more strokes when the area value is higher. **Tolerance** determines the minimum degree of color value similarity between neighboring pixels before the brush stroke affects them.

The Elements Color Replacement Tool isn't the most expert method for altering an image's color, and it doesn't always produce the desired effects. However, because it's such a simple tool to use and typically works well for basic jobs, it's worth trying before committing to more involved and time-consuming ways.

Do the following to use the Color Replacement Brush.

- After selecting the **Brush Tool** from the Toolbar, select the **Color Replacement Brush** from the Tool Options panel.

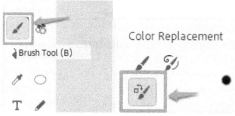

- Determine brush size with the **Size Slider**, and the degree of tolerance with the **Tolerance Slider**. Available in **Mode** are just three blending modes, namely *Hue*, *Saturation*, *Color*, and *Luminosity*.

- The way Photoshop Elements sample colors in the image as you move the crosshair over them is controlled by the **Sampling Options**.

Continous

As you move the Color Replacement Tool around, **Continuous** continuously searches for new colors to replace the old ones. No matter how many other colors you move over, **Once** will only sample the color you initially click on (as long as you keep your mouse button held down). The color that is currently selected as your background will be replaced with **Background Swatch**.

- After you are done with tweaking other options in the Tool Options panel, you can make your edits with the Color Replacement Brush.

Now let`s move to the world of the Pencil Tool.

The Pencil tool's primary function is to produce freehand lines with a sharp edge.

Do the following to use the pencil tool.

- To paint a particular hue, first set the foreground color.

- Choose the **Pencil tool** from the **Toolbar**.

- To paint, drag the Pencil tool into the image after adjusting its settings in the Tool Options window.
  - From the **Brush Picker Presets**, pick the type of pencil you would love to use.

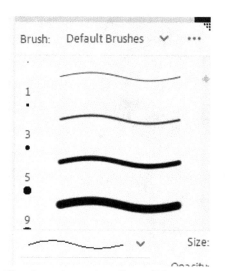

- To change the pencil's size, drag the **Size slider** or type a number in the text box. The transparency of the pencil tool can be changed by dragging the **Opacity Slider** or by entering an opacity value. **Mode** describes how the paint you apply melds into the picture's existing pixels.

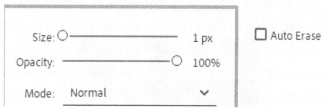

- You can use the current foreground and background color swatches to automatically change the painting color of the Pencil tool with the **Auto Erase** function.

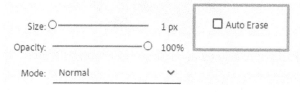

Gradient Tool, Paint Bucket Tool, and Fill Command

Starting with gradient, Using the Gradient tool or dragging within the image, you can apply a gradient to a selected area. The gradient type and appearance are determined by the distance between the starting point (where you first press the mouse button) and the finishing point (where you release the mouse button). The Gradient Tool uses the foreground and background colors to apply gradient to a layer or image.

Libraries contain gradients. By clicking the menu and selecting a library at the Tool Options panel, you can change which gradient library is displayed in the Gradient Picker menu. This option also allows you to save and load gradient libraries of your own.

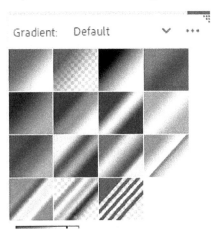

Do the following to apply a gradient using the gradient tool.

- Use one of the selection tools to select the area you want to fill with the picture. If not, the entire active layer is filled with the gradient (If you want it that way).
- Set the Foreground and Background Color Plate to the desired colors you want the gradient tool to apply.

- Choose the **Gradient Tool** from the **Toolbar**.

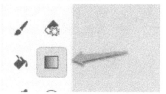

- Adjust the settings of the Gradient Tool in the Tool Options panel to apply your desired gradient.
  - ○ You can pick a gradient preset from the **Gradient Library.**

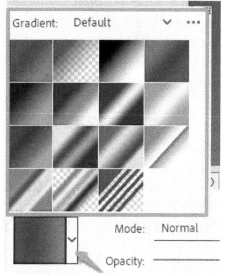

  - ○ Click on **Edit** to define the gradient you are applying.

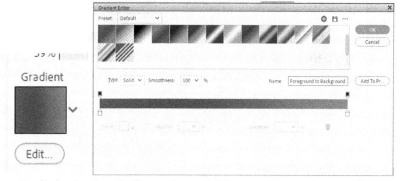

  - ○ *Linear, Radial, Angle, Reflected*, and **Diamond** are the gradient types available in Photoshop Elements.

Linear

- o The gradient's **Mode** describes how it combines with the image's existing pixels.
- o **Opacity**: Determines the gradient's opacity. Pixels beneath the gradient become visible when the opacity is set low.
- o **Reverse**: Modifies the gradient fill's color hierarchy.
- o **Transparency**: If there are transparent parts in the gradient, then those areas are used instead of any transparent portions in the image.
- o **Dither**: Produces a softer mix with subtler color bands.

Two or more colors, or one or more colors that fade to transparency, can be combined to create a gradient. To define your gradient is to determine the colors to combine and its opacity.

Do the following to define your gradient.

- After selecting the **Gradient Tool** from the **Toolbar**, select the **Edit** from the Tool Options panel to display the **Gradient Editor Dialog**.

- Choose a gradient to serve as the foundation for your new gradient in the Gradient Editor dialog box's Preset section.

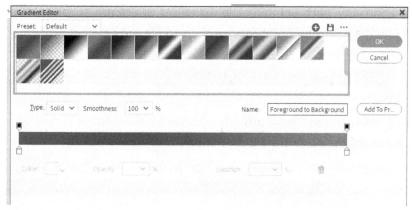

- Double-click the **Color Stop** to select colors for your gradient, or...

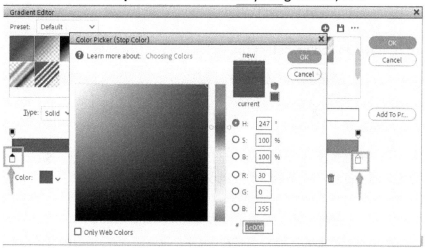

...click the **Color Swatch** to bring up the **Color Picker**. After selecting a color, click OK.

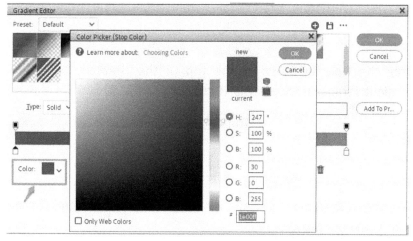

- Drag a **Color Stop** point left or right to change its placement.

- Click on any part beneath the Gradient Spectrum to add a new color to the gradient and a New Color Stop is created for the new color.

- Drag the diamond beneath the gradient bar to the left or right to change the position of the color transition midpoint.

- To remove any color, select the Color Stop of the color and click the delete icon.

- You can either drag the slider or input a percentage in the **Smoothness** text box to adjust the smoothness of the color transition.

- You can choose to either use **Solid Colors** or **Noise Colors** for your gradient.

- Drag the **Opacity Stops** at the top of the Gradient Spectrum to adjust the gradient's transparency levels, if desired.

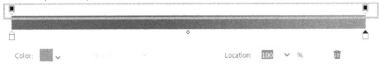

- Give the new gradient a name, click **Add to preset**, and the gradient will be saved in the gradient presets.

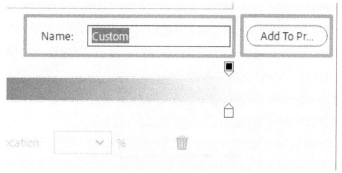

- Press **OK**. The freshly made gradient has been chosen and is prepared for usage.

Do the following to apply a noise gradient.

From the **Toolbar**, choose the **Gradient tool** and Click the **Edit** button in the Tool Options bar to open the Gradient Editor dialog box.

-

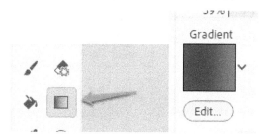

- From the Type menu, select Noise.

- Configure the gradient's settings.
  - **Roughness**: Defines the pattern's degree of softness in the color transitions.

  - **Color Model**: Indicates which color model will be applied to determine which color range will be included in the gradient. Drag the sliders for each color component to specify the color range.

322

- **Restrict Colors**: Prevents colors from becoming too vibrant.

- **Add Transparency**: This function gives random color transparency.

- Click the **Randomize button** to mix the colors at random until you get a gradient that you like.

- Give the new gradient a name and click **Add To Preset** to add your gradient preset.

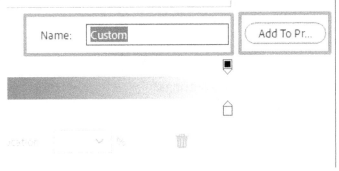

- To close the dialog box, click OK. Next, choose the just-made gradient.

When you click on pixels, the **Paint Bucket tool** fills in an area with a color value close to those pixels. A region can be filled with a pattern or the foreground color.

Do the following to use the Paint Bucket Tool.

- Pick a color for the foreground.

- From the toolbox, pick the **Paint Bucket tool**.

- Once the required settings have been made in the Tool Options menu, click the area of the image that you wish to fill.
  - Use **Paint** or **Pattern Fill**, select Paint when you want to paint over a layer with the foreground color and Pattern Fill when you want to fill the layer with a pattern layout.

Paint   Pattern

  - If you have decided to use the Patten Fill instead, click on the **Pattern Preset Picker** and select the pattern fill you want from the drop-down menu.

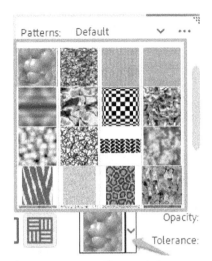

- o **Opacity**: Determines how opaque the paint you apply is. Paint stroke opacity can be reduced to reveal pixels beneath the stroke. You can enter an opacity value or drag the slider.
- o **Tolerance**: Defines how similar in color filled pixels must be. Pixels with a low tolerance are filled with color values that closely resemble the one you clicked. More color-ranged pixels are filled by pixels with a high tolerance.
- o **Mode**: Indicates how the paint you apply will mix in with the image's preexisting pixels.
- o **All Layers**: Fills comparable pixels that fall between the tolerance and contiguous thresholds on any visible layer.

Rather than utilizing one of the brush tools, you can apply a fill or pattern to your image by using a fill layer. You can alter the fill layer's mask to restrict the gradient to a specific area of your image, and you can also change the fill and pattern attributes.

Do the following to use a fill command.

- Choose a color for the background or foreground.

- Decide which space you wish to fill. In the **Layers pane**l, select the layer you want to fill in its entirety.

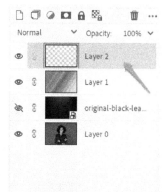

- Select either **Fill Selection** from the **Edit Menu** if you are filling up a selection or...

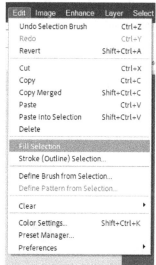

... **Fill Layer** from the **Edit Menu** if you are completely filling up a layer.

- Click OK after modifying the settings in the Fill dialog box.
  - **Contents**: Select a **Color** using the **Use menu**. Choose Color, and then use the Color Picker to choose a new color. Select Pattern to apply a pattern.

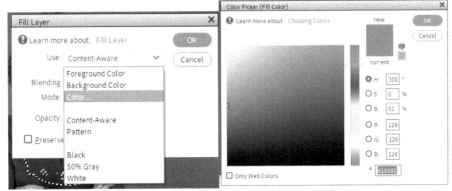

  - **Custom Pattern**: If you select **Pattern** from the **Use menu**, this specifies the pattern to be used. You have the option of making your own patterns or using ones from the pattern libraries.

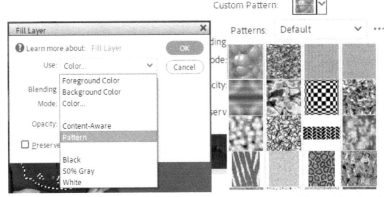

  - **Mode**: Indicates how your applied color pattern melds with the image's preexisting pixels.
  - **Opacity**: Determines how opaque the color pattern to be applied is.
  - **Preserve Transparency**: Exclusively fills opaque pixels.

The Stroke command in the Edit Menu can be used to automatically draw a colored outline around a selection or a layer's contents.

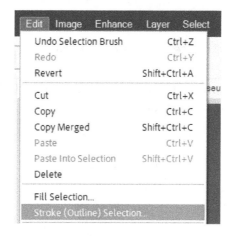

Do the following to use the *Stroke (Object) selection* command.

- Choose a region inside the picture or a layer within the Layers window.

- From the **Edit Menu**, select **Stroke (Outline) Selection**.

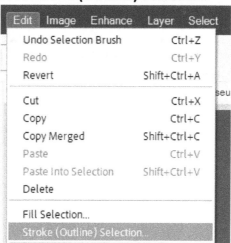

- To add the outline, select one of the following options in the Stroke dialog box, then click OK.
    - The **Width** of the hard-edged outline is indicated by this parameter. Pixel values can vary from 1 to 250.

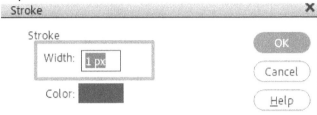

    - **Color**: Defines the outline's color. To choose a color in the Color Picker, click the color swatch.

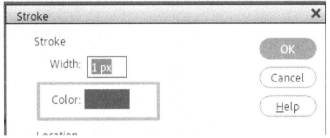

    - **Location**: Indicates if the outline should be centered over the selection or layer boundaries, outside, or inside of them.

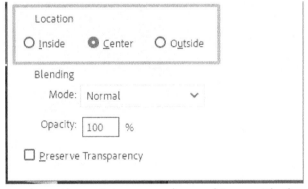

    - **Mode**: Indicates how the paint you apply combines with the image's pre-existing pixels.

- o **Opacity**: Determines how opaque the paint you apply is. You can drag the slider by clicking on the arrow or by entering an opacity value.

- o **Preserve Transparency**: Only parts of a layer with opaque pixels are stroked. This option isn't available if there is no transparency in your image.

Pattern Stamp Tool

Using the Pattern Stamp tool, you can create a design, or you can use one of the pattern libraries to fill a selection or layer. You can choose from a variety of patterns in Photoshop Elements. Using a pattern defined from your image, another image, or a predefined pattern, the Pattern Stamp tool paints.

Do the following to use the Pattern Stamp Tool to pattern a gradient fill.

- Choose the **Clone Stamp tool** from the toolbox, then click the Tool Options bar's **Pattern Stamp tool** icon.

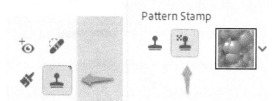

- From the Pattern pop-up panel located on the Tool Options bar, select a pattern.

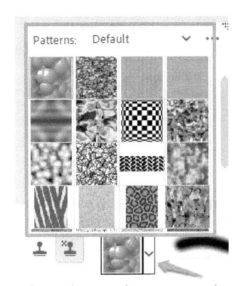

Choose a library name from the panel menu or select Load Patterns, then navigate to the library's folder to load more pattern libraries. Additionally, you can create your own pattern.

- To paint, drag the **Pattern Stamp tool** within the image after adjusting its settings in the Tool Options box. Any of the following Pattern Stamp tool settings can be specified:
  - Sets the tip of the brush. Select a brush thumbnail by clicking the arrow next to the brush sample, followed by selecting a brush category from the **Brush** drop-down.

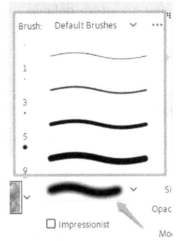

  - **Impressionist** uses paint daubs to apply the pattern, giving it an impressionistic look.

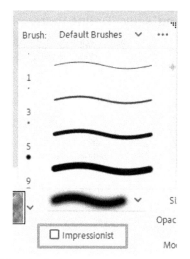

- o **Size**: Adjusts the brush's pixel size. You can enter a size in the text box or drag the Size slider.
- o **Opacity**: Determines how opaque the pattern you apply is. A pattern stroke's underlying pixels can be seen through when the opacity is set low. You can input an opacity value or drag the slider.
- o **Mode**: Indicates how the paint you apply will mix in with the image's preexisting pixels.

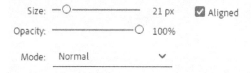

Do the following to create a custom pattern.

- Open the image you want to create the pattern from.
- Make a rectangular selection with Feather set to 0 pixels to extract a portion of the image for a pattern or deselect everything in the image to make a pattern out of it all.

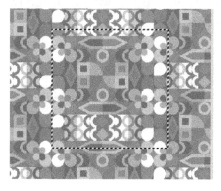

- From the **Edit Menu**, select **Define Pattern From Selection**.

- In the **Pattern Name dialog box**, give the pattern a name and click **OK**.

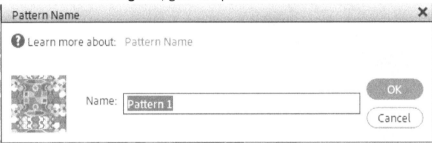

- From the **Select menu**, click **Deselect** or use **Ctrl+D** to remove the initial selection.

Eraser Tools and Smudge Tool

Among the numerous tools in the Photoshop Element, the Eraser feature should not be disregarded. The Eraser tools allow you to fully remove photos or selections. *Eraser Tool, Background Eraser Tool*, and the *Magic Eraser Tool* are the erasing features we have in Photoshop Elements.

Eraser

Now let us examine each eraser tool one after the other.

Using the **Eraser Tool**, you can erase your image to the color of the backdrop (mostly white, except manually changed). To use the Eraser, adhere to these instructions.

- Select the **Eraser tool** from the **Toolbar**.

- From the Layer option, choose the desired layer.

- Choose the desired type of eraser from the **Brush Preset Picker** menu.

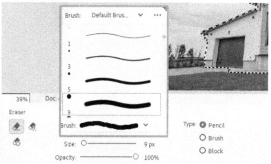

- Using the **Size slider**, adjust the eraser tip's width and use the **Opacity slider** to adjust the color's transparency level.

- Available in the **Type Section** are *Pencil, Brush* and *Block*. pick the optimal brush type you want.

- You can click and drag the image and apply the existing backdrop color to erase using the current settings.

The **Background Eraser tool** can be used to remove or erase the backdrop. Using this tool, you may quickly erase an object from its background by converting color pixels to transparent pixels. This tool does not affect the foreground or the objects on it. This tool eliminates a layer's transparency backdrop. The program also allows you to layer images with just a background.

To use this tool, adhere to the instructions below.

- From the **Toolbar**, select the **Eraser Tool**...

...and select the **Background Eraser Tool** from the Tool Options Panel.

- Select the layer you want to apply the tool on.

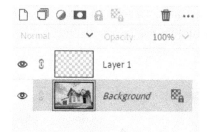

- In the Tool Options panel, adjust the following to your taste.
  - ○ **Brush Settings**: The brush tip settings, including Size, Hardness, Spacing, Roundness, and Angle, can be adjusted here.

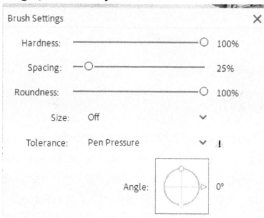

  - ○ **Limits**: You have the choice to select either *Contiguous* or *Discontiguous* in this case. Whereas contiguous removes all similarly colored pixels that are next to the ones beneath the hot spot, discontiguous eliminates all similarly colored pixels wherever they appear in the image.

  - ○ **Tolerance**: With the use of this option, you can specify the percentage that defines how close the colors must match the color beneath the hot spot for the Photoshop element to erase it.

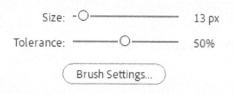

336

- After adjusting the tool options, you can now erase your unwanted parts. The end product will look like the image below.

Use the **_Magic Eraser tool_** if you need to modify two neighboring pixels in an image. When you drag a pixel inside a photo, the Magic Eraser tool modifies all matching pixels. The transparent pixels will either change the background color or be erased to transparency when you use this tool on a backdrop layer or a layer with locked transparency, which prohibits you from modifying the transparent pixels. The only pixels that can be deleted with this tool are those that are adjacent or have similar hues. The Magic Eraser tool is useful for photos where the background color is different from the subject color. Do the following to use this selection.

- Select the layer you want to edit from the **Layer Panel**.

- From the **Toolbar**, select the **Eraser Tool**...

...and select the **Magic Eraser Tool** from the Tool Options Panel.

Magic Eraser

- In the **Tool Options** panel, adjust the tool's settings in the Tool Options panel to your satisfaction.

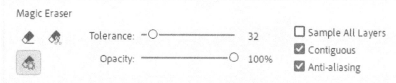

- After the adjustment, you can now make your edits. The image below is an example of what the end product will look like.

The Smudge tool mimics the feeling of running a finger over paint that has been dampened. Where the stroke starts, the tool detects it and pushes the color in the direction you drag. You can smear the foreground color onto the image or distort the colors that are already present.

Smudge

Do the following to use the Smudge Tool.

- Select the **Blur Tool** from the Tool bar and select **Smudge Tool** from the **Tool Options** panel.

Smudge

- To smudge color, select an option in the Tool Options box and drag inside the image.
    - Set the size with the **Size Slider**, set the blending mode with **Mode**, pick the type of brush to use from the **Brush Section**. Adjust the Size of the tool with the **Strength Slider**. Use **Sample All Layers** when you need your edit to apply to multiple layers.

CHAPTER TWELVE

TEXTS AND SHAPES

Working with Texts in Photoshop Elements

Learning how to use texts and the concept of typography is an important skill in the design world. In this chapter of this book, we will be acquiring this skill.

Introduction to Texts

Using the Photoshop Element, you may easily add text or words to your image in a variety of styles, colors, and effects. To edit these texts, use the relevant Photoshop Element tools. The Text tool can be found in the Toolbar

Before we can utilize the type tool to add text to your image, you need to understand *Tools, Modes* and *Formats* in concept of texts.

Horizontal Type, Vertical Type, Horizontal Mask, Vertical Mask, Text On Selection, Text On Shape, and *Text On Path* are the **Text Type Tools** available in Photoshop Elements.

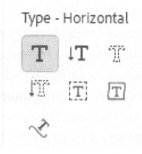

The methods by which Texts are included in the image are called **Modes**. In Photoshop Elements, you may enter text in three different ways: *Paragraph, Point,* and *Path* mode.

- **Paragraph**: This technique works great if you want to add more text to your image within a restricted block. To enter your texts in this mode, click and drag the type tool to form a text bounding box. Entering text does not extend past the bounding box; if a line of text does, it wraps to the following line inside the bounding box.

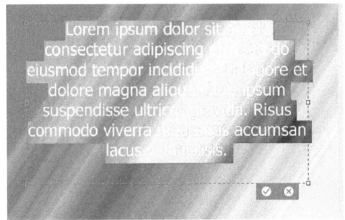

- **Point**: If you want to type a few words on your image, utilize this option. When input, text in this area may extend beyond the edge of your image. Go to the Tools Panel, choose the photos to begin typing, then click the n-Type tool to use this mode.
- **Path**: Here, you can utilize three special tools to input your texts on a path. After doing a double-click on the path, type the appropriate text.

The Photoshop Element's appearance and print quality are controlled by **Formats**. You choose the format to use according to your tastes. **Vector** and **Raster** formats are the two distinct file types in Photoshop Elements which also apply text operations.

- **Vector**: This is the default setting for texts of a type. With this format type, the diagonal stroke has resizable ascendable outlines without any jagged edges. This format type can also be changed with a higher-quality print.
- **Raster**: This is the kind of unchangeable text format. Converting the vector to pixels results in the texts being rasterized automatically. Put otherwise, a raster image has taken the place of the text. The raster format is most useful when you wish to include text with an image or apply a filter to your text. Every time the raster image is resized, it either loses quality or has jagged edges.

All that is mentioned in this section will also be of use when using Adobe Photoshop.

The Text Tool Options

Before we move into how to use the text tool for different purposes, we must journey through the setting options in the Text Tool for a seamless operation while using the text tool.

Set the following Type tool options in the options panel.

- **Font Family**: This open gives new or existing text a font family.

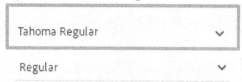

- Apply **Font Styles**, like bold, to newly created or updated text.

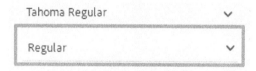

- Apply a **Font Size** to newly created or updated text.

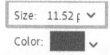

- **Color menu**: Selectable or new text can have a color applied to it.

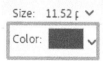

- **Leading menu**: This option adjusts the distance between lines of newly added or chosen text.

- **Tracking**: This option adjusts the distance between newly typed or chosen characters.

- **Faux Bold**: Gives newly written or already written text a bold look. If the Font Style menu does not offer a real bold style for your font, use this option.

- **Faux Italic**: Gives new or existing text an italicized appearance. If the Font Style menu does not offer an oblique or true italic style for your font, use this option.

- **Underline**: Either a new text or a portion of an existing text is underlined using this method.

- **Strikethrough**: This inserts a line through a portion of the current text or adds a new one.

- **Align Text**: Defines the alignment of the text. Text can be aligned left, center, or right if it is horizontally oriented. Top, center, or bottom for text-oriented vertically.

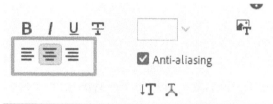

- **Toggle Text Orientation**: Flips text from vertical to horizontal and vice versa.

- **Warp text**: On the chosen layer, warp text.

- **Anti-aliased**: Text appears smoother when anti-aliasing is applied.

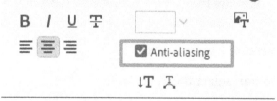

Baisc Texts Operations

Right here, we will be learning a few but basic operations that you can carry out with the text tools.

Do the following to create a horizontal Text.

- From the **Toolbar**, select the **Text Tool**.

- Make sure **Horizontal** is selected in the **Tool Options** panel.

Type - Horizontal

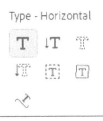

- Using the Tool Options bar, adjust the type parameters, such as font size, style, family, etc.

- Click any part of the image window, enter your texts, and click on the Marked icon to apply your texts.

Do the following to create a vertical text.

- From the **Toolbar**, select the **Text Tool**.

- Make sure **Vertical** is selected in the **Tool Options** panel.

Type - Vertical

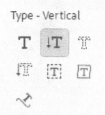

- Modify the type parameters (font size, style, family, etc.) using the Tool Options bar.

- To apply your texts, click the Marked button after entering your text in any area of the image window.

Do the following to create a paragraph type.

- Select the **Type Tool** from the **Toolbar**.

- Select a tool that is either **vertical** or **horizontal** in shape.

Type - Vertical

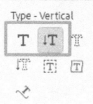

- Using your mouse, click and drag the boundary box's edge.

25.8M/27.8M

- From the **Tool Options**, select the formatting options.

- Enter text in the bounding box.
- To implement the modifications you have made, click the **Commit** button. Alternatively, to undo modifications, click the Cancel button.

Creating selection zones that resemble written type is made easier with the help of the *Type Mask tool*. The Shape Selection's fill effects can also be applied to the Text Selection. This option may be applied with a background or foreground color. To create a type mask, use the same procedures as for creating plain text.

Do the following to use the Type Mask Tool to create a type mask.

- Choose the layer on which you wish to build the type mask from the **Layer Panel**.

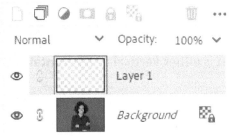

- Choose the Type tool from the Toolbox.

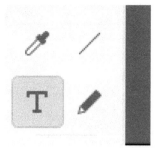

- In the Tool Options bar, choose the **Horizontal Type Mask** or **Vertical Type Mask** tool.

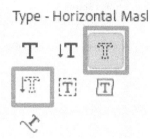

- In this case, a mask is made over the layer, and either point or paragraph text styles are used to form the text.

- In the **Tool Options**, adjust the type options, such as font family, style, size, etc.

- Go to **Edit** and click on **Fill selection** to apply any desired fill effect or strokes to the produced selection.

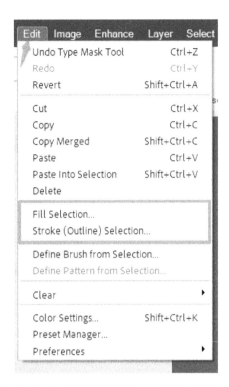

Using the **Text on Selection Tool**, add text to a path's outline that was formed from a selection. A selection is transformed into a path where content can be typed when it is committed.

Do the following to use the Text on Selection Tool.

- Select the **Type Tool** and click on **Text On Selection Tool** from the **Tool Options** panel.

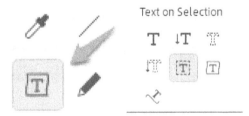

Text on Selection

- To make the selection you want, point the cursor to the object in the picture and drag it around...

...The Offset slider allows you to change the selection's size.

Offset: ————O———— 0

- Once the selection has been established, click inside of it, and then click the **Commit button** to make it into a solid line.

- Move the mouse pointer over the line at the desired spot to begin adding text to add them. At this point, the mouse pointer shifts to the I-Beam character, which is where you start adding text

- Once you've finished typing, press the **Commit** button. As an alternative, you can reject all changes by clicking the **Cancel** option.

The *Text on Shape tool* allows you to add text to the shapes that are available. Do the following to use this particular text tool.

- Choose the **Text tool** from the **toolbar**, then on the **Tool Options** Panel, choose the Text on Shape tool.

- Choose the shape that you wish to add text to from the ones that are available.

- To build the shape, drag the pointer over the image.

- Hover your mouse cursor over the path until the cursor icon turns to text mode to add text to the image. Press the pointer to include text.

Text can be altered in the same manner as regular text using the Tool Options panel.

- It is necessary to write the text within certain forms. You can use the keyboard shortcut **Cmd/Ctrl** key to click and drag the mouse to move the text inside or outside of the path (The text appears in a small arrow). The text route can go both inside and outside of an area, and you can drag the cursor into the area you've chosen.

- Upon completion, click the **Commit button**. You can also select **Cancel** to reject all changes.

Along a custom path, text and drawings are possible with the use of *Text On Custom Path Tool*. Do the following to add text along a custom path.

- From the **Toolbar**, select the **Text Tool**, and select **Text On Custom Path** from the **Tool Options** panel.

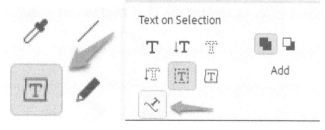

- The mouse pointer transforms into a pen icon at this point. Click and drag to draw the route where you want the text to appear. The route that was sketched solidifies when the mouse is released. then to approve the path, select the **Commit** Button.

- Move the mouse pointer over the line at the desired location to start entering your texts. The mouse pointer changes to the I-Beam character as you begin entering text.

- Once the work is complete, click the **Commit** button. You can also select **Cancel** to reject all changes.

Text in the text layer can be warped to apply universal forms to all of the texts. For example, applying the arc shape to a text layer will make the text arc like a rainbow.

Do the following to wrap a text.

- Create a Text Layer by clicking the **Text Tool** to add a text.

- Select the text layer from the layer panel.

- Navigate to Tool Options, then select the **Warp Text button** to initiate the warp effect.

- Configure the Warp Text dialog box's parameters.
  - **Styles**: This shows a drop-down menu where you may choose the text's shape that will be bent.

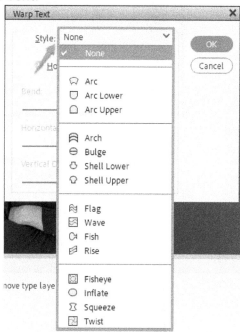

  - **Horizontal** and **Vertical** gives you the option to reposition your texts in a horizontal or vertical arrangement.

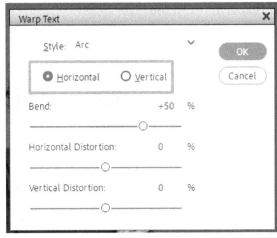

o **Blend**: This is how the amount of warp is set.

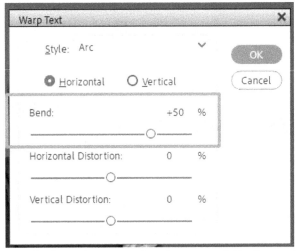

o Perspective is applied to the warp by the use of **Horizontal** and **Vertical Distortion**.

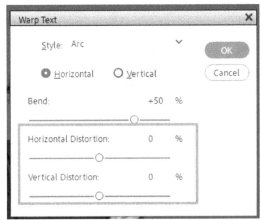

- After you are done tweaking the option, next, select **OK**.
- To unwarp your text, select None from **Style**.

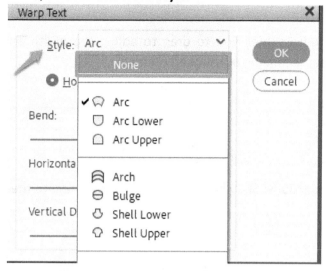

Working With Shapes

Shapes are vector graphics, meaning that rather than being composed of pixels, they are made up of lines and curves that are defined by their geometric properties. Because vector graphics are resolution-independent, they may be reproduced at any resolution and scaled to any size without sacrificing clarity or detail. A shape's fill layer can be edited, and layer styles can be applied to it to alter its color.

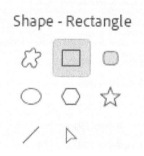

Shape layers are used to build shapes. Depending on the shape area choice you choose, a shape layer may include one or many shapes. It is up to you how many shapes to include in a layer.

Custom Shape Tool, Rectangle Tool, Rounded Rectangle Tool, Ellipse Tool, Polygon Tool, Star Tool, Line Tool and ***Shape Selection Tool*** are the shape tools available in Photoshop Elements, and we will be treating their operations in the preceding sections.

You can tweak the settings of each Shape Tool in the Tool options panel. The options listed below apply to all eight shape tools while the unique ones will be treated subsequently.

- **Unconstrained**: Enables you to drag to adjust the width and height of a custom shape, ellipse, rectangle, or rounded rectangle.

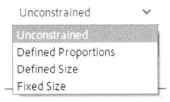

- **Defined Proportions**: Sketches a unique form according to the dimensions used in its creation.

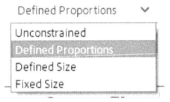

- **Defined Size**: Determines the size at which a custom shape was produced while drawing it.

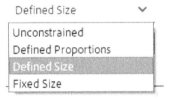

- **Fixed Size**: Based on the values you specify in the **Width** and **Height** text boxes, a bespoke form is drawn as a fixed shape.

- **From Centre** allows you to draw a unique shape starting in the center.

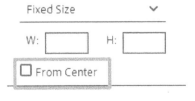

- Determine the shape's hue using **Color**, then use the **Layer Style** to apply the layer style effect.

- **Simplify**: Produces a raster graphic from the drawn shape. When a shape is transformed to raster form, it may appear pixelated and have jagged edges when it is shrunk or expanded.

-

Custom Shape Tool

You can design a wide variety of shapes with the Custom Shape tool. You can access these forms in the settings menu by selecting the custom shape tool.

Do the following to use the custom shape tool.

- Select the **Shape Tool** from the **Toolbar** and select the **Custom Shape Tool** from the **Tool Options** panel.

- Choose a shape from the **Custom Shape picker pop-up** in the options bar. To view a list of the shapes you can select and how to display them, click the arrow located at the upper right corner of the panel.

Heart Card

- You can modify the settings of the tool in the Tool Options bar

- To draw the shape, drag inside your image, after modifying your tool in the Tool Options panel.

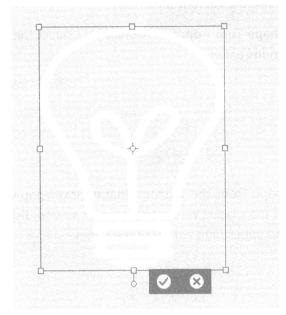

Rectangle and Rounded Rectangle Tool

The only difference between the Rectangle and the Rounded Rectangle Tool is the nature of the edges of the shape they form. The Rectangle Tool forms a rectangle with sharp edges while the Rounded Rectangle tool forms a rectangle with rounded edges.

Do the following to use the rectangle tool.

- From the **Toolbar,** select the **Shape Tool** and click on the **Rectangle Tool** from the **Tool Options** panel.

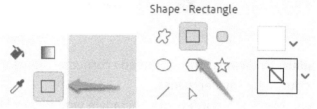

- Modify the settings of the tool to your desired taste in the Tool Options panel.

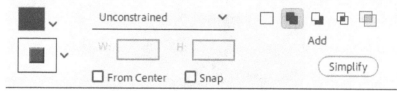

- ○ **Snap:** Aligns a rectangle's edges with its pixel bounds.
- To draw the shape, drag inside your image.

Do the following to use the rounded rectangle tool.

- From the **Toolbar,** select the **Shape Tool** and click on the **Rounded Rectangle Tool** from the **Tool Options** panel.

Shape - Rounded Rectangle

Radius:

- Change the tool's parameters in the Tool Options window to suit your preferences.

Shape - Rounded Rectangle

Radius: 10 px   Unconstrained   Normal

☐ From Center   ☐ Snap   Simplify

  - o **Radius**: Indicates the rounded corner's radius. Sharper corners are produced by smaller values.
  - o **Snap**: Aligns the borders of a rectangle with its pixel boundaries.
- Drag within the image to draw the shape.

Ellipse and Polygon Tool

The Ellipse tool allows you to create circular shapes while the polygon tool allows you to create polygonal shapes.

Do the following to use the ellipse tool.

- From the **Toolbar**, select the **Shape Tool** and click on the **Ellipse Tool** from the **Tool Options** panel.

Shape - Ellipse

- In the Tool Options window, adjust the tool's parameters to your liking.

Shape - Ellipse

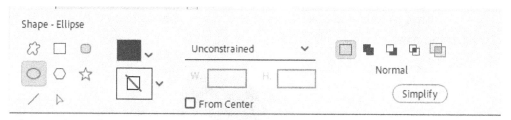

- After making the necessary adjustment to the tool in the Tool options panel, to design the shape, drag inside the image.

Do the following to use the Polygon tool.

- From the **Toolbar**, select the **Shape Tool** and click on the **Polygon Tool** from the **Tool Options** panel.

- Make any necessary adjustments to the tool's parameters in the Tool Options window.

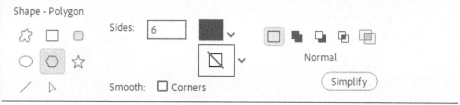

- o **Sides:** Insert the number of sides for the polygon into this box,
- o **Smooth:** Check the **Corners checkbox** to smoothen the corners of the shape and uncheck it to leave it unsmooth.

- To design the shape, drag inside the image, after adjusting the tool in the Tool Option panel.

Line and Star Tool

The Line tool is used to create line shapes while the Star tool is used to create star shapes.

Do the following to use the line tool.

- From the **Toolbar**, select the **Shape Tool** and click on the **Line Tool** from the **Tool Options** panel.

- In the Tool Options window, modify the tool's parameters as needed.

  - **Arrowhead**: This allows you to determine if your line will have an arrowhead, and its position.

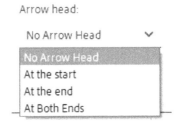

363

- Once the tool has been adjusted in the Tool Options window, design the shape by dragging inside the image.

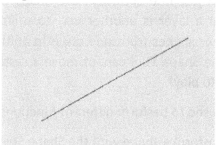

Do the following to use the Star Tool.

- From the **Toolbar**, select the **Shape Tool** and click on the **Star Tool** from the **Tool Options** panel.

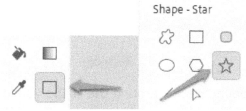

- Adjust the tool's parameters in the Tool Options window as necessary.

  - **Sides**: Insert the number of pointed edges you want the star to form.
  - **Smooth Corners**: It renders the corners of the star shape smooth.
  - **Indent Side By**: Indicates the depth of the indentations made by the star.
  - **Smooth Indents**: It produces a smooth indented polygon in the shape of a star.
- After modifying the tool in the Tool Options box, create the shape by dragging inside the picture.

Shape Selection Tool

To choose shapes with just one click, use the Shape Selection tool. Repositioning a particular shape within a layer is another way to utilize the shape selection tool. It allows you to move your shapes from one place to another as long as they are still in their vector format (The Shape Tool cannot move a rasterized shape and this is where the Moe Tool comes into play).

The Shape tool can be used to perform different functions like transforming.

Do the following to transform a shape with the Shape Selection Tool.

- Select the **Shape Tool** from the **Toolbar**, and click on the **Shape Selection Tool** from the **Tool Options** panel.

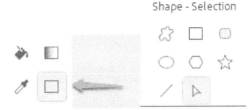

- To make the bounding box around the shape visible, mark the **Show Bounding Box.**

- To transform the shape, select the bounding box around the shape.

- Select the transformation style from the Tool Options panel.

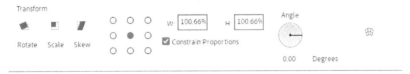

- After transforming the shape, click the **Commit** Button to apply the transformation.

BOOK SECTION 4

WORKING WITH FILTERS AND THE CAMERA RAW

CHAPTER THIRTEEN- CHAPTER FOURTEEN

❖ **FILTERS IN PHOTOSHOP ELEMENTS**

❖ **THE CAMERA RAW PLUGIN IN PHOTOSHOP ELEMENTS 2024**

CHAPTER THIRTEEN

FILTERS IN PHOTOSHOP ELEMENTS

What Filters Are

Photos can be retouched or cleaned up using filters. Additionally, you can utilize filters to apply distortion effects to produce unique transformations or unusual art effects. Some third-party developers' filters are available as plug-ins in addition to those supplied by Adobe. When these plug-in filters are installed, they show up at the bottom of the Filter lists.

Filter Menu, *Filter Panel*, and *Filter Layer* are the three ways of applying filters in Photoshop Elements.

The Filter Menu is located at the Menu Bar comprising multiple filter options.

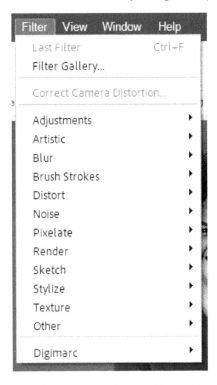

The Filter Panel is located on the lower right-hand side of the workspace.

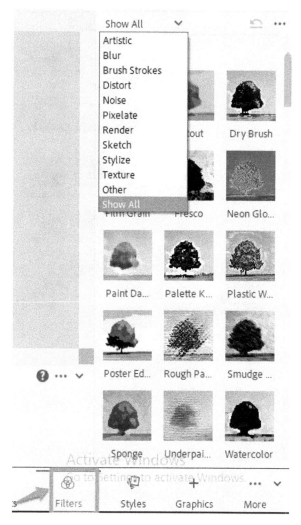

The Filter Menus are the filter thumbnails available in the Filter Panel. To accomplish your objectives, you can rearrange the filters and change the filter gallery's parameters. But not every filter available in the Filter menu is in the Filter Gallery.

To apply a filter, navigate to the **Filter Panel**.

select Filter Gallery, select a **category**, and...

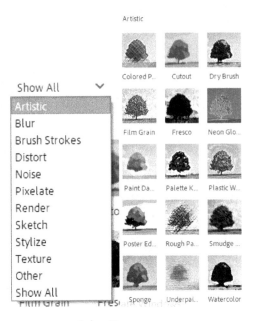

... then click on the layer that you wish to filter.

Filter Categories

Filter categories are groups of filter effects available in Photoshop Elements. They vary based on their purposes. Filter categories are found in the Filter Layer, Filter Menu and the Filter Panel. It's crucial that you understand the many kinds of filters before using them on your photos. The following are these categories.

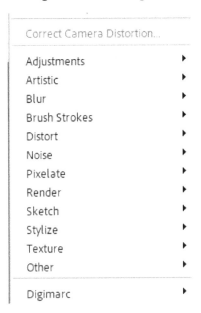

- **Correct Camera Distortion**: This filter category corrects vignetting, barrel and pincushion distortion, and other typical lens imperfections. In addition to correcting perspective issues brought on by vertical or horizontal camera tilt, the filter also rotates images.
- **Adjustments**: This filter modifies an image's pixel brightness, color, grayscale range, and tonal levels. Transform color pixels into monochromatic versions.

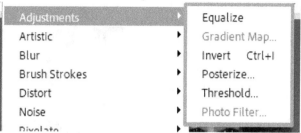

- **Artistic**: On conventional media, artistic filters evoke a painterly appearance and produce a distinctive look.

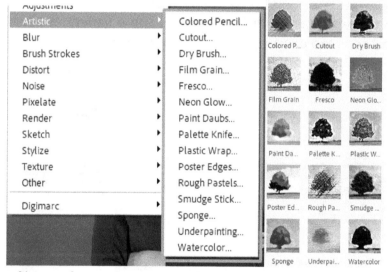

- **Blur**: blurry filters soften a picture or a selection. helpful for touch-ups.

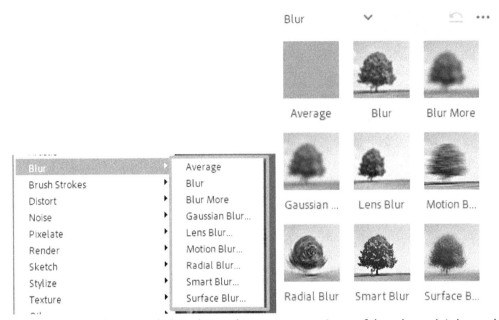

- **Brush Strokes**: filters with brush strokes Use a variety of brush and ink stroke effects to create a painterly or fine-arts appearance.

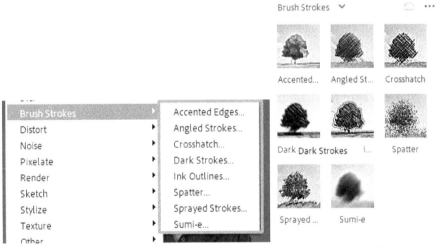

- **Distort**: Using the distort filters, a picture can be geometrically distorted to produce three-dimensional effects and other reshaping effects.

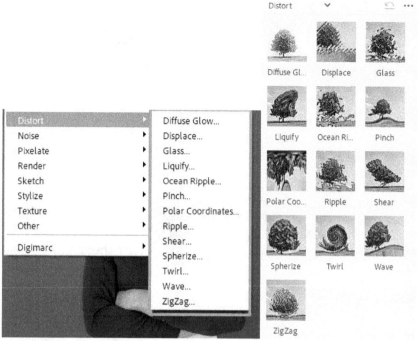

- **Noise**: It filters for noise in order to eliminate trouble spots like dust and scratches, and blend a selection into the surrounding pixels.

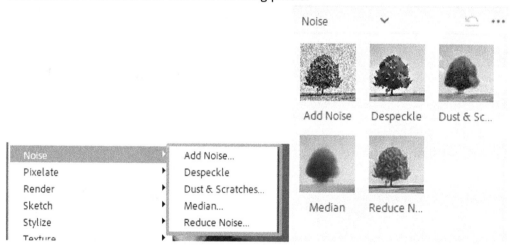

- **Pixelate**: Pixelate filters cluster pixels with similar color values to strongly define an image or selection.

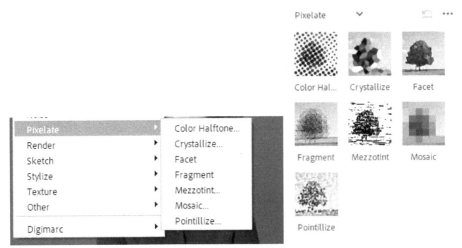

- **Render**: This category adds effects like fibers, lightning, lens flare, and cloud patterns

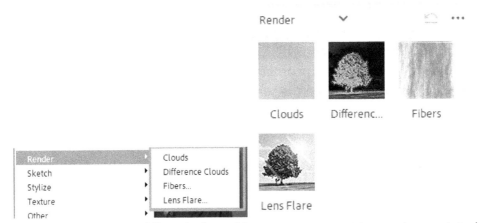

- **Sketch**: This category modifies pixels and increases contrast to create a painted or impressionistic look.

- **Stylize**: By shifting pixels and boosting contrast, stylize filters create an impressionistic or painted look.

- **Texture**: filters for textures Add an organic aspect, or give the impression of depth or substance.

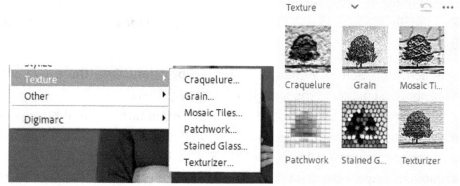

- **Other**: With the use of other filters, you can quickly adjust color, offset a selection inside a picture, tweak masks, and build your own filter effects.

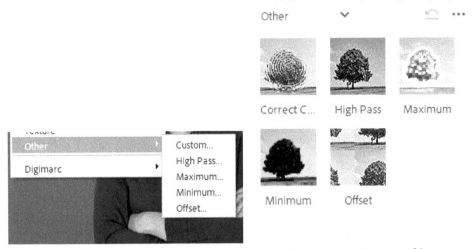

- **Digimarc**: You can read a Digimarc watermark by using a Digimarc filter.

Rules of Engagement in Using Filters

The following details will assist you in comprehending the filter application process for your photos.

- Only the active portion of an image is affected by filters. Only the active, visible layer or a specific portion of the layer is impacted by filters.
- Not all photographs can be processed by filters. Certain filters cannot be applied to grayscale photos, and none can be applied to bitmap or indexed-color images. A lot of filters don't function with 16-bit photos.
- It is possible to reapply the prior filter. The Filter menu's top row displays the most recent filter you used. To further improve the image, you can reapply it using the same parameters as before.
- Check out the filter's outcome. It can take a while to apply filters to a huge photograph. Viewing the filter's action in the Filter Gallery is faster.

Use the following methods to apply filters to create unique visual effects:

- By using the same filter on every image in a series, you can improve or mask flaws in the photos or create a uniform appearance.
- Apply filters one after the other to create effects. To create an effect, you can apply filters one at a time or to multiple layers consecutively. The effect can be

blended by selecting various blending modes in the Layers window. A layer needs to have pixels in order to be visible and affected by a filter.

Applying Filter Effects and Photo Effects

The Effects panel allows you to apply image effects from a single location. Normally, the Effects panel appears on the taskbar in the Quick and Expert modes. Thumbnail examples of the artwork and effects you can apply to enhance an image are displayed. For most parts, a menu with options for categories and related subcategories is provided. Three effect categories are available to you: *Color Match, Classic*, and *Artistic*.

Shown below are filters from *Artistic Effect*.

Do the following to apply filters from **Artistic**.

- Select Artistic from the Effect drop-down menu.

- Select any filter thumbnail of your choice from the Effect Panel.

- Adjust the following to edit the filter application to your taste.
  - **Keep Original Photo Color** enables you to preserve the original colors of your image in the Photo Bins.

  - **Intensity Slider** allows you to adjust the quality of the filter applied.

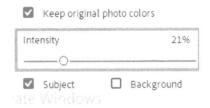

  - Mark **Subject** if you want the filter to be applied to the prominent element in the image and unmark if you want otherwise.

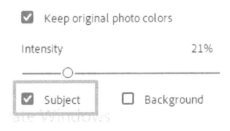

379

- o Mark **Background** if you want the filter to be applied to the background in the image and unmark if you want otherwise.

- After applying the filter of your choice, the filter effect is applied as a layer mask in the Layer Panels. Afterwards, you can save your file.

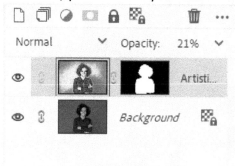

Contained in **Classic Effect** are eight filter categories namely **Faded Photo, Glow, Monotone Color, Painting, Panels, Seasons, Textures**, and **Vintage**. You may easily create various appearances for your photographs with photo effects. Select a subcategory from the Effects panel.

Do the following to apply any photo effect.

- Choose the picture to which you want to apply the effect, choose **Effect** by clicking on the Effect symbol located in the workspace's lower right corner.

- On the workspace's right side is the **Effect panel**, select **Classic** and choose any subcategory of your choice.

- Choose an effect, then apply it to the picture.

381

- The effect applies to your image automatically, then save your file after applying the filter effect.

Another effect option in the Effect panel is the ***Color Match*** Effect. The major purpose of this filter effect is to colorize an image.

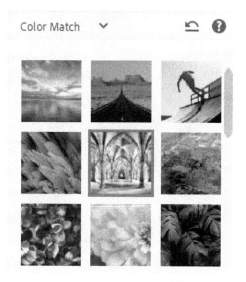

Do the following to apply a filter effect from the Color Match.

- Select the image you wish to apply the effect to, then click the **Effect symbol** in the lower right corner of the workspace to select the effect.

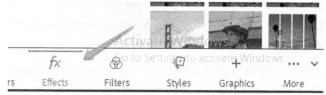

- The **Effect panel** is located on the workspace's right side; pick **Color Match** and select any filter effect.

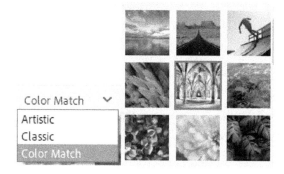

- Another way to add filter to your photographs is to import an image from the file manager.

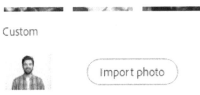

Custom

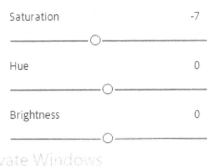

Import photo

- Use the **Saturation, Hue**, and **Brightness slider** to adjust the impact of the colors from the filters/images.

Saturation	-7
Hue	0
Brightness	0

- After applying the filter, you can now save your image.

Working with the Graphic Panel

With the tool in the Graphics Panel, you may add eye-catching artwork, theme decorations, frames, shapes, and text styles to your image. The artwork or effects that you can add or apply to an image are shown in thumbnail form in each component. A selection of categories and their accompanying subcategories are available for most sections.

Backgrounds, Frames, Graphics, Shapes, and *Text* are the categories of filter effects in the Graphics Panel.

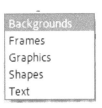

Backgrounds
Frames
Graphics
Shapes
Text

These effects in the Graphics Panel are classified By *Type, Activity, Color, Event, Mood, Object, Seasons, Style, Word*, and *Show All*.

Do the following to apply any effect from the Graphics Panel.

- From the lower right-hand side of the workspace select **Graphics**.

| Filters | Styles | Graphics | More |

- From the **Graphics Panel** category menu, and choose a **Category**

- To apply a filter effect, click the thumbnail twice or drag the image to the thumbnail.

384

- After you are done applying the filters, save your image.

Applying Layer Styles

Using the Layer Styles, you can apply various effects to a layer's content, such as light, shadows, embossed edges, neon, plastic, etc. The layer Style may only be applied to the entire layer; it cannot be applied to a particular object or element inside a layer.

Do the following apply a layer style to an image.

- Choose the picture or layer to which you want to apply the styles.
- Navigate to **Window** and choose **Styles**.

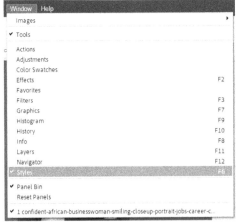

- As an alternative, you can use the styles by selecting **Styles** from the workspace's lower right-hand corner.

Filters	Styles	Graphics	More

- Using the drop-down menu at the top of the panel, choose the **style categories**.

- From the Style Panel, choose the desired style.

- Navigate to **Layer**, Select Layer Style, and then select any choice from the drop-down list that best fits your needs. A layer style can be copied and pasted, scaled, hidden, or shown to modify its settings.

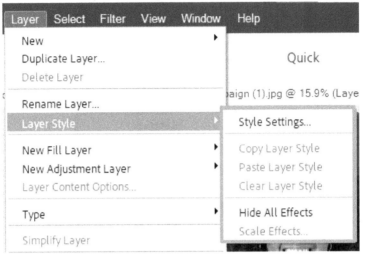

Photomerge Edits in Guided Mode

Complex photo modification is made simple with this set of guided adjustments. With Photomerge's capabilities, you may create stunning composites by combining two or more photos into one. The main use of the Photomerge command is to combine images; in this session, we'll learn how to accomplish this.

Keep in mind that you may only use the Photomerge features in the Guided Edit mode. There are six Photomerge edits in the Guided Mode namely, *Photomerge Compose, Photomerge Exposure, Photomerge Faces, Photomerge Group Shot, Photomerge Scene Cleaner*, and *Photomerge Panorama*.

PHOTOMERGE GROUP SHOT

Make sure everyone in your group shot is
smiling and has their eyes open by blending
multiple shots into one.

PHOTOMERGE SCENE CLEANER

Easily remove moving objects, like cars, from
a series of photos.

PHOTOMERGE PANORAMA

Create a panoramic photo by stitching
together multiple photos.

Photomerge Compose

With the **Photomerge Compose tool**, you can swap out parts of an image. Two photos
are required: a source and a destination. To achieve the most natural result, you can cut
a section of the source image, paste it into the destination image, and then make
adjustments to its color and proportion.

PHOTOMERGE COMPOSE

Extract an object from one photo and add it to
another.

Do the following to use Photomerge Compose.

- In the **Guided Edit mode**, select **Photomerge** and press **Photomerge Composure**…

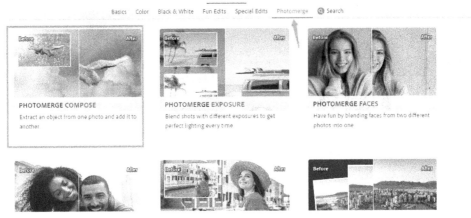

...after selecting two or more photographs from the **Photo Bin** or using the Open command in the File Menu.

- To extract an element from an image, drag it from the Photo Bin and into the photo editing area.

- Next, select an option using one of the Selection tools,
  - **Quick Select**: This allows you to quickly select the desired element by sweeping over your image.

  - **Outline Select**: This tool allows you to draw a circle around the desired image element.

389

extract.

- o Use the **Refine Selection Brush** tool to make your selection more precise.

extract.

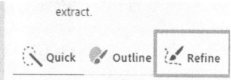

- o Use **Selection modes** to refine the selected portion.

- o Click on **Advance Edge refinement** to set the background.

- After making your selection, then click the **Next** button.

- To make sure the content that has been pasted is proportionate to the rest of the image, use the mouse to move the selection around and drag the coach marks to resize it. Then, click **Next**.

- To merge the extracted image's color with the new background, use the **Auto Match Color Tone** feature or adjust the Adjustment Sliders to manually tune the images.

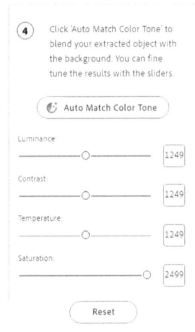

- Click **Next** to save your changes, **Continue Editing**, or **Share** them after you've finished.

Photomerge Exposure

Using the background and foreground, you can use the **Photomerge Exposure command** to reveal an image that has an exposure issue. To obtain a correctly exposed picture, you might combine two images into one.

PHOTOMERGE EXPOSURE

Blend shots with different exposures to get perfect lighting every time.

However, Photomerge Exposure can be used in two ways: Both *Manual* and *Automatic Photomerge Exposure*

Do the following to manually use Photomerge Exposure.

- Open 2-10 images in the Photo Bin.

- Select **Photomerge** from the **Guided Mode** and click on **Photomerge Exposure**.

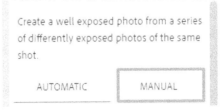

- Turn on **Manual mode** under the Photomerge Exposure option.

- select both the source and final images from the Photo Bin, then drag them to the Final window.

- Use the **Pencil tool** to sketch over the well-exposed region that you want to preserve or save.

- Use the **Eraser tool** to remove any place that the Pencil tool selected.

- Assign the subsequent
  - **Show Strokes**: This option shows the pencil stroke that is indicated in the original image.
  - **Show Regions**: This displays the areas that were chosen for the finished picture.

- o **Opacity Slider**: This tool is used to adjust the chosen regions' transparency so they blend in with the background appropriately.
- o Smoothing the blended edges is accomplished by **edge blending**.

☑ Show Strokes

☐ Show Regions

Opacity:

―――――――――――――――○ 100

Optionally, you can use the Opacity slider
to fine tune how much of each source
photo is blended into the final image.

☐ Edge Blending

- Once the changes are made, select Next to **Share**, **Save**, or **Continue Editing**.

Do the following Automatic Photomerge Exposure.

- Choose two or more pictures to utilize.

- Click on **Photomerge Exposure** after choosing the **Photomerge tab** in the Guided Edit mode.

- Choose the **Automatic mode** under the **Photomerge Exposure** option.

Create a well exposed photo from a series of differently exposed photos of the same shot.

AUTOMATIC   MANUAL

- Choose any of the following choices.

Click either Simple or Smart Blending to create a well exposed photo from the photos selected in Photo Bin.

○ Simple Blending ● Smart Blending

- ○ **Simple Blending**: This option shows the combined image but does not let you change the Photomerge Exposure parameters.
- ○ **Smart Blending**: This function enables you to modify the Photomerge Exposure parameters, including Saturation, Highlights, and Shadows, before combining the picture.

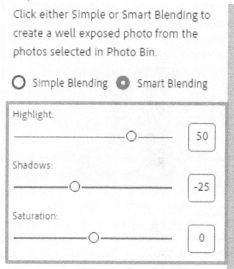

Click either Simple or Smart Blending to create a well exposed photo from the photos selected in Photo Bin.

○ Simple Blending ● Smart Blending

Highlight: 50

Shadows: -25

Saturation: 0

- Once the changes are made, select **Next** to **Share**, **Save**, or **Continue Editing**.

Photomerge Faces

To build a composite face, use Photomerge Faces to mix various facial traits. Do the following to use this feature.

- Open 2-10 images in the Photo Bin.

Show Open Files ⌄

- Select **Photomerge Faces** from **Photomerge** in the **Guided mode**.

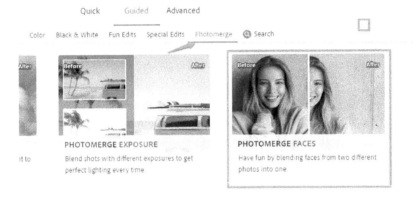

- Select a face photo to use as your base image, then drag it into the **Final window** from the Photo Bin.

- Select the **Alignment tool** by clicking on another image in the Photo Bin.

- Click **Align Photos** after positioning the three alignment markers on the lips and eyes in both the source and finished images.

- To view more pictures, click the Photo Bin (color coded to help you keep track). Mark the areas you want to incorporate into the final image using the Pencil tool. Use the Pencil and Eraser tools to add and remove information, respectively, to fine-tune the final image.

- Assign the following:
  - **Show Strokes**: To view the Pencil strokes you annotated in the original image, select this option.
  - To make the selected regions visible in the final image, use the **Show Regions** option.

- Once you have the desired outcome, select your preferred course of action by clicking **Next**:

  - **Save** - Save / Save As: Save the newly-created image in any compatible format.

398

Save:

- ○ **Continue editing** - In Fast / In Proficient: Select whether you want to work in Expert or Quick mode to continue editing the image.

Continue Editing:

- ○ **Share via Twitter / Flickr**: Select one of the social media or sharing options that Photoshop Elements offers to post your photo online.

Share:

•• Flickr

Photomerge Group Shot

Photomerge Group Shot allows you to merge several images into a group photo.

Do the following to use this feature.

- Open 2-10 images in the Photo Bin.

Show Open Files ⌄

- Select **Photomerge Group Shot** from **Photomerge** in the **Guided mode**.

- Drag the group photo that you think is the greatest from the Photo Bin into the Final window.

- Mark the areas you want to include in the finished picture using the **Pencil tool**. Use the Pencil and **Eraser tools** to add and remove information, respectively, to fine-tune the final image.

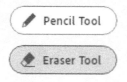

- Select one of the following options:
    - **Show Strokes**: To view the Pencil strokes you annotated in the original image, select this option.
    - To make the selected regions visible in the final image, use the **Show Regions** option.

400

- Click on the **Advanced Settings** to use the **Alignment Tool** and **Alig Photo**.

- Use **Pixel Blending** to blend the pixels of the merged images.

☐ Pixel Blending

- Choose **Next** to **Share**, **Save**, or **Continue Editing** after making the necessary adjustments.

Photomerge Scene Blender

By deleting unnecessary elements from the picture, such as cars and bystanders, the Photomerge Scene Cleaner command allows you to combine many photos into a flawless photo scene.

PHOTOMERGE SCENE CLEANER

Easily remove moving objects, like cars, from a series of photos.

To process of using Photomerge Group Shot also applies to the Photo Scene Blender.

Photomerge Panorama

The Photomerge Panorama tool allows you to combine many photos into a single image. The images used in this command must have shared and overlapping areas for them to be stitched together.

PHOTOMERGE PANORAMA

Create a panoramic photo by stitching together multiple photos.

Do the following to use this feature.

- Choose the pictures you want to use.

Show Open Files

| Photo Bin | Tool Options | Undo | Redo | Rotate | Organizer | Home Screen |

- Choose the **Photomerge** tab in the **Guided Edit** mode, then click **Photomerge Panorama**.

- Choose one of the following options from the **Panorama Settings**.

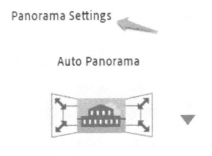

- **Auto Panorama**: This option applies a perspective or cylindrical arrangement after analyzing the source image.
- **Perspective**: By designating one of the source photos as the reference image, this creates a steady composition.
- **Cylindrical**: This technique makes a single image appear like an unfurled cylinder, which helps to lessen the bow-tie distortion that can occur when utilizing the Perspective layout.

- o With **Spherical** mapping, images can be repositioned and aligned as though they were inside a sphere.
- o **Collage**: This matches overlapping content, aligns the layers, and modifies them to any of the source layers.
- o **Repositioning**: This matches overlapping material and aligns layers as well, although it doesn't alter them from the source image.

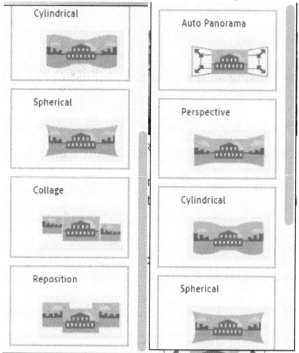

- •

- o **Blend Images Together**: This determines the best borders between the images in order to match the images' colors and construct seams based on those borders. Blend Images Together is turned off, and a straightforward blend of a rectangle is made. If you plan to manually adjust the mixing masks, this might be better.
- o **Vignette Removal**: This corrects exposure problems brought on by defective lenses.
- o Fisheye, barrel, and pincushion distortions are all corrected with **Geometric Distortion Correction**.
- o **Content-Aware Fill Transparent Areas**: This technique seamlessly inserts comparable image content into the transparent area.

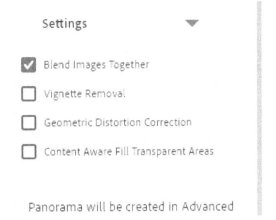

Settings ▼

☑ Blend Images Together

☐ Vignette Removal

☐ Geometric Distortion Correction

☐ Content Aware Fill Transparent Areas

Panorama will be created in Advanced

- After making all the necessary adjustments, select **Create Panorama**.

Create Panora...   Cancel

- At this point, you can either save the picture or carry on editing.

CHAPTER FOURTEEN

THE CAMERA RAW PLUGIN IN PHOTOSHOP ELEMENTS

About Camera Raw

This program was first launched in 2003 and is compatible with Adobe Photoshop Elements, Adobe Photoshop, and Adobe Lightroom. Professional photographers have found that Adobe Camera Raw, which allows you to import and edit raw photographs, is an essential tool.

Adobe Element comes with a plug-in program called the Camera Raw Editor that enables quick and excellent image editing. This program enhances and lets you import raw photos. With the Camera Raw Plugin, users can alter their raw camera photographs in several ways, such as:

- **White Balance**: The process of adjusting an image's overall color balance is known as white balance. Users can ensure that their photographs look natural and consistent by altering the white balance.
- **Exposure**: The amount of light that the camera sensor records is known as exposure. Users can change the brightness or darkness of their photographs by adjusting the exposure.
- **Contrast**: The difference between an image's light and dark parts is called contrast. Users can alter the contrast of their photographs to make them look more washed out or detailed.
- **Saturations**: The intensity of a color in an image is known as saturation. Users can alter the saturation to make their photographs appear more muted or brighter.
- **Sharpness**: The sharpness of an image's edges is known as sharpness. Users can alter the sharpness of their photographs to make them look either more detailed or fuzzier.
- **HDR Merging**: The technique known as HDR merging involves combining many exposures of the same scene to produce an image with a greater range of tones. A variety of HDR merging techniques are included in the Camera Raw Plugin, which can assist users in producing beautiful HDR photographs.
- **Noise Reduction**: The technique of eliminating undesired noise from an image is called noise reduction. Users can reduce noise in their photographs without sacrificing quality by using the various noise reduction features included in the Camera Raw Plugin.

- *Lens Correction*: Correcting for optical distortions caused by the camera lens is known as lens correction. The Camera Raw Plugin comes with a variety of lens correction features that users can use to enhance the clarity and sharpness of their photos.

And many more features...

The changes done to the photos are likewise non-destructive, which implies that the original files are preserved in their original state and that the changes can be reversed. The Camera Raw Editor opens in a distinct window each time a raw file is opened.

Understanding Raw File Formats

An image file is created when a digital camera's image sensor takes a picture. Usually, a picture file is compressed and processed before being saved to the memory card of your camera. Cameras may, however, also keep an image as a raw file, meaning they don't need to process or compress it. Consider raw camera files to be negatives for photos. Instead of depending on the camera to process the information, you may open a raw file in Photoshop Elements, make changes, and save it. You can adjust the white balance, tonal range, contrast, color saturation, and sharpness while working with camera raw files.

The following formats are available for saving the Camera Raw files:

- Nikon (. NEF)
- Pentax (. PEF)
- Olympus (. ORF)

- Hasselblad(.3FR)
- Panasonic(.RW2)
- Sony (.ARW, .SRF)
- Canon (. CRW)

Working with Camera Raw

To launch the Camera Raw in Photoshop Elements do the following.

- Go to **File**, then choose to **Open with Camera Raw Editor.**

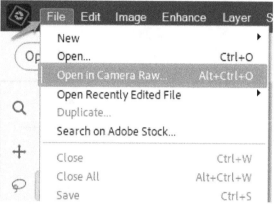

- The Camera Raw Editor is visible on this page.

The Camera Raw`s Workspace

Toolbar: The workspace's right side is where you'll find the Toolbar. The different editing tools in the Camera Raw Editor are found on the Toolbar. These tools are

408

comparable to those in Photoshop Element. Among these tools are the Spot Removal Tool, Crop Tool, Hand Tool, Zoom Tool, and so forth.

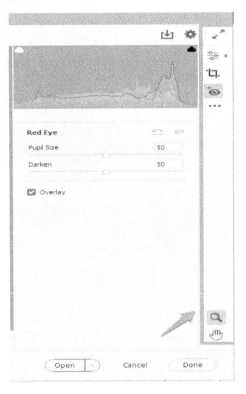

- **Hand Tool**: With this tool, you can move the image in the preview window comfortably when the zoom level of the image is higher than 100%.When using another tool, you can access the Hand tool by holding down the spacebar. To fit the preview image in the window, double-click the Hand tool.

- **Zoom Tool**: With this tool selected you can zoom in and out of an image. To zoom out, use Alt-click (or, on Mac OS, Option-click). To magnify a specific area in the preview image, drag the Zoom tool over it. Double-clicking the Zoom tool will bring it back to 100%.

- **Crop Tool**: With this tool, you can erase a portion of a picture. To pick the area you wish to keep, drag the tool inside the preview image and hit Enter. You can use the tool options in the panel to adjust the settings of the crop tool.

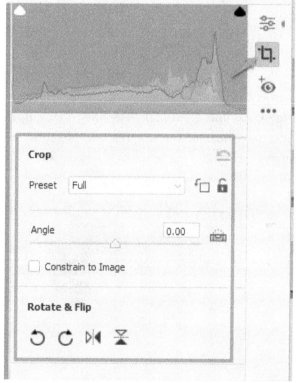

- **Red Eye Removal**: This tool can be used to remove green or white eyes from dogs and red eyes from people in flash images. Modify your tool in the panel

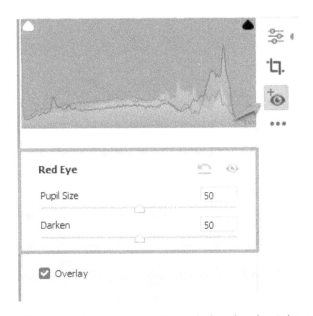

Histogram: This may be found in the Camera Raw dialog box's right corner. With the help of this tool, you may monitor the raw file's whole tonal range while working on it. The Histogram displays an image's current brightness level.

Panels: In the Camera Rae dialog, on the right-hand side, beneath the Histogram, are the Panels. Every tool in the workspace has a panel unique to it, displaying its tool options when selected. Much like Elements' panels, the Camera Raw Editor's panels are used for a multitude of tasks. Because they are all in one place, the panels in the Camera Raw are simpler to operate.

A few panels appear in the panel area when you pick the **Edit button** in the toolbar. These panels are essential for modifying any photographs in the Camera Raw Workspace. Let's now examine these panels.

- **Basic**: The majority of the tools required to edit the Raw files are available in this panel, which is the first to be shown. This panel's top section has control settings for things like white balance and color temperature. It also has a series of sliders for adjusting exposure, contrast, highlights, and shadows, as well as setting the major white and black points. To adjust the contrast in the midtones, move the

412

Clarity slider located at the bottom of the Basic panel. The Vibrance and Saturation slides, which are used to adjust color saturation, are the last ones.

- **Detail**: The Camera Raw Editor's second panel is this one. You can sharpen your image using the top half of this panel, and you can decrease any brightness or color noise using the bottom half.

- **Calibration**: In contrast to other iterations, Photoshop Elements 2024's Camera Calibration tool set includes enhanced and sophisticated functionalities under the name "Calibration panel." There are six process versions in the calibration panel. Photoshop Elements 2024 is currently on version 6, as opposed to the version used for Photoshop Elements 2023.

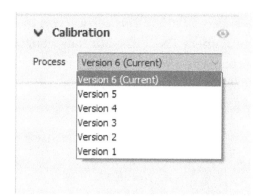

Process Versions in the Calibration Panel: Process Version is the method that Camera Raw uses to alter and produce photos. Depending on the process version you are using, you can access different options and settings under the Basic tab while making local adjustments. The calibration panel presently contains six different variations of the technique.

- ○ ***Process Version 6***: Version 6 of Process was first released in Camera Raw 15.4 June 2023 and is designed to minimize banding while utilizing the Color Mixer and B&W Mixer settings.
- ○ ***Process Version 5***: Process Version 5 is used for newly altered photos in Camera Raw 11. Higher ISO rendering in PV 5 helps eliminate purple color casts that occasionally appear in the shadows of photos taken in poor light. An enhanced Dehaze slider is another feature of PV5.
- ○ ***Process Version 4***: Camera Raw 10 is used to make the first image edits using procedure version 4. PV 4 includes Range Mask capability as well as a more robust Auto Mask that effectively reduces picture noise. PV 4 will automatically update any images from PV 3 (2012) that have not had any Auto Mask adjustments made to them.
- ○ ***Process Version 3 (2012)***: Using Camera Raw 7 for the first time, images are adjusted using version 3. For high-contrast photos, PV 3 has new tone adjustments and tone-mapping algorithms. Highlights, Shadows, Whites, Blacks, Exposure, and Contrast can all be changed in PV 3's Basic panel. Additionally, local adjustments for highlights, shadows, noise, moiré, and white balance (temperature and tint) are available.
- ○ ***Process Version 2 (2010)***: By default, Camera Raw 6 modified images utilizing PV 2. Comparing PV 2 to PV 1, the prior process version, sharpness, and noise reduction are enhanced.

- ○ **Process Version 1 (2003)**: This version was the first that came with the first version of Camera Raw. Camera Raw versions 5x and prior utilized the original processing engine.

To switch between process versions, select **Process** in the **Calibration Panel**.

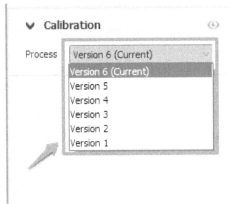

The Camera Raw`s Preference Settings

This part of the workspace allows you the modify the entire functions of the Camera Raw. To access this, select the *Settings Icon* at the upper right-hand of the workspace.

Displayed below is the Preference dialog box.

Basic Operations in the Camera Raw Editor

Camera Raw image representation of colors and tones varies by profile. A starting point for image changes is provided by the **Profile**.

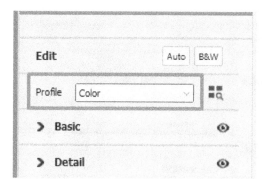

While modifying a raw profile, the following profile groups appear.

- **Adobe Raw**: This profile is meant to bring out the colors in your photos and lay a solid editing base. When raw photographs are imported into the Camera Raw Editor, they are assigned this default profile.
- **Camera Matching**: The model or make of the camera used to capture your raw image determines which profile is shown. When you want to match what's visible on the camera's display screen with your raw photos, the Camera Matching profile works best.
- **Legacy**: In the previous iteration of Adobe Camera Raw, this profile was visible.

To view the current Camera Raw profile in Photoshop Elements, click the **Edit button** on the Toolbar to the right of the Camera Raw dialog box.

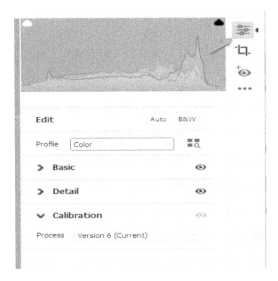

By choosing the Camera Raw profile from the **Edit panel's Profile drop-down** menu, you can further confirm that it is the one being used.

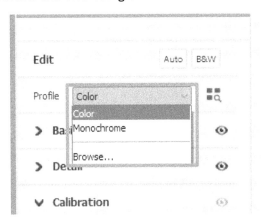

Understanding Creative Profiles

A creative profile is one designed to project a particular vibe or style onto your image. You can find them through the **Browse** Option in the **Profile** section.

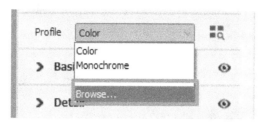

Any file can be utilized with these profiles, and some of them handle raw pictures, JPEGs, and TIFF files. The creative profiles are listed below.

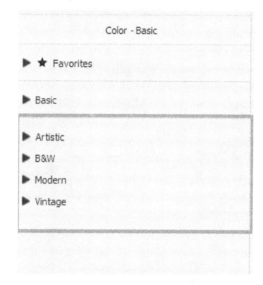

- **Artistic**: The term "artistic" refers to the utilization of significant color changes and a tighter color rendering in your photo.
- **B&W**: For a black-and-white project, this profile works well when you need to obtain the ideal tone shift.
- **Modern**: The amazing impression that this profile offers is most appropriate for modern photographic styles.
- **Vintage**: The effect of a vintage photo is shown in this profile.

The steps listed below will allow you to add a profile to your image.

- To view the profiles, navigate to the **Edit Panel** Camera Raw dialog box and select the **Profile Option** from the drop-down menu.

- Click **Browse** to view other available profiles.

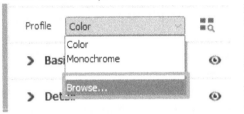

- To see the profiles that are available in each group, expand the profile group.

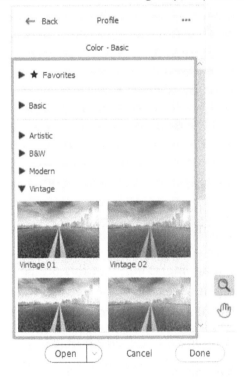

- To apply a profile to your image, click the one you want after moving the pointer over it to see how it will appear in the picture.

Do the following to add a profile to your favorite.

- Click the star icon that appears in the thumbnail's top corner after selecting the profile to add it to your favorites.

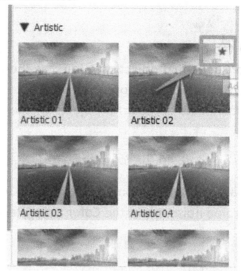

Aside from applying effects from the color profile, other basic operations can be performed with the Camera Raw Editor like Adjusting Sharpness and Noise Reduction.

Sharpness Adjustment

The sharpness slider, which modifies the image's sharpness, gives you the desired edge definition. This adjustment increases the contrast of pixels by a specific amount based on the threshold you set. It identifies pixels that differ from surrounding pixels.

To apply the sharpening to photographs in Raw files, follow these steps:

- The preview image should be zoomed in to at least 100%.
- Select the Detail tab.

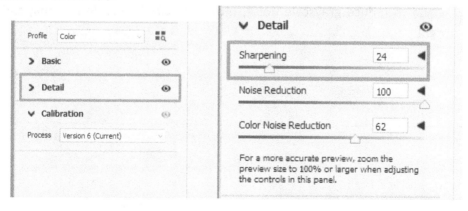

You may adjust the sharpness by moving the slider to the right to sharpen more or to the left to sharpen less. Sharpening is switched off when the slider reaches zero. Thus, let the Sharpness slider be set to a lower value for a clearer image.

Noise Reduction

A slider on the Detail tab of the Camera Raw dialog box reduces image noise. Picture noise is a visible, inconsequential object that reduces the quality of the image. Image noise can be classified into two categories: luminance noise (grayscale) and chroma noise (color), which manifests as colorful objects in the image and gives it a gritty appearance.

To lessen the noise in an image, do the following.

- The preview image should be zoomed in to at least 100%.
- To minimize chroma noise, move the **Color Noise Reduction slider** to the right...

...and to reduce grayscale noise, move the **Luminance Smoothing slider** to the right.

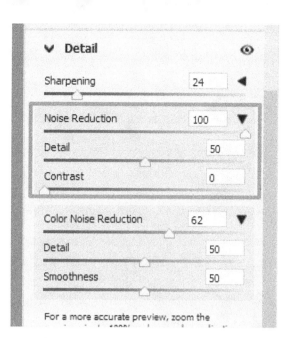

BOOK SECTION 5

TIPS AND TRICKS
CHAPTER FIFTEEN- CHAPTER SIXTEEN

❖**TIPS AND TRICKS ON PHOTOSHOP ELEMENTS**
❖**DRAWING THE CURTAIN**

CHAPTER FIFTEEN

TIPS AND TRICKS ON PHOTOSHOP ELEMENTS

Troubleshooting In Photoshop Elements

Adobe has improved its tools, and Photoshop Element is unquestionably one of them with unique features. But without fail, there will be an issue or two.

In this section of this book, a number of problems that you may encounter and how to fix them will be addressed in this section.

System errors may arise from an incomplete or damaged Photoshop Elements installation. Some signs of system failures include the following: An empty or fluttering dialog window, a stuck cursor or display, an Azure screen, unexpected restarting as well as an error message.

Troubleshooting Catalog issues

In the Photoshop Element, a database known as the catalog contains information about your photographs and other pertinent media assets. The computer's hard drive automatically stores the catalog.

Use Catalog Manager's Optimize tool to optimize your catalog's performance and reduce the amount of space it takes up. Optimizing a catalog also fixes Elements Organizer thumbnail problems.

Do the following to optimize your catalog.

- Make sure you have closed Photoshop Element Editor.
- In the Organizer, select **Manage Catalog** from the **File Menu**.

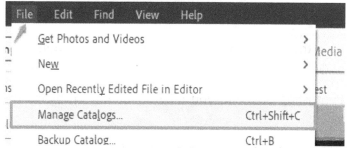

- Choose the catalog that needs to be optimized when the Catalog Manager dialog box appears, then click **Optimize**.

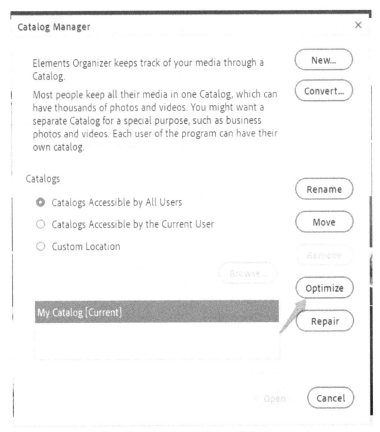

- You will be told when this has finished loading; click **OK** to close.

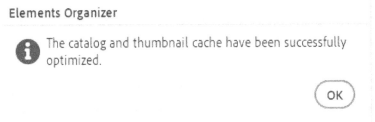

- Optimizing the catalog is a surefire method to fix thumbnail problems with the Element Organizer.

When using Photoshop Element, you may encounter problems that cause damage to the catalog file.

Catalogs that are damaged should be repaired using the procedures given below.

- Navigate to **File** > **Manage Catalogs.**

- Choose the catalog to be repaired when the Catalog Manager dialog box appears, then click **Repair**.

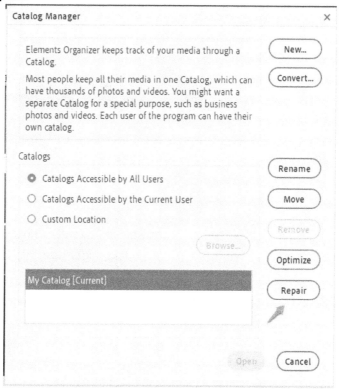

- After the Photoshop Element has finished checking for problems, select **Repair Anyway** after marking the **Re-index Visual Similarity Data**.

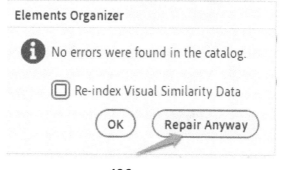

- Once this is finished, click **OK** to close the dialog box.

Every now and then, a catalog sustains damage to the point where the Optimize and Repair features are unable to fix it. Use the latest recent backup of your catalog to restore it if you have made one.

Do the following to restore a backed-up catalog.

- To access the Restore Catalog, navigate to **File** and select **Restore Catalog**.

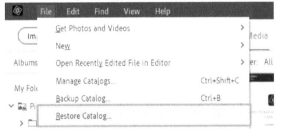

- From the dialog box that appears, select **CD/DVD**, **Hard Drive/Other Volume**. If you selected a hard drive as your backup location, click **Browse** to locate it.

- Once the backup file has been chosen, click **Browse** in the **Restore Files** and Catalog to specify where the backup file should be restored.

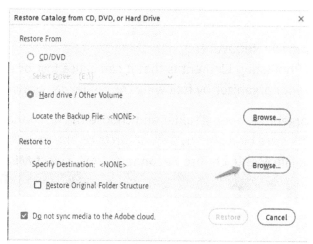

- If you want to keep the files in the catalog, you can select **Restore Original Folder Structure**.

- Next, press the **Restore button**.

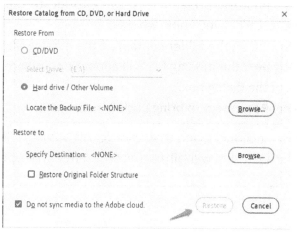

428

Troubleshooting File Recovery

One issue with Photoshop Element is that it can cause lost or disconnected files. Locate any lost files in your organizer by following the guidelines provided below.

- In your organizer, open a folder and choose the disconnected or missing file. (Any missing files are indicated by a small circle on the corner of the file.)
- From the **File Menu**, choose **Reconnect**. Next, select **Missing File**.

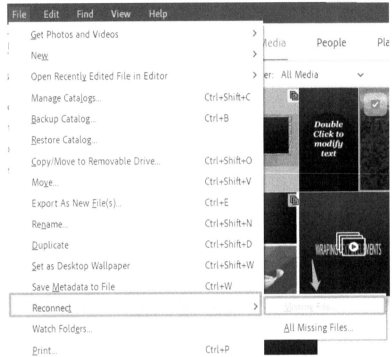

- This page's Photoshop Element is trying to locate the missing. Click **Browse** to locate the lost file if you know where it is.
- When you click on the folder containing the missing file in the R**econnect Missing Files dialog box**, the missing file will appear under **Locate the Missing File** on the right side of the dialog box.
- Next, select **Reconnect** to bring back the absent

Go to File, choose Reconnect, and then click on **All Missing Files** if you need to locate all missing files. The lost files will all be rejoined after this operation, which could take some time.

Date Correction for Different Time Zones

Inaccurate dates can cause problems for you when searching for photos in Photoshop Element. Even when both the time zone and your own time are correct, you may still receive inaccurate search results.

To modify the date for various time zones, adhere to the steps listed below:

- Select the files whose dates you wish to change by opening the Organizer.
- Right-click the image and select **Adjust Date and Time** to adjust the date and time.

- Click Shift by a set of hours in the Adjust Date and Time of Selected Item dialog box (time zone adjust).

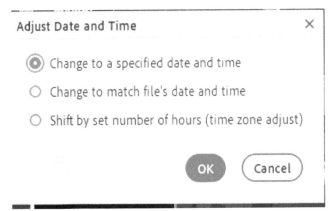

- Choose the desired time period using the Ahead or Back choices in the Time Zone Adjust dialog box, then click OK.

If any problem you may encounter while using Photoshop Elements is not aforementioned, be sure to report it to Adobe when you encounter it.

A Few Tips and Tricks

In this section, we'll go over some tips and tricks for working with the Photoshop Element. Several pointers and strategies are being presented in to promote a culture around the utilization of the Photoshop Element.

Now let's examine some tips and methods with Photoshop Element.

Displaying An Image in Two Windows

You can select between two alternate versions of an image with the Photoshop Element. This feature can come in handy when you need to enlarge an image to carry out some intricate tasks.

Do the following to do such.

- To view your image in two distinct windows, go to the **View menu** and pick **New Window**.

- When the aforementioned methods are followed, the image eventually appears in two windows.

Increasing The Number of Files in Recently Edited List

In a manner similar to the History panel, you can access the list of the last 20 files you opened. Choose **Recently Edited File** from the **File menu** to view these files.

To increase the number of files listed in Open Recently Edited Files, do the following.

- Select **Preference** from the **Edit Menu**.

- Click on **Saving Files** in the Preference Dialog box.

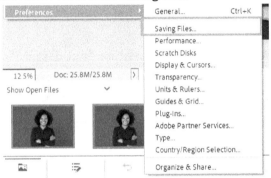

- Change the number of files you want displayed by inserting a new figure in **Recent File List Contains__ files.** Then click Ok.

Additionally, by accessing the Photoshop Elements menu, choosing Preferences, and clicking on Saving Files, you can browse up to thirty files and modify the figure to your liking.

Extending The Background of An Image

One of the edits that is made available in the Guided Mode is to extend the background of an image beyond its original size.

Do the following to do such.

- In Guided mode, open your photo. Click **Extend Background** after selecting **Special Edits**.

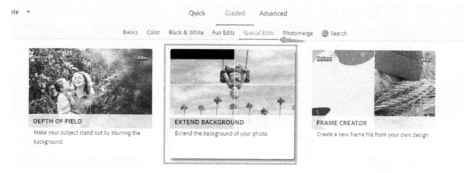

- Choose **Customized** to build your own size, or pick one of the predefined options in **Set Canvas Size**.

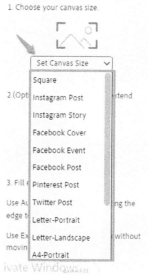

- Choose the photo's edges that you want to extend.

2.(Optional) Choose side(s) to extend.

- Do the following to fill the expanded area.
  - Choose **Autofill** and allow artificial intelligence to work its magic in the background or **Extend** to stretch the image without stretching the subject.

3. Fill expanded area.

Use Autofill to clone content along the edge to fill the expanded area.

Use Extend to stretch the photo without moving the subject.

Autofill

Or

Extend

  - The **Healing Brush** or **Clone Stamp tool** can be fine-tuned to remove any repeated patterns with a few clicks, not strokes.

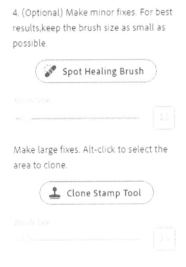

4. (Optional) Make minor fixes. For best results,keep the brush size as small as possible.

Spot Healing Brush

13

Make large fixes. Alt-click to select the area to clone.

Clone Stamp Tool

- After making your edits, click on Next and Save your work.

Dialogue Box Reset Without Closing

You should know by now that most of Photoshop Element's adjustment options are found in the dialog box. While making modifications to the dialog box, you might need to close it and open it again to get started. This time, all you have to do is click the **Reset button**. Still, dialog boxes do not always display the Reset button. All you have to do in these situations is hold down the Alt key until the Cancel button turns into the Reset button.

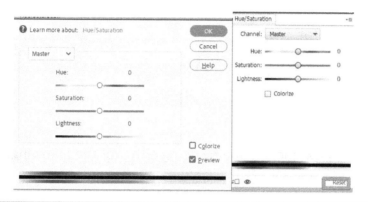

Removing The Background of An Image

Easily erase a background and swap it out for a preset, a different color, or another image with the Replace Background Guided Edit. Do the following to get it done.

- In Guided mode, open your photo. Click **Replace Background** after selecting **Special Edits**.

- To automatically choose your subject, click the **Select Subject button** or manually select your subject using the selection tools.

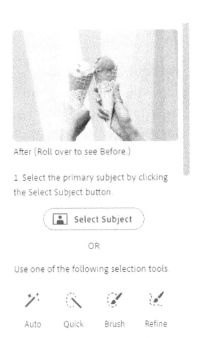

After (Roll over to see Before.)

1. Select the primary subject by clicking
the Select Subject button.

[Select Subject]

OR

Use one of the following selection tools

Auto   Quick   Brush   Refine

- Choose a new background by doing either of the following.

2. Choose a new background

Import a   None   Color   Adobe Stock
photo

OR

Choose Presets

- To add a photo to replace the background, click **Import A Photo**.
- To create a transparent background, select **None**
- To add a color to the backdrop, click **Color**.
- You can also pick from **Adobe Stock**.

437

- To apply a background setting, click **Preset**.
- After selecting your background, click on **Next** and save your work.

Keyboard Shortcuts in Photoshop Elements

Welcome to the last lesson section and chapter of this book as we learn the various shortcuts in Photoshop Elements. Don't forget to fasten your seat belt as we land on a safe place after going through the journey of thorough learning.

Basic Shortcut keys

Shortcut Result	Windows	Mac OS
New	Ctrl + N	Command + N
Open	Ctrl + O	Command + O
Undo	Ctrl + Z	Command + Z
Redo	Ctrl + Shift + Z	Command + Shift + Z
Copy	Ctrl + C	Command + C
Cut	Ctrl + X	Command + X
Paste	Ctrl + V	Command + V
Delete	Del	Del
Duplicate	Alt + Up/down button	Option + Up/Down button
Deselect	Ctrl + D	Command + D
Deselect All	Ctrl + Shift + A	Command + Shift + Z
Save	Ctrl + S	Command + S
Save As	Ctrl + Shift + S	Command + Shift + S
Save for Web	Alt + Ctrl + Shift + S	Command + Option + Shift + S
Export	Ctrl + E	Command + E

Shortcut Keys for The View Menu

Shortcut Result	Windows	Mac OS
Smart Guides	Ctrl + U	Command + U
Convert to Path	Ctrl + 8	Ctrl + 8
Intersect	Ctrl + Alt +I	Command + Alt +I
Text Threads	Ctrl + Alt + Y	Command + Alt + Y
Exclude Overlap	Ctrl + Alt + X	Command + Alt + X

Shortcut Keys for The Layer Panel

Shortcut Result	Windows	Mac OS
Apply value and keep	Shift + Enter	Shift + Enter

the text box active		
Delete without confirmation	Alt-click Trash button	Option-click Trash button
Load layer transparency as a selection	Control-click layer thumbnail	Command-click layer thumbnail
Add to the current selection	Ctrl + Shift-click	Command + Shift-click layer thumbnail
Subtract from the current selection	Ctrl +Shift + Alt-click layer thumbnail	Command +Shift + Alt-click layer thumbnail
Intersect with the current selection	Ctrl + Shift + Alt-click layer thumbnail	Command + Shift + Option-click layer thumbnail
Merge Layers	Ctrl + Shift + E	Command + Shift + E
Set layer options	Alt-click New button	Option-click New button
Create a new empty layer with a dialog	Alt-click the New Layer button	Option-click the New Layer button
Create a new layer below the target layer	Control-click the New Layer button	Command-click the New Layer button
Activate the bottom/top layer	Alt+(period)/ ,(comma)	Option+(period)/ ,(comma)
Select the next layer down/up	Alt + [or]	Option + [or]
Move the target layer down/up	Ctrl + [or]	Command + [or]
Merge a copy of all visible layers into the target layer	Ctrl + Shift + Alt + E	Command + Shift + Option + E
Merge down	Ctrl + E	Command + E
Copy the current layer to the layer below	Alt + Merge Down command from the panel pop-up menu	Option + Merge Down command from the panel pop-up menu
Copy all visible layers to the active layer	Alt + Merge Visible command from the panel pop-up menu	Option + Merge Visible command from the panel pop-up menu

Show/hide all other currently visible layers	Alt-click the eye icon	Option-click the eye icon
Copy the mask from one layer to another, and ask to replace it if the mask is already present	Alt + drag layer mask	Alt + drag layer mask
Toggle lock transparency for the target layer, or the last applied lock	/ (forward slash)	/ (forward slash)
Select all text; temporarily select the Type tool	Double-click the text layer thumbnail	Double-click the text layer thumbnail
Create a clipping mask	Alt-click the line dividing the two layers	Option-click the line dividing the two layers
Rename layer	Double-click the layer name	Double-click the layer name
Add to layer selection in the Layers panel	Shift + Alt + [or]	Shift + Option + [or]

Shortcut Keys for the Arrangement of Layers

Shortcut Result	Windows	Mac OS
Bring to Font	Ctrl + Shift + [	Command + Shift + [
Send to Back	Ctrl + Shift +]	Command + Shift +]

Shortcut Keys for Text Usage

Shortcut Result	Windows	Mac OS
Tabs	Shift + Ctrl + T	Shift + Command + T
Glyphs	Shift + Alt + F11	Shift + Options + F11

Select word	Double-click	Double-click
Select 1 character left/right	Shift + Left Arrow/Right Arrow	Shift + Left Arrow/Right Arrow

Select 1 line down/up	Shift + Down Arrow/Up Arrow	Shift + Down Arrow/Up Arrow
Select 1 word left/right	Ctrl + Shift + Left Arrow/Right Arrow	Command+ Shift + Left Arrow/Right Arrow
Select characters from the insertion point to the mouse click point	Shift-click	Shift-click
Move 1 character left/right	Left Arrow/Right Arrow	Left Arrow/Right Arrow
Move 1 line down/up	Down Arrow/Up Arrow	Down Arrow/Up Arrow
Select 1 word left/right	Left Arrow/Right Arrow	Command + Left Arrow/Right Arrow
Select line	Triple-click	Triple-click
Select paragraph	Quadruple-click	Quadruple-click
Scale and skew text within a bounding box when resizing the bounding box	Control-drag a bounding box handle	Command-drag a bounding box handle
Align top or bottom	Vertical Type tool or R	Vertical Type tool or R
Align centre	Vertical Type Mask tool + Control + Shift + L, C	Vertical Type Mask tool + Control + Shift + L, C
Return to the default font style	Ctrl + Shift + Y	Command + Shift + Y
Turn Underlining on/off	Ctrl +Shift + U	Command +Shift + U
Turn Strikethrough on/ off	Ctrl + Shift + /	Command + Shift + /
Decrease or increase the type size of selected text 1 pt/px	Ctrl + Shift + < or >	Command + Shift + < or >
Move type in Image	Ctrl + Drag when the Type layer is selected	Command + Drag when the Type layer is selected.

Shortcut Keys for Layout Menu

Shortcut Result	Windows	Mac OS
Add Page	Ctrl + Shift +P	Command + Shift +P
Go to Page	Ctrl + J	Command + J

Shortcut Keys for Zooming

Shortcut Result	Windows	Mac OS
Fit Spread in View	Ctrl + Option + O	Command + Option + O
Fit Page in View	Ctrl + O	Command + O
Pan in View	Spacebar + Drag	Spacebar + Drag
Zoom in/Zoom out	Ctrl + +/ Ctrl + -	Command+ +/ Command I + -
Zoom (Drag mouse to Zoom)	Ctrl + Spacebar	Command + Spacebar

Shortcut Keys for Painting

Shortcut Result	Windows	Mac OS
Select the first/last brush	Shift +, (comma) or. (period)	Shift +, (comma) or. (period)
Select the previous/next brush size	, (comma) or. (period)	, (comma) or. (period)
Decrease/increase brush size	[or]	[or]
Decrease/increase brush softness/hardness in 25% increments	Shift + [or]	Shift + [or]
Delete brush	Alt-click brush	Option-click brush
Select background-color	Eyedropper tool + Alt-click	Eyedropper tool + Option-click
Switch to the Eyedropper tool	Any painting tool or shape tool + Alt (except Impressionist Brush)	Any painting tool or shape tool + Alt (except Impressionist Brush)

442

Set opacity, tolerance, or exposure for the painting	Any painting or editing tool + and number keys. When the airbrush option is enabled, use the Shift + number keys.	Any painting or editing tool + and number keys. When the airbrush option is enabled, use the Shift + number keys.
Cycle through blending mode	Shift + + (plus) or - (minus)	Shift + + (plus) or - (minus)
Fill selection/layer with foreground or background color	Alt + Backspace, or Ctrl + Backspace	Option + Delete (Backspace), or Command + Delete (Backspace)
Display Fill dialog box	Shift + Backspace	Shift + Delete (Backspace)
Display precise crosshair for brushes	Caps Lock	Caps Lock
Lock transparent pixels on/off	/ (forward slash)	/ (forward slash)
Connect points with a straight line (draw a straight line)	Any painting tool + Shift-click	Any painting tool + Shift-click

Shortcut for Selection

Shortcut Result	Windows	Mac OS
Add to or subtract from a selection	Any selection tool + Shift or Alt-drag	Any selection tool + Shift or Option-drag
Deselect a selection	Ctrl + D	Command + D
Intersect a selection	Any selection tool (excluding Quick Selection tool and Selection Brush tool)+ Shift + Alt-drag	Any selection tool (excluding Quick Selection tool and Selection Brush tool) + Shift + Alt-drag
Reposition the marquee while selecting	Spacebar-drag	Spacebar-drag
Constrain marquee to square or circle If	Shift-drag	Shift-drag

443

no other selections are active		
Draw a marquee from the centre (If no other selections are active)	Alt-drag	Option-drag
Constrain shape and draw marquee from the center	Shift + Alt-drag	Shift + Option-drag
Switch from the Magnetic Lasso tool to the Polygonal Lasso tool	Alt-click and drag	Option-click and drag
Delete the last anchor point the for Magnetic or Polygonal lasso tool	Delete	Delete
Apply an operation of the Magnetic Lasso tool	Enter	Enter
Cancel an operation of the Magnetic Lasso tool	Esc	Esc
Move a copy of a selection	Move tool +Alt-drag selection	Move tool +Option-drag selection
Move selection area 1 pixel	Move tool + Right Arrow, Left Arrow, Up Arrow, or Down Arrow	Move tool + Right Arrow, Left Arrow, Up Arrow, or Down Arrow
Move layer 1 pixel when nothing is selected on layer	Control + Right Arrow, Left Arrow, Up Arrow, or Down Arrow	Command + Right Arrow, Left Arrow, Up Arrow, or Down Arrow
Increase/decrease detection width	Magnetic Lasso tool + [or]	Magnetic Lasso tool + [or]
Accept cropping or exit cropping	Crop tool + Enter or Esc	Crop tool + Enter or Esc
Toggle the crop	(forward slash) /	/ (forward slash)

shield off and on		
Switch to Move tool	Control (except when Hand or any shape tool is selected)	Command (except when Hand or any shape tool is selected)

Shortcut Keys for Objects

Shortcut Result	Windows	Mac OS
Text Frame Options	Ctrl +B	Ctrl + B
Centre to Content	Ctrl + Shift + E	Command + Shift + E
Transform again	Ctrl + Alt + 4	Ctrl + Alt + 4
Group	Ctrl + G	Command + G
Ungroup	Ctrl + Shift + G	Command + Shift+ G

CHAPTER SIXTEEN

DRAWING THE CURTAIN

As we conclude our exploration of the complex and dynamic world of Photoshop Elements 2024, it is clear that access to and empowerment in the field of digital creativity has never been greater. We have explored the wide range of functions and resources provided by Photoshop Elements in this in-depth book, enabling you to realize your creative potential in graphic design, photo editing, and artistic expression.

We've looked at the power of layers, the accuracy of selection tools, color grading, and retouching throughout the chapters. We've seen how adaptable text and typography can be, how filters can completely change an image, and how seamlessly photos may be included into b a project. Our investigation has not only concentrated on the software's technical features but also highlighted how crucial creative vision and inventiveness are to producing visually engaging stories.

It's important to understand that Photoshop Elements is more than simply a tool as we get to the end of this journey; it's a doorway to storytelling and self-expression. Photoshop Elements 2024 gives you the ability to realize your ideas in ways that were previously unthinkable, whether you're an aspiring photographer, digital artist, or just a hobbyist looking to gain new skills.

May you discover delight in every creation, inspiration in every click, and the satisfaction that comes from turning ideas into reality as you continue your adventure with Photoshop Elements. With Photoshop Elements 2024 as your guide, you may explore the enormous realm of digital creativity and its endless possibilities. Happy Digital Creating!

INDEX

449

U

V

W

Z

451

www.ingramcontent.com/pod-product-compliance
Lightning Source LLC
Chambersburg PA
CBHW060644060326
40690CB00020B/4516